Strategic Reframing

Traditional strategy assumes a stable and predictable context. Today's world is better characterized by turbulence, uncertainty, novelty, and ambiguity—conditions that contribute disruptive changes and which require strategy to be reframed, and new approaches to be tried and tested.

This book aims to become the premier guide on how to do scenario planning to support strategy and public policy. Co-authored by two experts in the field, the book presents The Oxford Scenario Planning Approach (OSPA). The approach is both intellectually rigorous and practical; methodological choices and theoretical aspects in practice are detailed in reference to the relevant literatures and grounded in six case studies the authors have been involved in.

The book makes several contributions to the field. It demonstrates how learning with scenario planning is supported by re-framing and re-perception; how this iterative process can be embedded in corporate, government, and multi-stakeholder settings, and how it helps those that it supports to thrive in today's world.

The book is written in an accessible style and will be a useful introductory text as well as a useful guide for the more experienced scenario planning practitioner and scholar.

Rafael Ramírez is a Senior Fellow in Strategy in both the Saïd Business School & Green-Templeton College as well as Director of the Oxford Scenarios Programme and has pioneered work in organizational aesthetics; the interactive design of strategy; and how scenarios work. He was Visiting Professor of Scenarios and Corporate Strategy at Shell International 2000–2003 and Chairman of the World Economic Forum's Global Agenda Council of Strategic Foresight. Rafael holds a PhD from the Wharton School, speaks Spanish, English, and French fluently, has lived in five countries, and has worked on scenarios and futures work in some 30 countries since 1980.

Angela Wilkinson is Strategic Foresight Counsellor, Organisation of Economic Cooperation and Development (OECD). With 30 years of experience in forward assessment, multi-stakeholder engagement, corporate strategy and policy advisory roles, she has contributed to over 100 foresight initiatives, worked in over 30 countries, and across a broad range of sectors. She works with senior executives, high-level policy makers, and other key change agents to address connected challenges and emerging global issues. A former member of Shell's global scenario team, Angela has a PhD in Physics. This is her second book on scenarios.

Strategic Reframing

The Oxford Scenario Planning Approach

Rafael Ramírez

Angela Wilkinson

OXFORD
UNIVERSITY PRESS

OXFORD
UNIVERSITY PRESS

Great Clarendon Street, Oxford, OX2 6DP,
United Kingdom

Oxford University Press is a department of the University of Oxford.
It furthers the University's objective of excellence in research, scholarship,
and education by publishing worldwide. Oxford is a registered trade mark of
Oxford University Press in the UK and in certain other countries

© Rafael Ramírez and Angela Wilkinson 2016

The moral rights of the authors have been asserted

First published 2016
First published in paperback 2018

Published in the United States of America by Oxford University Press
198 Madison Avenue, New York, NY 10016, United States of America

British Library Cataloguing in Publication Data
Data available

Library of Congress Cataloging in Publication Data
Data available

ISBN 978-0-19-874569-3 (Hbk.)
ISBN 978-0-19-882066-6 (Pbk.)

We dedicate this book to our families: Geneviève, Ivan, Louis, Noel, Ruairi, and Emer.

▨ FOREWORD

Why is this book important?

This is a book about *strategic planning*. Strategic planning is an approach to *business planning* aiming to be explicit about the value-creating principles that bring groups of people together in organisations to jointly pursue financial or other goals. The basis of the existence of organisations is the principle of economies of scale applied to production and transactions. This drives people together in order as a group to become more efficient in pursuing their shared aims. It leads to the need to organize things, driven by "general management" principles, which define goals and tasks to be performed to achieve the shared objectives. Under the influence of such driving forces emanating from general management things start to happen.

The organising and management activity becomes future oriented through an activity known as planning. Tasks are defined in advance and then allocated to people for execution. They become more articulate about achieving future goals, and so the future becomes important.

Management and planning have always been key ingredients of organisational life. The way planning was done, however, has changed significantly over the years in response to societal change in the business environment. For example, half a century ago planners based their activity on predicting the future and "making forecasts." Of course one knew that making predictions is difficult and things could turn out quite differently from the plans. Even if over time, with increasing turbulence in the business environment the discrepancy between forecasts and reality increased. This was not seen as a reason to drop forecasting altogether, as long as it was perceived as assisting management to maintain some control over affairs. But as time passed by and uncertainty increased planners became concerned about how much of the future can really be known. We assume that something about the future must be knowable. Why otherwise educate the young? Or reward leaders disproportionately? But this knowledge is limited; and over the years planners became concerned about where this knowledge about the future stops.

A watershed was reached around the mid-1970s, following the first global oil/energy crisis. Here was a major event that was not on the radar screen of most people, including many of the planners. The reaction to this was the rapid and decisive development of what became known as "strategic planning," in response to the growing awareness of the impossibility of forecasting this type of event. The reasoning of the strategic planners was as follows: if direct drivers such as demand and supply could not be predicted, but at the same time a total inability to predict anything would also not be a reasonable or useful assumption, then how might one engage the deeper driving forces underneath an apparently chaotic world of supply and demand at the macro-level? The answer of the strategic planners pointed to attending to these underlying value creation mechanisms.

Organisations were in the business of value creation driving demand. This was the traditional territory of economics which was now linked up with strategic planning. For example, Michael Porter's framework was based on the principle of "competitive advantage": if an organisation had competitive advantage demand would be attracted to it, and it would be successful, never mind what the rest of the market was doing.

Strategic planners became increasingly involved in refocusing their main attention from global demand statistics towards value creation. Attempts to articulate the principle of how any organisation (business or purpose driven) remains viable gave rise to notions such as the Business Idea as part of strategic planning (developed by R. Normann). Notions of this type proved helpful in describing the underlying success factors that lead to understanding successful performance. Strategic planning (and the strategic management that grew out of it) became based on understanding these principles.

Strategic management has been, and still is, in a state of flux. It is important to realize that its main focus of attention has been individual organisations and their competitive advantage considered from an economics perspective. Over time though, the field has expanded to bring into focus a much wider spectrum of stakeholders, moving the field towards an interest in the human perspective. The interest by many strategic planners in the socio-ecology field may be an outcome of that.

Strategic planning as it is practiced now would be unrecognisable to the planner of a half-century ago, involved in statistical aggregate demand at the macro-view. The last half-century has presented massive unprecedented change in the business environment, population has doubled, income quad-rupled, and the Western world has seen no wars on its territories. So why is it that instead of making us feel increasingly confident that we are starting to understand organisations we actually feel less secure, change seems accelerat-ing, control seems slipping out of our hands?

Some trends are obvious. For example, in global terms we are living closer and closer together, physically and informationally, highlighting cultural dis-crepancies with all the problems that come with it. Our ecological footprint now significantly exceeds available space and resource constraints are becom-ing evident. Beyond that there still are the great threats of our time. "We are approaching the greatest discontinuity in history," Ian Morris suggests, "dri-ven by nuclear proliferation, population growth, global epidemics and climate change."

This is the contextual environment in which we need to develop our approach to planning. It is all new and unprecedented. The old way of strategic planning will not deliver on this massive task. This is "turbulence" territory. As explained later in this book this means that while the environment will be driven by these new global issues we will all increasingly experience the turbulent planning repercussions at our own individual level.

Being aware of these dynamics drives home the need to think about strategic planning in a historical context. How was this done one hundred years ago, or fifty years? Is strategic planning now fundamentally different? The OSPA—the Oxford Scenario Planning Approach described in this book—is an attempt to map out what is happening, how effectiveness is defined and assessed, and where we see things moving into the future.

Turbulence

Causal Texture Theory (CTT), proposed by Emery and Trist and based on the field of socio-ecology, sets out to map the various changes as they observed these to include the human element. This required mapping out the various ways in which people saw strategic planning in relation to the way that the new turbulent contextual environment is understood. They decided to use connectivity as an organizing principle. Specifically, connectivity between the internal organisational world over which the strategist has some control, and the external world, which constitutes the environment that is outside any control of the strategist.

However, there are causal links between the internal and external worlds. For example, connectivity may be dominated from the personal, the internal self, and directed to the environment. Or the environment may drive what happens internally. Depending on the degree of dominance of any of the connections between these two worlds, Emery and Trist developed different models of what they called the "texture" of the environment that is relevant to the strategist.

For example, a world in which internal connectivity dominates would describe an old and mostly superseded strategy model, based on prediction of future developments of the contextual environment through statistical extrapolation of already available data. As discussed earlier, for quite some time now the applicability of this model has become increasingly reduced, as a consequence of increasing awareness of poor overlap between statistical forecasts and actual system performance.

This reduced applicability has brought forth the idea of turbulence, where the external environment and its effect on internal interactions have become much more salient, causing an increasing part of the world of the strategist to become unpredictable. The main theme of attention in this book is the accelerating drift from strategizing as a way to help bring about a more agreeable future towards new ways of strategizing, in turbulence, based on strengthening the adaptive capacities, and the resulting competitive state, of the organisation.

So over the last half-century we see a transition in which prediction has been becoming less dominant in the strategist's toolkit, and focus has increased on strengthening the organisation's skill to build human systems that will be able to cope with an unpredictable future. This type of environment is now called the turbulent environment, indicating the fact that strategists have less grip on what for them is autonomous change in the contextual business environment and an increasing need to find new approaches to allow organisations to develop skilful coping behaviour.

Looking ahead towards the future of strategic planning we are particularly focused on a world in which an increasing web of external linkages dominates. Uncertainty and novelty drive complexity that is becoming ever more dominant. This situation has major repercussions for the strategist. Specifically Ashby has suggested that the complexity of the internal management world has to keep up with the complexity of the world we are planning for. He formulated the following "law of requisite variety":

Only variety in the management system can deal successfully with variety in the system managed.

In other words our experience of turbulence in the environment and our diminishing ability to predict or forecast as part of the strategic planning for the future involves a level of complexity in the environment calling for a commensurate increase of complexity of thinking in the management system. If this level of variety is not forthcoming we will experience breakdown in our coping capability.

Where are we now?

A few key elements of the current state of play:

- The big macro issues in the environment are growing in importance and we are now in desperate need of new effective coping mechanisms.
- Our management systems are in need of redesign to restore the balance between the complexity of context of the system managed and that of the management system.
- A management system driven by macro-predictions and forecasts has proven too narrow to deal with turbulence. The alternative model the world needs has to be based on social ecology that can balance the increasingly complex web of both internal and external connectivity.

- This book suggests that such an approach to planning might be feasible, if grafted on to an approach to strategic planning known as scenario planning.

What does scenario planning have to offer?

Let's start from the observation that in essence we need to redesign the strategic management system to restore the balance between the complexity of the system managed and that of the management system. This need is not a new observation. So why is it often not happening? Especially why has social ecology not delivered on this? The answer to this question must be that the systems are too complex especially when we juxtapose the internal (bottom-up) and the external (top-down) connectivity networks as part of the same ecological system, as social ecology does.

In the future the world may come up with new approaches to such complex problematiques, perhaps if the promises of complexity theory start to deliver. We don't know, but in the meantime scenario planning appears to provide useful insights. In this book we have an opportunity to acquaint ourselves with the state of the art. But before diving in we must realize that scenario planning is not a finished field that has "all the answers." There is still a lot of work to do to fully understand why scenario planning does not always deliver.

How does scenario planning balance the multidimensional system consisting of "the system managed" and "the management system" that socio-ecology has failed to tackle? The answer is simple: it doesn't. Scenario planning does not try to map the entire contextual environment in one go. Instead it analyses a few (typically three or four) cuts through the future system which focuses on a few highly relevant and dominating issues of concern to the strategic planner. The decision of what constitutes such a key issue at the time of analysis is made on the basis of the intuitions of the stakeholders involved. Even though the scenario analysis does not cover all possible movements of the ecological system, generally the analysis will come up with one or more new insights based on mappings that have not been seen before, which may provide indications of new ways forward to create novel strategy on which coping behaviour can be based. And if these are not immediately forthcoming, as is common in this work, scenario planning provides for the possibility to add further iterations on the basis of a different cut through the system. The OSPA in fact provides for the possibility to add more iterations until participants feel that reasonable balance has been achieved between the scenarios and the ecological system issues in need of being addressed.

Scenario planning has proven helpful by taking a few alternative snapshot cuts through the ecological system of interest. However, in turbulence the validity of the outcome of any one iteration of the scenario planning cycle quickly shrinks over time. As a consequence most successful scenario planners now look at the activity as an ongoing set of iterations, rather than a one-off episodic activity. The OSPA is particularly suited for this as it is essentially conceived as an iterative learning process that may, but does not have to, come to an end.

A scenario planning approach starts with developing an understanding of the problematic situation. Understanding means having an articulated mental model of the way the main variables in the situation hang together, whether quantitative or qualitative.

Scenario planning then is in the first place a process of knowledge acquisition around the problematic situation. It involves exploration and learning in an iterative process. We call this the "strategic conversation" in which planners share insights and learn from each other, and learn jointly from the external world. Each iteration involves them in cutting through the group's understanding in a number of ways that provide new perspectives on the situation. At an appropriate point in time the group considers whether they are still making progress in developing understanding of the situation. If this is no longer the case the group launches a new iteration bringing in new variables that need more priority. The iterative process is the key to making the complex contemporary models manageable.

As long as scenario planning hangs on to the iterative learning imperative of the scenario planning process there is no upper limit to the size and complexity of the problematic situation that can be tackled. In this respect the scenario approach to planning offers the possibility to explore issues that have until now been inaccessible due to the size and complexity of the big global issues staring us in the face.

I welcome the idea of putting this complex material together in one place, as an attempt to gain an overview of where we are and where we are heading. I welcome this book as a statement of the current state of the art that allows us to take stock and then take it from there.

Kees van der Heijden

Heemstede, Holland
July 9, 2015

■ PREFACE

This book is for those who are interested in scenario planning.

While the experience of increasing change is not a new phenomenon, there is today a common perception of a quickening pace of more disruptive, large-scale changes that make the world less stable than "normal." There is thus a demand for approaches in strategic management that better prepare organizations for sudden shifts and rapidly emerging possibilities. Scenario planning, which emerged over sixty years ago, is one such approach which has remained a persistent feature of the strategic management toolkit. This book explores why this has happened, analyzes how scenario planning helps strategists, leaders, and decision makers, and provides guidelines for making it more effective.

The phrase "scenario" has become commonplace in today's world. It is used widely in the media and everyday life, but what it means varies considerably. People use the term "scenario" to describe all kinds of situations in the worlds of sport, war, business, economics, international relations, climate change science, movie making, and so on. This contributes to confusion and misunderstanding about the practice of *scenario planning*. A challenge we seek to address is to sort out an intellectually coherent and practical definition that can be shared across different communities of practice.

Scenario planning has become widely practiced, in no small part, because the world is more interconnected; connectivity has become the key driver of value and vulnerability. Many individuals and institutions feel they currently face, or will in future encounter, radically new challenges as they try to pursue their goals and interests (commercial or otherwise), in competition or collaboration with others. These challenges present as problematic situations or unprecedented opportunities that often cut across national borders, scales of intervention, sectors, departments, functions, professions, and policy domains; they cannot be easily understood from a single or disciplinary perspective. As we see in this book, new and better options can, however, be developed using scenario planning.

Many different approaches to scenario planning have emerged in the last few decades, and interest in scenario planning has increased following the unprecedented events of 9/11 and the 2008 financial crisis. This book introduces the distinctive approach to scenario planning that we the authors have developed together with Kees van der Heijden in the University of Oxford over the last dozen years: the Oxford Scenario Planning Approach (OSPA). Scenario planning, as we explain in this book, contributes to strategic management through an iterative process of framing, reframing, and reperception.

This usually represents an important shift in mindset, whose effectiveness lies not in terms of old to new, or wrong to right, but from closed to more open and more flexible. This is the central value proposition of our approach.

The OSPA is distinctive in several ways. We consider scenario planning as intervention: a set of social and intellectual processes that are designed for someone, or a group of people, and their specific needs. We position the role of the strategist as primarily a learner: effective and shared learning is enabled by directing attention to unexpected and less familiar changes in their wider context and with this, becoming able to challenge taken-for-granted assumptions. We use social ecology theory to explain and guide the effectiveness of scenario planning under what we call TUNA conditions—conditions of turbulence, uncertainty, novelty, and ambiguity—that characterize a more connected, plural, and multipolar world. This book explains these concepts and articulates the methodological and practical implications in an accessible and rigorous manner.

The OSPA is also centrally focused on learning *with* rather than *from* scenario planning. This stance involves attending to the learner's "sense of future." This is achieved in scenario planning by redirecting attention from self to context, and by mobilizing open systems thinking and model building in groups, to access and share tacit knowledge and to generate more than one future context so that assumptions about the future can be surfaced, tested, contested, questioned, and improved.

We maintain the stance that the future is a useful fiction and explain how scenarios as multiple images of future contexts are central to *framing and reframing* the present situation of the learner. Indeed, according to the OED, fiction is "the action of fashioning or imitating; an arbitrary invention; that which is fashioned or framed." While the OED allows that fiction can also be "feigning, counterfeiting; deceit, dissimulation, pretence," it signals that "[t]he action of 'feigning' or inventing imaginary incidents, existences, states of things, etc., (can be done) whether for the purpose of deception or otherwise." Most importantly for this book, the OED defines fiction as "that which, or something that, is imaginatively invented; feigned existence, event, or state of things; invention as opposed to fact."

We explain how scenario planning helps strategists and policymakers to better understand the frame that is being used—often automatically or implicitly—to make sense of observations and experiences; and how it opens up the possibility to *reframe* their situation by considering alternative frames. The framing and reframing process, in turn, helps the scenario learners to *reperceive* how their world works, the situation they are in, and the options that are available—and indeed, to generate new options—for action.

This approach to exploring, navigating, and creating new and different future possibilities is intended not just as an episodic intervention—that is, a one-off strategy cycle of reframing, reperception, new sensemaking, and decision taking—but as a fundamental part of an organization's culture and a foundation of its strategic capabilities to adapt in a more connected and rapidly shifting world. The quality of "strategic conversation" is a critical success factor in what we identify as the reframing-reperception learning loop at the center of this scenario planning process.

The journey of learning that led to this book

Each of us, the three people who co-developed the OSPA, has long experience and deep engagement with scenario planning—in corporate, public sector, interorganizational, and multi-stakeholder settings of the practice; in consulting with clients in those sectors; in teaching very experienced and often very demanding strategists and scenario planners; and in academic writings. Together, we offer over a century of scenario planning expertise, in which we have experienced the roles of initiating, commissioning, directing, contributing to, communicating, and reviewing several hundred scenario planning projects—or as we prefer to think of them, scenario planning-based interventions.

Each one of us can trace a different route to our interest in scenario planning, as well as a common experience of scenario planning with Royal Dutch Shell. Ramírez and van der Heijden first worked together in 1986; Wilkinson and van der Heijden in 1999; Ramírez and Wilkinson in 2000, first in Shell and then in Oxford. We have continued to collaborate on a regular basis and have worked together in various roles relative to each other, including commissioning client, consultant, colleague, teacher, co-researcher, co-author, and apprentice. This book shares what we have learned from our individual and shared experiences of success and failure in scenario planning. It aims to provide insights that are relevant to both novice scenario planners and those seeking to confirm their experience and gain greater mastery in working with scenarios.

All three co-developers of the OSPA have been intimately involved in the design, development, and delivery of the Oxford Futures Forum (OFF) and of the Oxford Scenarios Programme (OSP). The OSP is, at the time of writing in 2015, a week-long educational opportunity that started in 2004 as a much shorter introductory course, and is now offered twice per year at Oxford's Saïd Business School. The OFF is an invitation-only event that we (with other colleagues) have so far convened four times, where scenario planning practitioners and scholars confront their understanding of scenario planning with scholars and practitioners from another field. OFFs have related scenario planning to Causal Textures Theory and its analysis of turbulent environments in 2005; engaged with concepts of ambiguity and equivocality in sensemaking scholarship and practice in 2008; explored causality and emergence with complexity experts in 2011; and exchanged perspectives and experiences with design experts in 2014. We, along with those that have attended one or more of the OFFs, have learned much about scenario planning from these always stimulating events.

Part of our purpose in writing this book has been to systematize and consolidate our own learnings about the substance and pedagogy of the OSP and to make it more widely available. Thus, the OSPA that we present in this book has been tested and refined in the OSP. It is also the result of numerous joint presentations, publications, workshops, seminars, and engagements we have enjoyed (and sometimes struggled with) doing together. That the three of us also all worked at some point in the Shell scenarios team, in different roles, has provided a common experience with Shell's well-known scenario practices and philosophy, and that has enabled us to compare what we have learned in many other settings.

This extensive and intensive collaboration and sharing among ourselves, we have learned, does not mean we have always agreed with each other. Constructive disagreement has been a rich source of our learning, enabling us to notice errors and avoid repeating mistakes. Nor do we consider ourselves to be evangelists for scenario planning. None of us believes scenario planning can do everything for everyone, or that it "must" be carried out in all settings. We remain keen to clarify the conceptual conundrums and contingencies of the practice, lest this approach take on the hubris of "best practice," or worse, a faddish practice used indiscriminately. Yet at the same time, we have experienced the "might of might" whereby scenario planning interventions enable people to see their situation anew and, in doing so, discover new possibilities and more options for action. It is our hope that this book contributes to the continued coevolution of scenario planning with other fields, methodologies, and practices, and helps others experience and benefit from the opportunities it enables for strategic and policy learning.

The future is always in the here and now. Scenario planning enables us all to realize the new opportunities of learning with futures in order to recreate our future.

Rafael Ramírez
Angela Wilkinson

Oxford and Paris
July 2015

ACKNOWLEDGMENTS

Both authors contributed equally to writing this book, and the ideas we present are the product of our longstanding collaboration with our dear friend and colleague, Kees van der Heijden. Throughout the book "we" is used sometimes to refer to the two authors (e.g. "we direct the reader's attention to Figure 2.1") and sometimes to the three developers of the OSPA (e.g. "from experience we have found that about two thirds of an intervention's time should be devoted to client issues"). We kindly ask the reader to keep these two senses of "we" in mind.

Many other people have contributed to our learning over decades—too many to list by name. We direct our thanks to those who have contributed to our Oxford-based activities.

In terms of the scenario planning case studies in the Appendices, we would like to thank Shirin Elahi for co-authoring the UEG and EPO cases, and Esther Eidinow for co-authoring the Risk-World case. For reviewing and commenting on cases we thank: Prof. Michael Farthing for reviewing and commenting on the UEG case and Mr. Ciaran McGinley for doing the same on the EPO and Risk-World cases. We also want to thank Andrea Hernandez, Pauliina Tennilä, Rakesh Sarin, Jaakko Eskola, Mikael Makinen, and Christoph Vitzthum for reviewing and commenting on the Wärtsilä case study. Thanks to Jeremy Bentham and Cho Khong for reviewing and commenting on the Shell case and to Assaad Saab for doing the same on the Risk-World case.

We are very happy to extend our thanks to all the OSP and the Coaching and Consulting for Change Programme alumni/ae, and to the OFF participants for the learning we have been able to do with them. We particularly wish to thank the colleagues who have co-designed and co-hosted the OFF events with us: Yasser Bhatti, Kees van der Heijden, Lucy Kimbell, Roland Kupers, Diana Mangalagiu, Felix Reed-Tsochas, Cynthia Selin, John Selsky, and Kathleen Sutcliffe.

There is an army of "behind-the-scenes" staff who have contributed to the successes of the OSP and the OFF—colleagues who cater, clean and prepare rooms, provide administrative support, maintain the grounds, etc., and provide the enabling work environment which supports our research, education, and learning. We are very thankful to them.

We want to thank many colleagues in Templeton College (and thereafter Green-Templeton College), and in the Saïd Business School, the Smith School, and the James Martin School, for having supported our work in Oxford. Particular thanks go to Sue Dopson, Michael Earl, David Feeny, Gay Haskins, Elizabeth Howard, Janine Nahapiet, Jerry Ravetz, Steve Rayner, Keith Ruddle,

Marc Thompson, Peter Tufano, David Watson, Andrew White, Caroline Williams, and Marshall Young.

The librarians in Templeton College, Green-Templeton College, and the Saïd Business School have been ever helpful with the futures library collections: Debra Farrell, Chris Flegg, and Christopher Jones; and of course Napier Collyns and the late Jaap Leemhuis must be acknowledged for having donated the Pierre Wack Library, and Angela Wilkinson for having obtained the Boucher Futures Research Library. These resources attract visiting scholars and executives to Oxford.

Many graduate students and more experienced researchers have acted as teaching and research assistants to the OSP over the years: our lead teaching assistants—Andromachi Athanasopoulou, Yasser Bhatti, Malobi Mukherjee, and Trudi Lang—deserve special mention. More recent iterations have had Cho Khong and Cynthia Selin act as OSP faculty, contributing to our learning. Thanks also to the dedicated program administrators who have made things work as planned: Christina Lisgo, Elaine Pullin, Claire Stephens, and Rose Talbot.

Over the years, the OSP has benefitted from organizations whose leaders have lent themselves and their conundrums as live case studies to support the learning of OSP participants. Thanks are due to executives in: Atkins; BMW; the Basingstoke and North Hampshire Foundation Trust of the NHS; the British Psychoanalytical Society; CESPA; Chatham House; the City of Helsinki; Discovery; Global Footprint Network; the Koestler Trust; the Legal Services Board; the McConnell Foundation; Meggitt; Music World; the National Breast Cancer Coalition; Novozymes; Orange; the Organisation Internationale pour la Francophonie; Oxfam; Oxford Analytica; the Oxford NHS Trust; Royal Mail; Selex Galileo; SIG Canada; SRG-SSR Swiss Broadcasting Corporation; Titan; Unipart Automotive; and the University of Southampton.

We would like to acknowledge the contributions of the OSP reviewers, whose critical collegiality has also contributed to our learning. External reviewers of the OSP include: Robin Bourgeois, Prof. Ted Fuller, Susan Lansig, Jaap Leemhuis, Steve Morgan, Dr. Michael Oborne, Satish Pradhan, Alun Rhydderch, Dr. Teresa Ribeiro, Fiona Schwab, Kristel van der Elst, and Prof. Wei-Ning Xiang. We are also grateful to Oxford University colleagues who have acted as internal reviewers: Prof. Sonia Antoraz Contera, Prof. William James, Prof. Javier Lezaun, Prof. Ted Malloch, Prof. Paul Montgomery, Dr. Pythagoras Petratos, Prof. Mari Sako, Prof. Hiram Samel, Prof. Martin Seeleib-Kaiser, Prof. Victor Seidel, and Prof. Sonia Trigueros.

We are also most indebted to Dr. John Selsky, who for this project acted as our editor. John managed to weave our varied prose into coherent and insightful text and also kept us focused on our aim of contributing new and clarifying ideas. The production of this book benefited from funding from the Saïd Foundation and the Smith School for Enterprise and Environment. We are most thankful to David Musson and Clare Kennedy at Oxford University Press for their caring and frank guidance and help in getting this volume published.

We hope this book continues to extend the considerable interest in scenario planning scholarship and practice in Oxford and beyond.

We fully acknowledge that any errors in references to wider literature are our responsibility alone.

■ CONTENTS

■ LIST OF FIGURES

■ LIST OF TABLES

■ LIST OF BOXES

■ LIST OF ABBREVIATIONS

AiA	AIDS in Africa (case study Appendix D)
EDF	Electricité de France
EPO	European Patent Office (case study Appendix E)
G20	Group of 20 (an informal group of 20 leading national economies)
HSE	UK Health and Safety Executive
ICT	information and communication technology
IP	intellectual property
JPO	Japan Patent Office
NGO	non-governmental organization
OECD	Organisation for Economic Co-operation and Development
OFF	Oxford Futures Forum
OSP	Oxford Scenarios Programme
OSPA	Oxford Scenario Planning Approach
R&D	research and development
TUNA	Turbulence, Uncertainty, Novelty, and Ambiguity
UEG	United European Gastroenterology (case study Appendix C)
UN	United Nations
UNAIDS	Joint United Nations Programme on HIV/AIDS
USPTO	US Patent and Trademark Office

1 Introduction

Scenario planning—The Oxford Approach

Introduction

Scenario planning is a methodology that uses the inherent human capacity for imagining futures to better understand the present situation and to identify possibilities for new strategy. It is applied mainly in institutional planning contexts, such as businesses, government agencies, and intergovernmental bodies, as well as in not-for-profit and community contexts. In this chapter we describe the distinctive features of the Oxford Scenario Planning Approach (OSPA) methodology and its focus on supporting and informing new approaches to strategy and policy in contexts that exhibit turbulence, uncertainty, novelty, and ambiguity (TUNA—these terms will be explained in detail).

INTERVENING EFFECTIVELY IN AN UNPREDICTABLE WORLD

Since emerging in the 1950s/1960s, the persistence of scenario planning as a methodology is quite remarkable in a field of practice—strategy—notable for transient fads and fashions. In recent years there has been a growing *scholarly* interest in scenario planning as evidenced by the extraordinary rate of growth in related peer reviewed papers in English alone. It seems plausible that the growth is part of a search for new ways of surviving and thriving in a more globally interconnected world, with the potential for new and bigger surprises for entire communities, companies, and countries. These include various crises in public trust and national security, such as the 9/11 events and subsequent developments. Another example is the 2008 global financial crisis and its aftermath, which include impacts well beyond the financial system such as a Grexit situation and unprecedented high levels of youth unemployment. There is growing appreciation that more disruptions are waiting in the wings—a global migration crisis, a food-water-energy resource stress nexus, climate change, and asymmetric impacts of new technologies such as winner-takes-all outcomes of the digital economy. The list is endless but the diagnosis is common: we now all live in an era of connected challenges, and connectivity is the key driver of value and vulnerability.

For some people with responsibility for strategy or public policy, the wider environment is increasingly perceived as fast shifting and less predictable.

Traditional planning approaches seem inadequate. Uncertainty is unsettling and creates anxiety for the expert. For others with strategic responsibilities, the challenge is how to engage with fast moving and novel situations characterized by ambiguity. Relying on trend analysis and projection is not enough to guarantee future success in these conditions. For example, when looking at the implications of a combination of current trends—zero-marginal-cost businesses, the rise of the peer-to-peer economy, the automation of more and increasingly higher-skilled jobs—some suggest that we are entering a new era of self-generated work. The implications of this for the social contract between citizens and their governments is difficult to comprehend; what might this hold for income tax revenues, for markets, for pensions, for public institutions?

Any of the four TUNA elements can trigger a search for methodologies that enable new and better strategies. Many individuals and institutions feel they currently face, or will in the near future confront, disruptive changes as they pursue their goals and interests (commercial or otherwise) in competition or collaboration with others. While the experience of sudden, disruptive change is not a particularly new phenomenon, there are a number of reasons why the current era is, or seems to be, triggering a strongly felt need to develop new strategies not only to cope but also to do well in TUNA conditions. We argue in this book that the Oxford Approach to scenario planning is a promising and useful methodology for strategists and policymakers dealing with these conditions.

BALANCING COMPETITIVE AND COLLABORATIVE TENDENCIES FOR MORE EFFECTIVE FUTURE PREPAREDNESS

More broadly, research on turbulent environments has for decades suggested that the focus of attention for strategic managers shifts from tactics through to engaging a wider and more complex set of stakeholders in strategizing as turbulence becomes more salient. Social scientists Fred Emery and Eric Trist, in their 1965 paper, proposed that in "turbulent fields" (TUNA conditions) strategy requires collaboration and realignment of values.

Established collaborations can also, however, become misaligned with the complexity in the wider field they are meant to engage with strategically. World War II institutions such as Bretton Woods and the UN no longer appear capable of enabling sustainable value creation in an era of high-tech entrepreneurial capitalism, climate change externalities, or complex global issues such as tax avoidance. Many new technologies appear to be supporting the social need to collaborate—with virtual community, the proliferation of open-source systems, frugal and social innovation, and shared and circular economies. As Harvard's Martin Nowak (2006) declared in an overview of the evolution of cooperation, "Perhaps the most remarkable aspect of evolution is its ability to generate cooperation in a competitive world. Thus, we might add 'natural cooperation' as a third fundamental principle of evolution beside mutation and natural selection." Clearly we are in an era where the "rules of the game" not only need to be rewritten but are being rewritten from the bottom up, rather than through top-down reforms.

The proliferation of multi-stakeholder scenario planning by cross-sectoral social partners (such as those found in the Appendices for AIDS in Africa (AiA), the futures of risk, or the futures of gastroenterology) is one manifestation of the need to strategize anew in TUNA conditions. Many such initiatives operate as temporary institutions that seek to enable and sustain collaboration to transform field-level issues, practices, and relationships.

The OSPA offers strategists and policymakers the means to use scenario planning to find options that balance the competitive and collaborative tendencies that are now needed to survive and thrive in a world beset with TUNA conditions.

A SHIFT FROM PREDICTION TO REFRAMING

We suggest policymakers and strategists in TUNA conditions might be well advised to adopt a phenomenological approach to strategy development, which we contrast with the more traditional "predict and control" approaches (Selsky et al. 2007; Ramírez and Selsky 2015). A phenomenological approach to strategy is grounded in the lived experience of strategists, and gives higher priority to individual *and* organizational *learning* (Michael 1973; de Geus 1997) than to control or positioning. It is based on a creative and disciplined process of discovery, interactive immersion,[1] and invention. In many institutional settings the resulting strategy-as-learning process can clash with the dominant mode of time-bounded, project-based activities, so extra care needs to be dedicated to making the approach acceptable.

The essence of the Oxford Approach to this strategic learning process, we believe, lies in an ability to reperceive self-interest and options, and others' interests and options and experiences—all enabled through a process of reframing.

In the 1950s, economist Herbert Simon, a Nobel laureate, highlighted a form of limited reason that he characterized as "bounded rationality" and argued it applied across all professional fields. More recently, Donald Schön and Martin Rein (1995) highlighted another form of limited reason that they believe applies across all professional fields, as soon as one moves beyond mere analysis of facts to make professional recommendations. They call it "design rationality."

While Simon's notion of "bounded rationality" explains realistic cognitive constraints within which professionals act, Schön's notion of "design rationality"

> **BOX 1.1** FROM BOUNDED RATIONALITY TO FRAME REFLECTION
>
> In their 1995 book, Schön and Rein reviewed the theory base underlying the three most common means of dealing with intractable policy problems: (1) "rational" policy analysis, (2) power politics, and (3) mediated negotiation.
>
> The dominant tradition of policy choice is based on the rational actor model; it treats disputes as instrumental problems that can be solved through the application of a value-neutral policy science. The political perspective is a pluralist model in which policymaking is seen as a political game of multiple rational actors, each with his own interests, freedoms, and powers. Consensual dispute resolution through joint gains is the theme of mediated negotiation.
>
> A large and important class of policy disputes has proven resistant to these three main traditions. The authors proposed a fourth way of making sense of intractable policy controversies; it focuses on getting at the underlying structures of belief, perception, and appreciation, which they called "frames." The idea is that once actors in the dispute can get a better understanding of their underlying assumptions and frames, they can begin to shift their often tacit and untested ways of seeing the world and the issue. This fourth approach can lead to a better understanding of the arguments each side is making, and to a more reasoned approach regarding what "data" are relevant to the situation. They characterize this fourth approach as "design rationality."

also concerns limits but emphasizes the possibilities for developing exemplary practice, such as scenario planning (see Box 1.1).

THE REFRAMING-REPERCEPTION CYCLE IS AT THE HEART OF THE OSPA

Reframing helps people to become mindful of the frame they have been using to make sense of and intervene in the world, as well as what is left out of this frame. As we will explain, reframing occurs in the process of scenario planning when alternative scenarios describing future contextual environments are contrasted to reveal, test, and redefine the official future (given frame), to generate plausible alternatives, and in effect generate new shared knowledge and insights. By rehearsing actions with these alternative frames, new and better options for action can be identified and contribute to a reperception of the present situation. Thus, in the OSPA one learns about the present with views regarding the future—not about the future from the perspective of the present. Moreover, in the OSPA this learning is not just performed during an episodic intervention. Instead, scenario planning is a sustainable, iterative way of taking seriously the TUNA conditions in today's world—scenario planning is an interactive process. So in the OSPA strategists using a scenario planning intervention are considered *learners*. These learners seek to reframe strategy and reperceive options for action.

Although this learning process applies to individuals as much as to groups, scenario planning learning can be enriched when done in a social setting. This requires strategists to design, manage, and be articulate in the "strategic conversations" that matter (van der Heijden 2005).

In this book we explain how scenario planning enables this process of reframing and reperception to support distinctive approaches to strategy. We first reflect on some general misunderstandings about scenario planning and then describe the seven premises that underpin the OSPA. These premises structure the characteristics of the methodology.

NAVIGATING THE RICH HISTORY OF PRACTICE AND CHALLENGING THE POVERTY OF SHARED WISDOM

Surveys conducted by the US strategy consulting firm Bain and Co. show that a high level of satisfaction with the use of scenario planning combines with fluctuating rates of use, with periodic spikes in interest.[2] Influential players in the world of business and policy, such as the Secretary-General of the OECD, consider that scenario planning "is needed more than ever."[3] However, data on scenario planning use can be misleading, as the term "scenario planning" can be used to mean very different things in different organizations, thus making overall assessments of use or effectiveness practically impossible.

The sheer volume of publications on scenario planning makes it difficult for an experienced hand, let alone a novice, to navigate the relevant literature. The growing body of work—dealing with great differences in approach, criteria for effectiveness, techniques, and methods—appears to be increasingly fragmented, and is located within different scholarly fields and professional communities. In addition, there are no barriers to entry; everyone seems to be able to "do" scenario planning, and no professional qualifications are required. As a consequence many people don't know how to do it well. While evidence of allegedly effective engagements is becoming commonplace, so too are examples of much more questionable work with the label "scenario planning" attached to it. As in many other hybrid fields of practice-cum-scholarship, not every published paper on scenario planning claiming "good" or even "best" practice is of high quality, replicable, testable, usable, or even interesting.

As a consequence, a variety of methodological approaches have become established over the last sixty years. As we noted in the Preface, one such approach—the OSPA—has been developed by the authors of this book in collaboration with Kees van der Heijden during the last twelve years at the University of Oxford, in what is now Green-Templeton College, the Saïd Business School, and the Smith School of Enterprise and the Environment, with roots in the corporate scenario planning practices in Royal Dutch Shell. The results of this activity are evidenced in the semi-annual week-long Oxford

Scenarios Programme which has graduated over 500 executives, the tri-annual Oxford Futures Forum, in other programs and events delivered in Oxford, and in numerous publications and presentations.

Introducing the OSPA: seven key premises

The central purpose of this book is to lay out what has become known as the OSPA. It is our aim to make this approach available to a wider set of readers than those able to attend scenario planning and related programs offered at the Saïd Business School at Oxford. This book offers the benefits of more than one hundred years of combined reflective practice and expertise among the developers of the OSPA. It explains from our particular point of view why, how, and when scenario planning is helpful. The intention is to help scenario users (what we will call *scenario planning learners*), strategic planners, and scholars to develop good practice and to navigate common traps, hazards, and pitfalls that can turn good practice into bad—using "cats eyes" (see Box 1.2).

In this chapter we first outline key premises that underlie the OSPA. These are not characteristics or features of the OSPA, but foundational ideas that underpin the practice of scenario planning. Next, we outline the central social and cognitive features of the OSPA, features that distinguish it from other scenario planning approaches (see Box 1.3). Key premises and central features are the subjects of the next two sections.

Premise #1—Many organizations are facing unprecedented TUNA conditions.

People have always had the feeling that "change in our times" seems faster and more profound than in the past. So how seriously can one take contemporary

---

BOX 1.2 CATS EYES

In this book we distill a number of principles, articulate a number of concepts, and proffer a number of ideas that we consider guides to good practice in scenario planning. We think of these principles, concepts, and ideas as having the same role as "cats eyes"—beads of glass that are placed in steel-reinforced casings sunk into the asphalt along the painted lines of rich-country main roads, which reflect the headlights of cars at night. These bright spots of reflected illumination help guide the drivers and prevent them from going off the road. In a similar sense, the principles, concepts, and ideas found in this book are meant to help guide good work and prevent reflective practitioners from inadvertently leaving the road of good scenario planning practice to end up in the ditches of disappointments and dashed hopes, or become stuck in the muddy fields of what Bruno Latour (2010) called "methodological fetishism."

BOX 1.3 SEVEN KEY PREMISES THAT UNDERPIN THE OSPA

---

1. Many organizations are facing unprecedented TUNA conditions.
2. TUNA conditions require new approaches to strategic and policy planning that seek to balance competitive and collaborative opportunities.
3. An explicit and flexible sense of future is called for in TUNA conditions. It can be enabled by contrasting plausible, alternative future contexts through an iterative process of reframing and reperception.
4. The "aha" moment of impact is only realized once the reframing-reperception cycle has been completed. This can require several iterations.
5. A culture of learning supported by scenario planning can avoid the extremes of groupthink and fragmentation, which are pathologies preventing learning in organizational settings.
6. Reframing strategy is a distinctive capability that enables learners to identify new opportunities and more and better options.
7. Scenario planning can help develop new social capital to renew the license to operate.

---

claims of "more turbulence," typically expressed as an accelerating pace of change driven by more connections and technology,[4] and increasing disruptive and sudden surprises?[5]

There are plenty of time-series data indicating greater price volatility, or depicting the asymptotic potential of continued trends in resource consumption. But there are no widely agreed objective measures of turbulence (or of uncertainty, novelty, or ambiguity in a given strategic situation)—either experienced or perceived as potential—that can be used to benchmark the present with prior years, decades, or centuries; assessments often boil down to subjective and intuitive assertions. Relying on the supposed ubiquity of TUNA as a justification for scenario planning requires us to consider other ways to substantiate the claim.

First, support comes from studying the reasons given for the increased use of scenario planning that are cited within the literature and told to us by participants of the Oxford Scenarios Programme. These variously suggest reasons of accelerating change, increasing complexity, and unpredictable uncertainty as a strong impetus to replace earlier "predict and control" approaches to corporate strategy and risk management. These reasons are quite similar to the arguments for scenario planning made several decades ago by Pierre Wack, a highly influential corporate practitioner of this methodology (see Wack 1985a, 1985b). We refer to several of Wack's key ideas throughout this book.

Many attempts have been made to explain turbulence as a sense of faster paced, disruptive reality using causal lines of reasoning. Climate change is an example of this. The level of atmospheric carbon dioxide now exceeds that ever encountered in all of recorded human history. "Climate change" now looms large in our collective imagination, but (or because) its impacts and the timing of those impacts remain uncertain.[6] Other causal lines of reasoning concern possible tipping points leading to irreversible consequences associated with population aging, inequality, and the consumption of natural resources exceeding planetary limits. Neo-Malthusians offer compelling stories of water wars, famine, and energy blackouts. It is not unreasonable to consider these changes to be unprecedented, and to consider as novel how they manifest in the context of what companies and institutions are doing, trying to do, failing to do, or not doing.

For public sector organizations in particular, an important aspect of today's significant challenges and contemporary worries lies in the mismatch of fast moving, connected events and issues and the slow pace of institutional responses to adapt to the changing circumstances, and even to reinvent themselves. Given this mismatch between faster feedback loops and the slow pace of institutional innovation,[7] the anticipation of increasing TUNA disruptions does not seem outrageous.

Yet it is also essential for effective strategy to maintain a realistic sense of the hope for new and better possibilities in the future, and to seek to develop the new and unprecedented possibilities that new collaborations promise for realizing many of these. In the OSPA, we reject the concept of the future as all good or all bad and instead think of it as latent potential.

The Belgian Nobel Prize winning chemist Ilya Prigogine examined the origins of change in the reactions he studied. He concluded that all systems that are sufficiently complex can develop unpredictable emergent behavior. This includes *social* systems. The origins of this conclusion lie in positive feedback loops embedded in the system, producing boom and bust behavior that is difficult if not impossible to predict. From this he surmised that denser systems (for example, increasing population density and communication links) will produce more turbulence, that is, more complex interactions that produce virtually unpredictable emergent states and patterns of behavior. This has worrying implications for corporate strategists and public sector policymakers (see Selsky et al. 2007). Our colleague Mary Bernard (2008) introduced these ideas in the scenario planning field.

What do we mean by turbulence?

As we mentioned earlier in this chapter, the late social scientists Fred Emery and Eric Trist (1965) studied the options that organizations could consider in conditions of what they labeled "turbulent field environments." They were very specific in their definition of the "causal texture" of the environment an organization and its leaders might find themselves in. They noted that when a high rate of change combines with high complexity to produce high uncertainty for people inhabiting that environment, the resulting texture of turbulence would be unsettling. Turbulence[8] involves either the experience of actual change—or the expectation of it—so significant that it could fundamentally transform one's situation in ways that could overwhelm one's capacity to adapt (see McCann and Selsky 2012; Ramírez and Selsky 2015).

We extend their ideas on turbulence and associated uncertainty to also emphasize dimensions of novelty and ambiguity which help scenario planning to grapple with complexity (Wilkinson et al. 2013).

Our research is based on scenario planning as it relates both to single organizations (typically corporations such as Wärtsilä and Shell in the Appendices) and public, often multi-stakeholder situations (such as the AiA, Risk-World, European Patent Office (EPO), and UEG cases in the Appendices). In TUNA conditions even the single organizations benefit from extending their strategizing interactively (Normann and Ramírez 1993) to engage key stakeholders, as we show in this book, often helped by scenario planning. The OSPA is useful in both situations.

Premise #2—TUNA conditions require new approaches to strategic and policy planning that seek to balance competitive and collaborative opportunities.

Our experience of conventional strategic and policy planning processes is that, paradoxically, they focus attention on what happened in the past. In TUNA conditions we argue that success might require different ways of coping than those that were successful in non-TUNA settings. And we show that scenario planning is a good way to achieve this reallocation of attention so that the future in the present is given more priority, thereby helping strategists to avoid what would otherwise remain missed opportunities.

Premise #3—An explicit and flexible sense of future is called for in TUNA conditions. It can be enabled by contrasting plausible, alternative future contexts through an iterative process of reframing and reperception.

The sense of future is an aspect of our present—manifested perhaps as hopes and fears, as expected opportunities, and as plans. We call it a "sense" because emotion plays an important part in how the future is sensed in the present. As we explain, this sense of future can be enabled by contrasting plausible, alternative future contexts of a specific situation of a specific person or group of actors through a cyclical process of reframing and reperception repeated over multiple iterations.

In TUNA conditions, the motivation for scenario planning is not to find "the right answer" to "the" (already posed) "problem" that confronts the strategist. Instead, attention is redirected to reconsidering assumptions and to asking better questions through a process of discovery, interactive and immersive learning, and invention. This has several implications. First, this process enabled by scenario planning provides new conceptual frames to appreciate and interpret changes in the wider context that are relevant to a situation of concern facing a group of scenario learners. As is shown in Figure 1.1, with

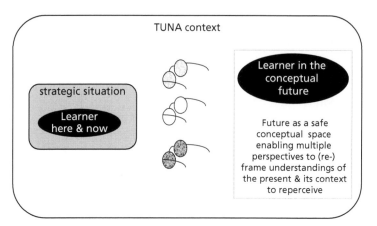

Figure 1.1. The "there and then" and "here and now" in scenario planning

scenario planning the learners temporarily consider the here and now from an imagined set of perspectives in the "there and then" of the future.

Second, this process enables the learners to develop their *capacity* for framing and reframing their situation in ways elaborated through the application of Premise #4.

Reframing is enabled by articulating plausible, often emerging stories, and supports the learners to *reperceive* their world and to bring forth new options for action. For this reason, as we explain in Chapters 2 and 3 respectively, scenario planning involves both social and cognitive processes. Scenario planning can be an episodic activity, like a one-off intervention or a project with a due date, but its reframing-reperceiving backbone implies that it is more effective if done iteratively.

> *Premise #4—The "aha" moment of impact is only realized once the reframing-reperception cycle has been completed. This can require several iterations.*

In conceptualizing any situation one has already "framed" it: something is in the frame and other things are left out. This happens whether one is attending to this explicitly or not. Reframing occurs more easily among people in conversation than individually (van der Heijden 2005). Reframing occurs through strategic conversations that explore new territory, and that accommodate disagreement and render it a productive asset. Scenario planning supports these with a combination of rigorous open systems thinking and imaginative storytelling. These help to co-create a set of plausible and contrastable future contexts that can, in turn, be used in a process of immersive learning to rehearse actions and stimulate reperception of the present situation. Reperception happens when people experience what the future frame feels like and what options it opens up (or closes down).

According to van der Heijden (2005), a strategic conversation sweeps in both attention to the context as well as to the business idea at play in a strategic situation. Scenario planning invites multiple framings of a situation into a strategic conversation. Each frame enables more and different options to be designed and tested and in turn helps strategists to develop a unique strategy.

Premise #5—A culture of learning supported by scenario planning can avoid the extremes of groupthink and fragmentation, which are pathologies preventing learning in organizational settings.

Scenario planning can sustain individual and organizational learning by redirecting attention to changes in the context and how these are framed, by whom, and for what purpose. This redirecting of attention helps to avoid the positive feedback loops that build up in groups and become the pathologies of groupthink and fragmentation that can hamper collective learning.

This recasts the role of the CEO, policymaker, and strategist using scenario planning processes as chief learning officers, rather than plan makers or commanders of predictable actions. The scenario planning process both embodies and supports the collective learning taking place in the process. This is not a trivial matter—De Geus (1997) underlined the competitive importance of securing a superior corporate learning capability. In company or government settings, for example, scenario planning helps to genuinely involve people with a wide range of relevant (or potentially relevant) knowledge, including planners, operational managers, functional and specialist experts, non-executive directors, trade union representatives, thinkers, and doers. External stakeholders can also be included, such as suppliers, distributors, and customers.

In scenario planning this learning is thus enabled through a combination of knowledge exchange (tacit becomes explicit) and new knowledge generation. Both redirect the learners' attention to examine the broader setting (the "contextual" environment) in which the more immediate business environment (the "transactional" environment) and the learner are situated. This is depicted graphically in Figure 1.2.

The new learning manifests how the transactional environment might be reshaped from a combination of the impact of the contextual factors. Possible disruptions of the established rules of the game that characterize the competitive-collaborative interactions can then be mapped.

Similar links between scenario thinking and strategic planning and action were first articulated by our colleague Richard Normann (2001). Figure 1.3 is an extended version of Normann's view of scenario-enabled strategic planning. The situation (where the strategist is located) is unfolding along the

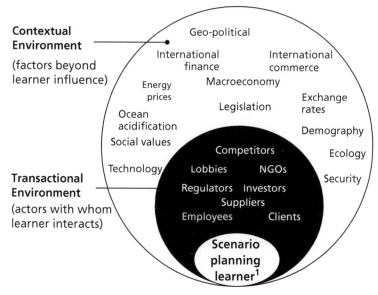

Figure 1.2. The contextual and transactional environments

[1] In this figure the central scenario planning learner is assumed to be top management. If it is a division head, then other division management teams, and HQs, would be in the transactional environment; if it is a government ministry (e.g. natural resources), then other ministries (finance, etc.) would be in the transactional environment.

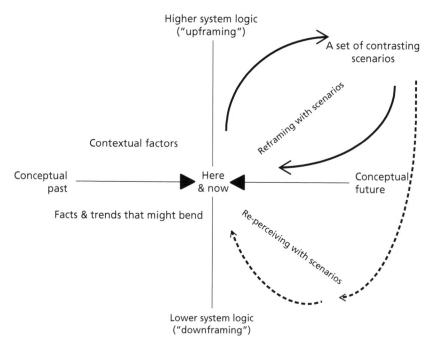

Figure 1.3. Reframing and reperceiving in scenario planning
Adapted from Normann 2001, p. 225

horizontal time axis. Knowledge and experience relevant to dealing with the situation are flowing into the present (here and now) from the past. As Kees van der Heijden puts it in the Foreword of this book, in the "predict and control" mode of planning which originated in more stable times, trends from the past were extrapolated and the forecasted future provided a more or less reliable point of reference to guide new decisions.

Scenario planning adds a different space which is orthogonal to the time line in the figure. It is a breadth dimension reflected in the vertical "upframing," which takes in the "bigger picture" and creates new "space." To access this new space, the strategists must broaden their perspective and look at the wider context of their immediate situation, *at the same time as* moving along the time dimension, that is, they must consider the future context(s). (Note also that in this new space the future is coming *toward* the here and now, as expectations, imaginations, and feelings such as hopes and fears, as indicated in Figure 1.3.) Normann considered that this upframed knowledge about the contextual environment operates at a higher-logic order and that it affords insights into connections among factors that are otherwise not envisioned by the strategists. *Downframing* then allows the scenario planners to immerse themselves in that possible future context to feel and work through existing and new courses of action, and to do so in detail with those who must work with the implications. With downframing, scenario learners rehearse the actions and reactions stakeholders might engage in under each plausible future context. These immersive experiences enable them to reperceive their situation, reassess the strategic options, and provide a new space for enabling design and experience of new and better options. This reframing-reperception cycle and how it supports learning in scenario planning processes are illustrated in Figure 1.4.

> *Premise #6—Reframing strategy is a distinctive capability that enables learners to identify new opportunities and more and better options.*

An explicit and more flexible sense of future can enable a shift from a reactive to a pre-active stance which supports strategic innovation. That is, more options can be considered, as well as how they might unfold. This can increase organizational adaptive capacities (having thought through an alternative plan makes it easier to shift if required). Teams and organizations can become better at engaging with unexpected, less familiar, and uncomfortable future developments, and by learning with futures can identify new opportunities and options to transform and create their future.

This is a distinctive capability for several reasons. Earlier we saw that the reframing-reperception cycles: enable the generation of new and shared knowledge; support tolerance for divergent thinking; and act to contain two "pathologies" that inhibit learning for people working in groups, namely, fragmentation and groupthink.

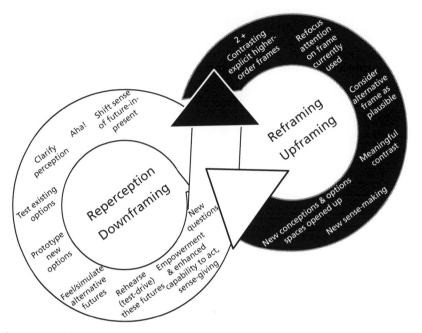

Figure 1.4. The interconnections between reframing and reperception

The effective learning among diverse participants is a key aspect of the scenario planning process. However, the process is about more than just knowledge sharing. It also involves rehearsing the new actions and the inter-actions that arise in each future context—i.e. in the newly created frames—and to do this through a process of immersive experiences which can deepen the understanding and implications about changing relationships and therefore new roles. These insights on new relations and new roles become unique strategic options in themselves.

Premise #7—Scenario planning can help develop new social capital to renew the license to operate.

By "license to operate," we mean the roles and functions that society tacitly allows any organization to play, not any formal legal agreement. The tacit license to operate is more easily lost in TUNA conditions, and as such an organization's existing license to operate cannot be taken for granted but can be redesigned and renewed or regenerated. The strategic conversation does not (or should not—or indeed often cannot) stop at the perimeter of the organization; it can support wider engagement that reaches out to encompass myriad external co-producers and stakeholders. Co-producers (Normann and Ramírez 1993) are those that play an active role in decision making and action; stake-holders are those potentially or actually affected by those decisions and actions.

The diffusion of power and authority in a more connected, socially complex, and multipolar world contributes considerable ambiguity. Disagreements within strategic decision-making groups on both means and ends are inevitable, and demands for direct participation in strategic decision making by such a diverse set of actors will arise. Strategic framing contests can become polarized between opposing ideological positions, or in the face of the contradictory certitudes held by individuals with different discipline-centered expertise. An inability to take in disagreeing frames can lead to back-handed power plays, whistle-blowing, community conflicts, and the demoralization of staff—particularly if there is no attempt to generate new shared understandings and in a manner that avoids unintentional "colonization of the future" by the existing status quo of power which is embodied by the "official future" of any organization.

Distinctive features of the OSPA

Having outlined the premises underlying the OSPA we suggest the three most distinctive characteristics of the practice that differentiate it from other scenario schools are:

- The emphasis on focusing the scenario planning engagement on the learner-centric experience. This combines social and intellectual processes. Each scenario planning engagement is designed and manufactured for the individual learners or group of learners; for the specific circumstances they inhabit; and for the purposes they want scenario planning to serve.
- The centrality of the reframing-reperception cycle which can benefit from several iterations in order to deliver real impact.
- The need for a balance of competitive and collaborative strategic action for surviving and thriving in TUNA conditions.

A PURPOSEFUL PRACTICE AND LEARNER-CENTRIC SCENARIO PLANNING METHODOLOGY

Our emphasis on purpose in the OSPA—in treating scenario planning as a purposeful practice—is crucial; it directs attention to the usefulness of scenario planning as a means rather than an end. The end has to be ascertained in advance. Examples include: is the learning obtained through scenario planning meant to inform what skills need to be secured for the future? Or is it instead going to help the learners to assess how robust existing options are? Or to seek the development of new options? Or to revisit the major risks faced?

Or will scenario planning help to attract and keep interesting partners? This emphasis on purpose is based on pragmatic observations from our day-to-day practice in working with clients.[9]

Whether scenario planning is effective can ultimately be decided only by those whose role we call in this book the "scenario planning learner." We define the learner as the individual or coherent group of people who have the power to launch or discontinue a scenario planning intervention, and for whose learning the scenario planning is designed. These roles may be held by different people, but in the OSPA all are learners. We discuss the role of the learner in scenario planning extensively in Chapter 4.

In our experience, too many scenario planning interventions are launched with inadequate definition of purpose (indeed, all too often also without identifying the intended learners). Insufficient attention to this is a major reason for frequent disappointment. In the OSPA we advise facilitators of scenario planning processes to be particularly attentive to the specification of the learner, and to the need to develop a definition of the scenario planning intervention's purpose together with the learner in advance. The art involved here is to find the best possible balance between clear-cut purpose definitions on the one hand, and keeping the intervention sufficiently open for the learning process to take place.

Purpose is also essential inasmuch as the success or failure of the scenario planning process is defined in terms of how well it meets the purpose, and this depends on the learners' judgment. It follows that a key success factor is to produce a clear-cut description of the purpose of the intervention, and put it on the table in advance as much as possible (see further discussion of these matters in Chapter 4), and to revisit and—if necessary—to "recontract" accordingly. The avoidance of clarifying multi-purpose intervention designs, if this implies a "fudge" or lack of clarity of purpose, is a good way to fail with scenario planning.

Empirical and independent analysis on how much of reported scenario planning work meets these criteria is rare. There is so far little agreement and considerable confusion in the literature on "what works." Much of the published scenario planning accounts seems to focus on the importance of the so-called "focal" question which we discuss in Chapter 4 (and all too often a related 2 × 2 matrix) in a fairly mechanistic way, with little attention paid to the needs of the learners or how reframing will contribute to meeting their organizational goals. Many publications also assume that a set of scenarios are the "final product" of the scenario planning process, which are "delivered" to the "scenario users." Issues of reframing and enabling learner reperception are frequently overlooked. In the OSPA, however, a final report or scenario book is not the purpose, nor the only product or most important outcome, of the scenario planning process.

THE RELATIONS BETWEEN REFRAMING AND REPERCEPTION
AND THE ITERATIVE PROCESS

The OSPA considers that a scenario planning intervention can work best iteratively, as opposed to being a one-off project, in successive rounds of reframing and reperception as depicted in Figure 1.5. Van der Heijden's work on Indian agriculture (2008) is an example of first- and second-generation scenarios, articulating an iterative learning process over time. Shell International and the Singapore Government are also examples of organizations that practice scenario planning iteratively, as indeed Wärtsilä's shipping division has done (see Appendix A).

Thus scenario planning as we see it in the OSPA is ideally not a linear "project" with a beginning, middle, and end, nor (ideally) a one-off intervention, but is instead an iterative process that enables and sustains organizational learning.

Taking this a step further, in the OSPA we see the relations between reframing and reperception as co-evolutionary. That is, they feed off each other, and as they do new knowledge is produced and learning evolves among those participating in the activity. This helps to forge shared understanding of the present and, in turn, enables more and better strategic options to be considered. The elements that make up the co-evolving learning that the cycles of reframing and reperception support are illustrated in Figure 1.4, where we have listed some of the key features involved in each component.

The reframing process provides contrasting alternative future contexts to enable a constructive exchange of perspectives. This typically happens in

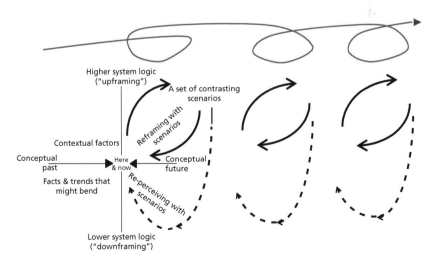

Figure 1.5. Iterative learning cycles of reframing and reperception

"strategic conversations" (van der Heijden 2005) which the scenario planners design and manage as places for disagreements to be aired safely, and made into an asset, as we explore in Chapters 2 and 3. This acceptance of difference and even disagreement supports the elicitation of tacit knowledge and the generation of new knowledge. It also helps to forge shared understanding of the present, and in turn enables more and better strategic options to be considered. Reperception results when a new course of action is identified.

THE LIMITS OF POSITIONAL STRATEGY: COLLABORATION FOR EVOLUTIONARY ADVANTAGE

As we will explain, evolutionary science is not predictive but does provide evidence that both competitive and collaborative strategies, as well as chance, have been key features of the co-evolution of living systems and their wider contexts. We will explain the value of scenario planning as a way to overcome this limitation by enabling strategists to consider new and better options, competitive and collaborative, by framing and reframing alternative future contexts to develop unique strategy. We build on the ideas of Emery and Trist, who also suggested that more collaboration among organizations sharing turbulent environments (whether in the same sector or across sectors) would help them to succeed under turbulent conditions.[10] This has more recently been supported by research indicating that in a turbulent environment, enhanced competition at the level of the firm can undermine the resilience of the entire field (see Selsky et al. 2007[11]).[12] This is consistent with Prigogine's view that to reduce turbulence it is advisable to reduce the number of relevant systemic interconnections.

We suggest that, over time, the institutional innovation produced from this field-level collaboration can either fail to reflect sufficient complexity (that is, lack requisite variety[13] of information on system functions and actors) and/or become inflexible. The result can be a form of new endogenous crisis which also cascades to other co-dependent fields. This is arguably what happened in the 2008 financial crisis, when regulatory oversight failed to keep up with field-level collaborations of the increasing number of intermediaries in the system. The resulting "toxic assets" undermined trust of the whole financial system, and knock-on impacts cascaded to the real economy and ripped through the fabric of many societies.

In the same way, our own research, teaching, and professional intervention experiences support the idea that scenario planning offers a way of thinking and acting strategically that is more suited to TUNA conditions than conventional "predict and control" strategic methods. This applies both to leaders of single organizations and to sets of them acting in concert, especially established regulatory agencies and international institutions, as well as through cross-sectoral scenario planning initiatives that comprise temporary institutions. We explain this in detail in Chapters 2 and 3.

Methodological choices in the OSPA

Having set out the foundational premises underlying the OSPA and its distinctive characteristics, the methodological choices scenario learners face in following the Oxford Approach are perhaps easier to appreciate and understand.

First and foremost, we are convinced there is *no single best or right method* or set of techniques or tools comprising "the" method in scenario planning. Instead, it is advisable to understand and navigate methodological choices in designing an intervention that effectively supports the purposes and capabilities of the specific scenario learner.

In addition, the impact in scenario planning comes from completing the reframing-reperception cycle at least once. While new knowledge is generated in the construction of the scenarios, the actionability of that knowledge is only realized in the uptake of new options that have emerged from the scenario planning process. Scenario planning is always part of a wider intervention—it is a means to an end. As such *scenarios are best thought of as services, not products*, in raising the quality of the strategic conversation, or inventing and testing new options and actions, etc.

The impact and return on investment of a scenario planning intervention cannot be determined from the measurement of "better" decision outcomes. In TUNA conditions it is impossible to attempt to calculate all decision options and predict their outcomes in advance. Instead, the *contribution of scenario planning learning processes needs to be assessed based on the explicit purposes of the intervention* (were these met? how well?). The contribution often also involves a broader set of criteria. These include its contribution to improving the quality of the pre-decision interpretive framework and judgment process, its effects on shifting the strategic vocabulary used or on clarifying strategic choices, the types of new questions brought forth, and the availability and prototyping of new options it has enabled.

We conclude this chapter by suggesting that it is incumbent on the scenario planning process facilitator (or "practitioner") to also act as a learner as well as an enabler of learning. In doing so, s/he becomes able to clarify for others the guiding principles of their practices, as well as to use these to inform methodological choices in designing more effective scenario-based interventions.

Organization of this book

This book discusses scenario planning in general, and develops an in-depth overview of what has become known as the OSPA. The subject is treated in seven chapters, as follows:

Chapter 1 describes the crux of this book: how scenario planning enables individuals and groups in organizations and multi-organizational bodies in TUNA conditions to enhance their understanding of a particular situation in which they find themselves, and to develop new strategies. We outlined seven key premises underlying the OSPA, as well as its three most distinctive features. The first is its emphasis on enabling specific users to learn with scenario planning. The second concerns the tight relations between reframing and reperception in the scenario planning process. The third is its explicit focus on supporting and informing more flexible and balanced (competitive and collaborative) strategies in TUNA conditions.

In Chapter 2, scenario planning is assessed as an inherently social process. We show how it acts to either interrupt the continuous, backgrounded sense (particularly one's sense of future) that underpins understanding of the present;[14] or acts to help people make new sense when they experience or expect interruptions in their context.[15] We explain that in the OSPA plausibility is co-produced by learners and supports their sensemaking. That is, when supported by scenario planning, co-produced plausibility involves social as well as conceptual iterations of reframing (sensemaking) and reperception (sense-giving). In Chapter 2 we also explore how scenario planning operates in situations where the future is one of the major playing fields where power is exercised.

Chapter 3 focuses on scenario planning as a designed and inherently cognitive process of inquiry. We explain how it helps people to mobilize existing knowledge and generate new knowledge by directing attention to the wider situation. It also helps people to develop ways to frame and reframe their understanding of what is happening now. This new co-produced and shared understanding, in turn, enables reperception in the form of new options for action to be identified and considered. We also outline three kinds of research that are pivotal for effective scenario planning work.

In Chapter 4 we focus on the purpose of the learner(s) as being pivotal in guiding the design of an intervention, and in choosing methods both for building reframing devices and for engaging different perspectives. We treat all those involved in and supported by scenario planning as "learners"—whether their role officially is that of client, user, strategist, policymaker, or facilitator. We explain that in the OSPA all are treated as co-learners, and that learning to reframe strategy is scenario planning's core role. We review several "matters of technique," including how to overcome attention and connection deficits in organizations undertaking scenario planning.

In Chapter 5, we explain the OSPA methodology in some detail. We propose heuristics and criteria that can act as "checklists" of factors to consider. These help scenario planners to select and deploy tools and techniques so they can work in harmony to contribute to the effectiveness of scenario planning in practice. We review eight aspects involved in designing a scenario planning intervention, beginning with defining purpose and use, and ending with evaluating the effort.

Chapter 6 provides insights for reflective practitioners about how scenario planning education can be designed to enable more effective practice. We focus on engaged scholarship, designing teaching/learning programs for individualized learning and for constructive feedback, and the role of errors and mistakes in learning scenario planning. We discuss the divides between practice and scholarship, and between scenario planning and other futures methods, and the potential role of scenario planning in bridging these divides.

In Chapter 7, we revisit the earlier chapters to recap the seven key premises and the differentiating characteristics of the OSPA. We then summarize its key ontological, epistemological, and methodological features. We highlight several issues that we see as unresolved in the field of scenario planning. We also propose two directions for further research in this field, namely, assessing the value of reframing and attention to case studies of failures.

In the Appendices we offer six illustrative case studies spanning corporate, public sector, and multi-stakeholder settings for scenario planning interventions. These six cases are referred to throughout the book. We also provide a Glossary to clarify some of the terms we use to explain the OSPA and its related concepts.

▦ NOTES

1. By "immersion" we mean that participants in a scenario planning process learn to experience the stories of the future that they create.
2. <http://www.bain.com/publications/articles/management-tools-scenario-and-contingency-planning.aspx> (accessed July 2015).
3. The Secretary General of the OECD noted that "scenario planning is needed more than ever" (quotation on book cover of Wilkinson and Kupers' 2014 book *The Essence of Scenarios: Learning from the Shell Experience*).
4. Such as Moore's Law.
5. See Peter Schwartz' *Inevitable Surprises* (2004); see also Selsky and McCann (2008).
6. Some impacts of climate change seem to be getting clearer. They include differential geographical effects, ocean surface acidification, more extreme weather patterns, and sea-level rises.
7. A term which threatens to be oxymoronic in the case of large bureaucracies.
8. Emery and Trist (1965) specified this more rigorously than the everyday use the term has taken on, such as in the media.

9. Recall that clients are treated as learners in the OSPA.
10. But not the collusive type of collaboration among companies engaged in the same business (e.g. price fixing among Internet service providers). Emery and Trist suggested that collaboration among functionally dissimilar organizations (e.g. companies, universities, NGOs, and public sector agencies all operating in the same region) would help to quell emerging turbulence. See also note 12.
11. Two segments of the US health care system were used in this study as an extended illustration of differential outcomes of contrasting perspectives of strategy making.
12. In Emery and Trist's approach, a "referent organization," such as a regulatory body operating in the public interest, would not only ensure a level playing field and safeguard against monopolistic behavior but also would balance this with the need to ensure the resilience of the whole sector by collaborating with relevant stakeholders to manage turbulence. In the case of the recent financial crisis, efforts by regulators to calm turbulence and prevent the collapse of the global financial service sector have been evident in innovative, macro-prudential risk management policies (such as quantitative easing), the separation of retail and investment activities in banking, and the increase in the level of capital stock held by banks. Building buffers and slowing down transactions are thus examples of collaborative strategies that can calm turbulence.
13. W. Ross Ashby's (1956) *Law of Requisite Variety* implies that the degree of control of a system is proportional to the amount of information available. This means one needs an appropriate amount of information to control any system, whatever it is. Scenario planning enables actors to co-create shared understanding of plausible alternative states of their wider system context and thus generate more knowledge of their wider system and overcome their limited perspective of their situation.
14. Which would otherwise remain implicit, untested, and unchallenged.
15. An example of the former type of interruption is the scenario planning of the EPO in Appendix E, which assessed how the growth of patenting might be interrupted. An example of the latter type of interruption is the AiA scenario planning work in Appendix D, which assessed various ways of making sense of how the AIDS pandemic might interrupt the flow of life on that continent and how that might unfold.

2 The OSPA as social process

Introduction

In this chapter we explain scenario planning as a social process, or more exactly, as set of social processes. It builds on the key notion we introduced in Chapter 1, that a sense of future shapes understanding, attention, and action, whether or not this sense of future is made explicit or operates on a tacit basis. Developing a more explicit and flexible sense of future is neither easy nor straightforward. Cognitive, behavioral, cultural, and institutional barriers need to be overcome. As management guru Peter Drucker has been widely attributed to have said:

The most common source of management mistakes is not the failure to find the right answers. It is the failure to ask the right questions. Nothing is more dangerous in business than the right answer to the wrong question.

In this chapter on scenario planning as a social process we explain, in effect, how people in efficiency-driven, consensus-seeking, problem-solving modern business organizations and public agencies can learn to ask better questions.

As noted in Chapter 1, uncertainty creates anxiety and ubiquitous information can be interpreted in many different ways, bringing forth ambiguity. Here we explain how this contributes to strategic framing contests and determines what "facts" and "data" are relevant to the "official future."

The logic of the OSPA as a social process, and a roadmap to this chapter, is represented in Figure 2.1. Thus, we begin by describing how social processes are triggered when a group of people encounter TUNA conditions. Their individual and collective sense of future influences their perceptions of their current situation, and, in turn, these affect the choices and options they consider.

Second, we explain how the scenario planning social process contributes a prospective reframing of a situation by opening up a safe space in the present, so that disagreements about what might happen in the future can be surfaced and explored; and how it helps to avoid some common pathologies in organizational learning. The safe spaces created in the scenario planning process afford and support enhanced strategic conversations that dissolve zero-sum strategic framing contests and enable institutional learning (van der Heijden 2005).

Third, we discuss how looking forward is a socially conditioned process, and especially so in organizational settings. Typically today an individual does not make strategic decisions alone but within groups of people—and affecting many people; and issues relating to which time horizons are used and social

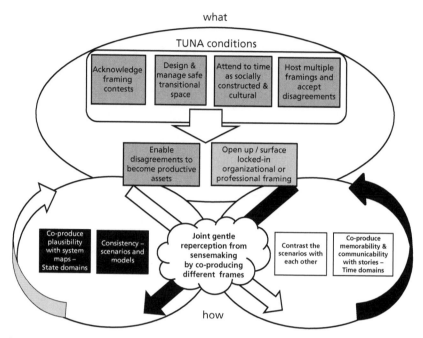

Figure 2.1. The OSPA as social process: reframing and reperception in TUNA conditions

aspects of time framing matter. We contrast the OSPA's "arrows of time" framework with the more conventional concept of using time horizon(s). We also highlight that in the OSPA a set of scenarios is both an output of the scenario planning process and—very importantly—also an input to other processes. Effective use involves linking scenario planning with those other social and organizational processes, and requires that the schedules of each be matched.

Fourth, we describe how the OSPA involves a social process of iterative and immersive learning. Framing and reframing are enabled by people working together in groups to co-create plausible, relevant, challenging, and memorable future contexts using methods of storytelling and open systems thinking. The resulting *co-production of plausibility* of alternative future contexts resets the sense of future in the present, enabling new signals of change to be noticed and to become accepted as legitimate.

Fifth, we describe how scenario planning yields wider social benefits that extend beyond the conventional focus on decision support tools. These include overcoming the "locked in" sense of future which has become engrained in organizational norms and routines,[1] and accelerating the development and uptake of a new and shared strategic vocabulary, which can enable people to engage in joint sensemaking and build new social capital. We also explore how a setting beset with TUNA conditions is also characterized by *social* complexity and diffuse power and influence. So in TUNA conditions, organizations can more easily lose their social "license to operate."

We conclude with reflections on some ethical challenges that can arise in scenario planning processes.

Strategic situations are always socially constructed

The challenges we are interested in exploring using scenario planning are those that arise in TUNA conditions, which are often puzzling and in some way "problematic" because they point to uncomfortable issues and questions. The motivation for using scenario planning to find new ways of dealing with these puzzling situations can vary. It might involve seeking an opportunity, improving a business that is doing well, or preparing a successful strategy for a new environment; or it might involve avoiding losses, reducing conflict, dealing with power grabs, etc.

Persistent problems or emerging issues are often discussed as threats to established organizations, whether in the private, public, or civic spheres; or they might entail new business opportunities. These threats and opportunities are always talked into existence, that is, they are socially constructed.

The "talk" involves references to the past as well as fears and hopes regarding the future. It comprises a mix of facts (that is, the "hard" data), anecdotes (story snippets), and values (normative judgments)—all interpreted with the help of some lens, such as a scientific theory or ideology. Those situations constructed as "problems" may come with an already available and widely acceptable "solution"; those taken to be "problematic situations," "wicked or intractable problems," "problematiques," "messes," or "orphan issues" do not correspond to available problem-solving approaches. They typically imply uncertainty and not manageable and quantifiable risks; they can trigger dispute about the nature of the causes and may bring forth conflict when solutions are applied, rendering the future a "playing field of power" (van Asselt et al. 2010). Indeed, the future may be empty of facts, but it is full of opinions, expectations, and emotions that lead to contradictory certitudes (Chapman and Thompson 1995, 26) and present as ambiguity.

In all cases, the scenario planning intervention revisits the sense of future that underpins the official future—that is, the existing strategy and vision of the organization—and invites alternative sensemaking.

Within organizations the individuals involved in making decisions do so with and for groups of people (Vennix 1996). Team-based decision making involves sensemaking processes whereby people tell each other stories to make sense of what is going on (Weick 1979). While even in organizations

---

BOX 2.1 PEOPLE DON'T LEARN FROM CRISES

The very act of calling an event or situation a "crisis" is an exercise of power that closes down an expected future (Wilkinson and Ramírez 2010). Organization theorist Bill Starbuck, who has extensively studied how people learn (or don't) in crises (2009), noted that the emotional aspects in cognition make it difficult for people to learn from events considered "one-off exceptions" or "rare." As he put it, "reactions to the uncertainty (of and in rare events) include wishful thinking, substituting prior beliefs for analysis, biasing probability distributions towards certainties, searching for more data, acting cautiously, and playing to audiences." (But sometimes people learn *in* crises; see Box 3.4 on the Cuban missile crisis of 1962.)

The OSPA suggests that scenario planning can be used to support better shared sensemaking. In crisis situations this shared sense often does not have the time to arise. Because scenario planning allows disagreeing views, it can reveal, compare, and test alternative framings that can help to prevent premature foreclosure on the crisis problem definition, and to instead promote learning as inquiry and reflection.

---

sensemaking is undertaken by individuals, it is inherently and inevitably "social and systemic" (Weick et al. 2005, 412): people make sense together, not alone.

Ongoing sensemaking processes are often tacit and implicit, and are rarely questioned until an interruption occurs—the shock of a scandal, an accident, a failure, or an externally induced crisis. Unexpected events force a "brutal audit" of sensemaking (Weick and Sutcliffe 2007). Yet not every crisis presents an opportunity for effective learning, as we see in Box 2.1. Moreover, we argue that dealing with the novelty of something we imagine might happen prior to it erupting as a "crisis"-type interruption, and doing so with the help of scenario planning, is a more effective way of preparing for the sudden and disruptive changes that occur under TUNA conditions. Clearly, we are not advocating scenario planning as a way to better predict a specific crisis, but rather as a way to bolster an organization's capability and culture for being more prepared for strategic surprises.

And as we learned in Chapter 1, organizations co-evolve with their context and can only be understood through the interaction of the many different parts. As there is still no such thing as a predictive, scientific theory of this evolution, knowledge of possible future situations cannot be derived solely from direct observations. Knowledge regarding the future in TUNA conditions is often "uncomfortable" knowledge (Coulson 1985).[2] Weick (2006) suggested that uncomfortable knowledge can be related to an inability to act, thus affecting what one allows oneself to see and talk about. This difficulty has also been canvassed in the scenarios literature. For example, Hodgkinson and Wright (2002, 955) argued that scenario practices may cause "dysfunctional stress levels" among decision makers if the dangers of the future are perceived as being too difficult to address. Thus, effective scenario planning helps people as learners to question some, but not all, of their assumptions

(Ramírez et al. 2015). This is not easy for them to do. As Chris Argyris (1991) observed, many highly trained professionals prefer to remain focused on what they know and/or can influence. That is, they like to continue working in what for them have become comfortable forms of knowledge about their situation and wider context. They would rather not engage with irreducible uncertainty and its implications for loss of control, which Weick suggested involved a highly uncomfortable "letting go" of one's professional role.

"GENTLE" REPERCEPTION AS SENSEMAKING HELPED BY CONTRASTED FUTURE CONTEXTS

For some people, in some settings, the insidious turbulence, uncertainty, novelty, and/or ambiguity roiling in business landscapes can be experienced as making strategic decisions in a *permanent* crisis (Heifetz et al. 2009) rather than one-off extraordinary events after which "normalcy" can be expected. The approach to scenario planning we have developed in Oxford offers a more effective means to triggering and accelerating sensemaking—through dialogue, strategic conversation, and reframing—compared with the brutal reperception that is otherwise inevitable when facing or following a crisis.

Pierre Wack (1985a) suggested that scenario planning enables "*gentle* reperception"—a means of engaging with the inner "microcosm" or mental model of the decision maker by bringing in alternative "macrocosm" external possibilities to the mind. Although he never developed a theory of reperception, others have suggested it is triggered when the uncertainty in the organization's environment "stops being predictable" in the minds of the managers (Ramírez et al. 2008b, 22). A perceived lack of predictability leads to anxiety and confusion about how to act (Weick refers to an acute version of this as a crisis of identity), but with the help of scenario planning this can in turn trigger a search for new ways of coping.

Scenario planning interventions are one way that people in organizations can initiate a process of explicit and purposeful sensemaking. This process is prospective, in that it invites explicit consideration and contrast of alternative future possibilities to frame and reframe a situation that would otherwise continue making people increasingly anxious and less able to cope. It is also retrospective, because the sensemaking is made from imagined future frames that link "retrospectively" back into the present. Sensemaking occurs from rehearsing actions in alternative future contexts. By contrasting the implications of plausible alternative futures with their present situation people engage in *backcasting*—from imagined possible futures to appreciate the implications for action options today.[3]

This particular means to support sensemaking can help to evolve the organization (Weick et al. 2005).[4] Having an alternative coping mechanism such as scenario planning enables people in TUNA conditions to become more willing to address their (growing) inabilities to act on their problems (Westrum 1994, 340). In turn they are more open to revisit and to review their mission, identity, and core capabilities with the help of alternative future framings. For example, Charles Perrow's (1984) analysis of the 1979 Three Mile Island nuclear plant accident shows how easy it is for those confronting a crisis to believe mistakenly that what is unfolding has been planned for.[5] This refers to what behavioral economists call "anchoring," that is, the human habit of relying on the familiar (and thus on the past) to judge something, thus attaching one's interpretation of new signals to past, proven events and accompanying frameworks (see Tversky and Kahnemann 1986). It is difficult to let go of anchors, and to recognize that what one is facing is entirely unprecedented; but this difficulty can be reduced by having imagined versions of these new events beforehand with the help of scenario planning.

As we saw earlier, when referring to the possibility of conflict erupting, learning in crises can also be impaired if the situation deteriorates into a "strategic framing contest" in which opposing factions propose what in their view is the (only) "correct" view regarding what is going on, and deride any alternative on the "other side" as "unrealistic" or wrong. Framing contests can reflect overt or hidden power dynamics, and often raise questions about judgment and authority, such as who decides, when decisions should be made, what to think about the future and on what basis? Examples of framing contests are offered later in this chapter.

In the next four subsections we take each of the TUNA characteristics described in Chapter 1 and explicate their social-process aspects.

TURBULENCE AND UNPREDICTABLE UNCERTAINTY

As we explained in Chapter 1, turbulent contexts can be seen in sudden and game-changing transformations that overwhelm the relations between an organization and the parties with whom it regularly transacts business. Turbulence in complexity theory terms would be seen as an emergent property of a field (see Selsky et al. 2007; Bernard 2008). A "field" in Emery and Trist's view is an environment shared by many different organizational actors; for example, the financial services field is a field shared by the many types of financial field companies, hedge funds, private equity firms, banks, finance ministries, and regulators involved in the North Atlantic financial crisis that started in 2007–8. Emery and Trist believed that strategic situations in a turbulent environment could not be addressed using conventional competitive strategic moves—those focused on zero-sum competition. In fact, they suggested that such moves would exacerbate the emergence of turbulent environments. They suggested instead the benefits of formulating joint adaptive strategies in turbulent conditions. Ramírez and van der Heijden (2007) investigated how such collaborative strategies could help those involved to come together and create a "larger actor" that in turn could decrease the uncertainty of the contextual turbulence for all involved. A classic example of such a strategy is the formation of the VISA card payment system by banks, telecom companies, retailers, device makers, and consumer groups (see Ramírez and Wallin 2000). This is quite a common practice: in business ecosystems many firms are simultaneously competitors in relation to each other in one arena, but partners with each other in other arenas (Normann and Ramírez 1993).

The OSPA reflects Emery and Trist's Causal Textures Theory in practice (see also Emery and Trist 1965; Ramírez et al. 2008a; Ramírez and Selsky 2015). A basic premise of Causal Textures Theory is that both individual and collective perceptions are crucial in assessing whether a context is turbulent, notably manifested by a growing sense that one's capacity to cope is becoming diminished (Selsky et al. 2007). In the OSPA this "perceptual differentiation" is inbuilt, inasmuch as scenario planning interventions help people to compare how their own perceptions (and their respective framings) differ, and in comparing these differences jointly assess what would be considered as their shared environment by an "external" viewer.[6]

The OSPA encourages and supports scenario learners to engage with uncertainty by having them attend to and model the possible linkages among factors in their contextual environment. We explore how this is done in Chapter 4. The social process in the OSPA involves people sharing knowledge and perspectives about these linkages in a way that does not simply stick with the comfortable facts, perhaps manifesting as today's trends or simply confirming the "official future" narrative. Moreover, it helps them to surface tacit and less comfortable knowledge and listen for alternative stories that are emerging. These stories describe other plausible future contexts that reflect how linkages in the environment *might* unfold. By opening up a safe space for sharing different stories and contrasting these to clarify meaningful differences, new knowledge about the current situation is co-generated. See Chapter 3 for further explanations of the OSPA as a knowledge generation process.

In this respect, scenario planning helps strategists engage with turbulent contexts by helping the scenario learners to attend to the factors in their contexts that they consider relevant and yet beyond their direct control and influence. This brings the unpredictable uncertainty in the world "out there" closer to the learners' mental models of how the world should or ought to work. With the scenarios, strategic actions are analyzed and rehearsed, as well as experientially played out, through simulations (or "war games") in the transactional environment. This social inquiry process supports better quality strategic framing contests. This renders them constructive as individuals gain a better understanding of other perspectives, and this encourages respect for different perspectives and points of view. We return to these disagreements later in this chapter.

Situations of turbulent change characterized by unpredictable uncertainty can also involve disruptions that are unique and novel, rather than simply being faster/slower, or higher/lower, extensions of changes which have happened in the past. We turn to such novel situations next.

NOVELTY AND UNIQUENESS

It can be difficult to describe what is imaginable but not yet experienced to someone else. Similarly, when facing situations that are unprecedented in the totality of human history, such as living in a world facing higher average temperatures due to human-induced climate change, communication and action is difficult for policymakers. Emery and Trist suggested that the development of a new shared vocabulary and new units of analysis would help strategy in such novel situations.

For example, the convergence of new computer-enhanced technologies—including nanotechnology, artificial intelligence, biochemistry, robotics, programming, and communication—heralds for some a new era of self-generated work, "local capitalism," and "circular economy" that may become very different in scale, speed, and nature from both the recent era of global financial capitalism and earlier industrial-scale job creation. The UEG scenario planning intervention in Appendix C explores what these new future developments might imply for the professions involved with gastrointestinal medicine; for example, if scientists develop the capacity to re-engineer the genetic building blocks of food and nutrition, what might that mean for a healthy diet? For others, such developments are the makings of a Frankenstein world.

Similarly, in the Risk-World scenario planning intervention (Appendix F), experts in the field of risk grappled with a new vocabulary, looking at terms such as "global," "emerging," and "systemic" risk and what they mean for different professional communities of risk management, such as the technical, financial, social, and environmental. What these emerging concepts mean also depends on who asked which questions and for what purposes. The focus on the scenario learners and their purposes (in this case, to reconsider the assumptions on which "risks" might matter for the executives in the four sponsoring organizations) is a distinctive characteristic of the OSPA, as we explained in Chapter 1 and will return to in Chapter 4.

Almost by definition, unique and novel situations cannot be described effectively without the invention of new concepts and terminology. For example, ten years ago no one had heard of Twitter and now even presidents tweet. Concepts such as "peer-to-peer" business models and the "shared economy" are no longer unimaginable but reality, as is evident in the rapid growth of businesses such as Uber and Airbnb. Similarly, strategic concerns about "sustainable development" and "inclusive growth" would be impossible to express, never mind address, without the invention of new measurement frameworks, images, and vocabulary.

In 2015 there are five times as many words in the English language as there were when William Shakespeare authored his plays and sonnets in sixteenth-century England. Language and vocabulary provide the means by which humans relate the external world of experiences (observations) to their inner world of thought (concepts).[7] Thus, it is hard to imagine how one might explain an airplane to someone living in those times, without them assuming sorcery or magic were involved. Indeed, Henry Ford purportedly commented that if he had asked people what they wanted they would have said "faster horses," but what he imagined and realized with the mass production of the automobile resulted in a new culture of consumerism. This is a good example of a concept that never existed before but is now commonly understood. That novel concept in turn has generated its own evidence base, facts, and measurable trends such as consumer price indices.

The history of human development has always involved the development of new concepts and the language with which to articulate them; in the OSPA shared meaning about novel situations is developed through the use of imaginable (but not yet predictable) future contexts that often involve new terms.

AMBIGUITY

Ambiguity arises when there are different interpretations of the same event or phenomenon. In the OSPA, the aim is not immediately to resolve ambiguity to facilitate problem solving. Instead, the scenario planning process is designed to understand why ambiguity arises and how it can help reveal the different interpretive frames that are enabled, suppressed, or dismissed in the strategic framing contests which have become common in power-laden organizations.

For example, in the AiA scenario planning intervention (Appendix D), forging a shared strategic vocabulary was pivotal in enabling effective engagement and communication among a very complex set of scenario learners. They comprised a diversity of experts and stakeholders within and beyond Africa, and spanned domains of medical research, public health, development, security, and economy. For example, in some African cultures there is no equivalent word for the medical term "virus." Moreover, each policy community worked only within its own specialized language. As a social process, the UNAIDS-led scenario planning initiative consciously sought to avoid having the strategic vocabulary of any one community dominate others so as to hear all the participating stakeholders, help them to forge new common ground, and enable more collaborative action.

BOX 2.2 SOURCES OF AMBIGUITY IN STRATEGIC DECISION MAKING

- Ambiguity of purpose—in what terms can action be justified? What are the goals of the organization? This can challenge established forms of strategic practice (Ramírez and Selsky 2015) and decision making.
- Ambiguity of power—can challenge established forms of social order and control.
- Ambiguity of experience—raises questions such as how people make inferences about their experience and how they can challenge learning and adaptation patterns.
- Ambiguity of success—raises questions of how it is established and when and by whom, inviting motivation and pleasure to be questioned.

(March et al. 1976)

Strategic decision situations in TUNA conditions, such as the AiA case, relate to what Rittel and Webber (1973) called "wicked problems." They coined the term to describe situations in public planning characterized by ambiguity—they have an ambiguous definition, ambiguous stakeholders, and ambiguous criteria for judging success. West Churchman characterized wicked problems as:

a class of social system problems, which are ill-formulated, where the information is confusing, where there are many clients and decision makers with conflicting values, and where the ramifications in the whole system are thoroughly confusing. The adjective "wicked" is supposed to describe the mischievous and even evil quality of these problems, where proposed "solutions" often turn out to be worse than the symptoms. (Churchman 1967, 141)

Ambiguity is manifested by the apparently irreconcilable differences in framings. The relevance of ambiguity to the OSPA as a social process is made evident by the different sources of ambiguity that arise in strategic decision making and planning (see Box 2.2).

Assessing the plausible futures of a context with the help of scenario planning can effectively engage ambiguity and help people to reveal their deeply held worldviews. Such views reflect less visible, often taken-for-granted myths that underpin any organized body of expertise, such as academic disciplines or professional practices.

EXAMPLES OF TUNA-INDUCED STRATEGIC FRAMING CONTESTS

TUNA-induced strategic framing contests and how these were transformed by scenario planning interventions are illustrated in each of the six real-world case studies that are referred to throughout this book and detailed in the Appendices.

In the Wärtsilä energy and shipping scenario planning (Appendix A) there were differences within the leadership team on whether incumbent fossil-based energy systems would prevail or whether a global energy transition to a low carbon economy was accelerating. These contrasting perspectives might have resulted in a strategic framing contest. The scenarios articulated the implications of each existing frame, and enabled the co-generation of a new third frame that avoided the "either-or" nature of the uncertainties implied by the other two perspectives.

The Shell Global Scenarios 2001 case study (Appendix B) looks at the development of Shell's scenario planning since it first started using scenarios in the 1970s to grapple with a new source of uncertainty, namely, political risk. Since then, the increasing number of actors and factors shaping the company's context has contributed to greater complexity in interactions and to unpredictable uncertainty globally as well as in regional and localized markets. This set of 2001 scenarios described plausible future developments from the perspective of two different worldviews, each held by constituencies across the corporation at the time. The two scenario frames reflected different assumptions about the pattern of globalization that might emerge (avoiding a polarization between more/less, yes/no) depending on which sets of interests came to the fore: those conveyed by the globally interconnected elites, or the cultural and identity values manifested in national preferences in different parts of the world.

The UEG professional association scenario planning case study (Appendix C) examines the way in which the viability of the post-World War II social welfare funding model was being challenged by technological advances, demography, financial limits, and societal expectations. That model underpins the delivery of medical care in many European countries. These changes combined to create a more turbulent context for the gastrointestinal professions and related medical specialties. Experts disagreed about what these changes meant for the relevant professions (that is, ambiguity), how they might influence each other (unpredictable uncertainty), and whether the identity of the professions in the future would remain unchanged (turbulence).

AiA (Appendix D) was a multi-stakeholder scenario planning intervention initiated in a cross-sectoral partnership. Different communities of expertise— for example, medical professionals and economic development professionals— did not agree with each other about the effective priorities needed to prevent the spread of the AIDS epidemic across Africa, nor about whether an AIDS-free generation was possible within the next twenty years. Cultural and linguistic diversity contributed to ambiguity about the meaning of the HIV/AIDS situation in Africa. There were also unpredictable uncertainties concerning the evolution of the virus itself due to the complexity of vectors of transmission and, for example, the roles of poverty, transportation, security, and cultural taboos in addressing some of these issues. The scenario planning process helped different professionals and stakeholders jointly to explore ambiguities on what the different groups involved might consider priorities— as well as what would be acceptable compromises and what might become unviable positions to change, up to the year 2030.

In the EPO intergovernmental scenario planning case study (Appendix E) we see how TUNA conditions for the EPO came from a convergence of new forces around the turn of the millennium. These included new societal demands (e.g. access to medicines, transparency of information), new trans- disciplinary technologies (e.g. genetic engineering), new social-movement politics, the rise of the "knowledge economy," and disruptive business models. There was ambiguity regarding what these new forces meant and how they might come to relate to each other, potentially threatening the very legitimacy of conventional intellectual property. The environment in which the EPO operated was rendered highly unpredictable. As an example, a strategic fram- ing contest erupted between the anti-intellectual property (IP) position of Greenpeace and the IP-centric view on the future of Europe manifested in the Lisbon Agenda. The intervention's social processes allowed for these positions to be jointly assessed: the "Green" scenario articulated the plausible context in which a Greenpeace expectation might logically emerge, and the "Gray" scenario critically examined what might arise if a context that fitted the expectations of the Lisbon Agenda were to unfold.

The Risk-World interorganizational scenario planning initiative (Appendix F) followed a recent series of very public risk-related crises and scandals (e.g. the UK "mad cow" crisis of the 1990s). There were concerns about the ambiguity brought forth by novel technologies such as nanotechnology, and unpredict- able uncertainties relating to wider societal, national security, and economic impacts of the ICT (information and communication technology) revolution and social media. The co-creation of scenarios relevant to the different inter- ests of the four organizations involved (two private sector, two public sector) enabled tacit knowledge on the governance of new risks to be shared and made explicit. This new shared understanding was reflected in the development of the scenario storylines and contributed to the learners in the four organiza- tions framing and reframing their understandings of the plausible landscapes and trajectories of specific risks facing each organization.

CREATING AND SUSTAINING A "SAFE SPACE" TO AVOID SOCIAL LEARNING DYSFUNCTIONS

In essence, the social processes in scenario planning interventions create a "safe space" in which more and different perspectives can be revealed, and alternative frames compared, to generate new and shared understanding to test and develop options for action. This safe space is the key to:

- Surfacing and sharing new (tacit and often uncomfortable) knowledge about the current situation.
- Revealing and clarifying the dominant strategic frame (that is, the "official future") underlying the existing action plan, and enabling this to be safely tested and constructively challenged.
- Creating or enhancing strategic conversations where contrasting framings can be compared in a way that enables new and different options to be considered.
- Hosting a set of alternative strategic frames that enable leaders to ask better questions about what is happening now.
- Supporting individuals to recalibrate their respective mental frames.
- Reconsidering whether the assumptions relating to context and core capabilities that underpin the existing "social license to operate" are still and will remain valid. For example, the way Shell uses its Global Scenarios as "door openers" to build better relations with wider stakeholders and retain its license to operate in different countries or regions; or the engagement by the EPO of academics as well as policymakers; or the way that Wärtsilä developed its scenario planning process to better relate to its customers' customers.

So how does this safe space operate? It does so by preventing two types of dysfunction.

Janis and Mann (1977) identified errors made by groups when making decisions collectively, which of course affects strategy.[8] They coined the term *groupthink* to describe the tendency of some groups to try to minimize conflict in the rush to reach consensus. When this occurs, there are cycles of insufficient testing, analyzing, and evaluating of alternative ideas, so the group ends up converging on a single solution which, when it sets in, can no longer be questioned. Shy of reaching the lock-in of actual groupthink, social pressures for conformity tend to restrict the breadth of options any decision-making group will think of, sometimes leading the group to conclusions that no single member wants.[9] Groupthink processes promote superficial, simplistic, and stereotyped views and stifle creative and independent thought.

The opposite, equally nefarious group process is *fragmentation*, where every individual gets to see only their own view and refuses to even acknowledge that other alternatives are just that—viable alternatives.

Groupthink and fragmentation are important sources of judgment biases in group decision making. Our colleague Paul Schoemaker (1993) suggested in a highly cited article that scenario planning can help groups to address such judgment biases. Consistent with this, our research and experience suggests that scenario planning interventions and the reframing they manifest can be carried out so as to help individuals working in groups to avoid groupthink and fragmentation in their strategy work. To achieve this, the scenario planning process has to be designed to create a safe space for disagreements to be managed productively as assets.

Ramírez and Drevon (2005) explored how scenario planning creates "transitional spaces," which is what psychologists call these safe learning spaces. They did so using Winnicott's pioneering research on how young children use teddy bears as "transitional objects." That idea helped researchers in the Tavistock Institute of London to build "transitional spaces" from their earlier experiences during World War II with "therapeutic communities" (for example, to help battle-weary soldiers resettle into war-torn British civilian life) (Bridger 1990). More recently, social psychologists have developed the notion of "transitional dynamics" (see Amado and Ambrose 2001) to design and hold spaces for learning that are safe, as we do in our scenario planning interventions and as was explored in the 2014 Oxford Futures Forum.

Time matters

Given the prospect that in TUNA conditions the future can become a playing field of power, looking forward can of itself become an act of power. Whose timeframe will be used and challenged in a scenario planning engagement? Who decides when the future begins, or how far to look ahead?

In the OSPA we pay attention to the social constructions of time, where time is not a physical given (as in the development of a butterfly's life cycle) but a set of conventions and arrangements that govern social life. In the OSPA we deliberately unsettle how forward time framing is determined (and can become locked in) by organizational routines, social norms, or professional training. To enhance the impact of scenario planning, in the OSPA we open up important considerations about time that are often taken for granted in conventional strategic planning approaches.

SOCIAL CONSTRUCTIONS OF TIME

In our executive education programs, we ask participants these questions:

- Do you think there is one future or many?
- Do you think the future is in this room or not yet in it?
- How are the past, present, and future related in your organization?

We then ask participants to draw three circles—one for the past, one for the present, and one for the future. The resulting diagrams never fail to create an "aha" moment by revealing the very different ways organizations order and weight "past," "present," and "future."

The answers to these questions also reveal choices people may not have realized they were making. These choices, in turn, reflect assumptions about the way the world works—assumptions deeply held and often below the level of conscious thought (see Normann 2001 for more on this).

Many people have never really questioned the social conventions about time that govern their lives. In modern societies, the march of time is measured by the clock and that time must be "saved" or "cut" ("being faster to market," or as the consultancy BCG put it several years ago, "competing against time"). Just think of the compression of transaction time in quantum shares trading.

The concept of time varies across cultures. In some it is linear, where tomorrow follows from today and today from yesterday in a straight line. In others time it is circular. In yet others it is a combination of these, with time being cyclical; an example may well lie in the culture of contemporary commodities trading.

The study of time involves many disciplines, not only anthropology and sociology, but also others such as astronomy. The field of fundamental physics offers several explanations for the origins of the universe, taken by many as starting with the Big Bang, followed by an expanding universe, which suggests one cannot physically travel back in time. According to that theory, the universe is moving from a state of order to a state of randomness or chaos, and in the resulting process of entropy the conversion of matter into energy cannot be reversed. This story reflects the "arrow of time," in which time flows in one direction, from past to future, through the present. In contrast, alternative theories in other fields of science offer different possibilities for time travel by shifting assumptions about the origins and nature of the universe to include the possibility of its origin in cosmic dust, a living universe, and a multi-verse—not to mention wormholes. Our point is not to advocate for any particular scientific view, but to illustrate that the convention of time is socially constructed even in the field of scientific endeavor. It depends on the story that is used to make sense of the wider reality—whether this is the origins of the universe, the next big thing in the market, or everyday life (see Box 2.3).

TIME CULTURES SHAPE HOW ONE "LOOKS FORWARD"

Jameson (2002) noted a reduction of attention to the present in the postmodern era. There is a sense of a contracting future, possibly as a result of a build-up of intractable societal problems (persistent poverty, climate change), combined with rampant short-termism of political election cycles and the growth of the global financial system. Civil society and leaders in the business world insist that "we must act to address what is urgent now!" Thus,

---

BOX 2.3 CULTURES OF TIME

In 1998, management consultants Fons Trompenaars and Charles Hampden-Turner published their "Seven Dimensions of Culture" model to help explain national cultural differences in organizations and to show how managing these differences in a heterogeneous corporation can be a major challenge for international managers. They gathered data over ten years using a method that relied on asking subjects to respond to certain dilemmas or contrasting tendencies. Each dilemma consisted of two alternatives that were interpreted as indicators for basic attitudes and values. The authors identified three different cultures of time:

- In *past-oriented* cultures, people view the future as a repetition of previous events and experiences. Characteristics include respect for ancestors and collective historical events.
- *Present-oriented* cultures don't attach great value to the past or future. Instead, individuals are directed by the daily demands of everyday life.
- *Future-oriented* cultures are concentrated on future prospects and do not deem the past to be significant for future events. Planning is a major activity among individuals in this culture.

The implication for scenario planning is that one must be very attentive to the time orientations of the cultures of the people and of the organization hosting the scenario planning intervention, and how easily (or with what difficulty) this culture's views on time will accommodate scenario planning and its temporal ontology and epistemology.

---

what is urgent now comes to dominate what is important in the future and contributes to a syndrome of eternal firefighting. Pervasive short-termism in political and economic life would logically imply disabling and delegitimizing a sense of future in which more attention would be given to prospective possibilities.[10] In a similar way, this attention to "now" can also exclude history from one's consideration in situational analyses. In turn, this could contribute to blind spots, making the urgent a higher priority than the important, with people spending too much time firefighting and too little time thinking and designing prevention. The urgency of dealing with Heifetz et al.'s (2009) permanent crisis mentioned earlier, which has been inherited from the recent past, in turn justifies the denial and exclusion of other framings of the situation. Recent scenario planning work by one of us with one of the world's premier financial regulators showed how senior officials can, with some effort, reallocate their own time to devote more to the future and less to the present and past, which they can delegate to their staff.

Many before us have engaged such issues. Ackoff (1981) contrasted five positions in relation to the future: reactive, which is past oriented; inactive, which is present oriented; pre-active, concerned with *predicting* the future; proactive, concerned with *creating* the future; and interactive, *engaging and working with* the future. Adam and Groves (2007) proposed two contrasting frames regarding the future. With the "futures-present" frame, assumptions of the future shape the understanding of the present; with the "present-futures" frame, the future is taken to be an extension of what has happened in the past. In the OSPA, these contrasting frames are represented by two of the different arrows of time described later in this chapter. In a different way, Kahane (2012) contrasted what he called two stances to the future which can underpin inquiry on and intervention in social systems. His "reactive stance" assumed the future cannot be changed but can be better anticipated; his "pre-active stance" assumed the future can and should be changed. The OSPA resists this type of time framing, leaving the discussion of action to the process of developing strategic options within each scenario and using these to help clarify strategic choices.

NEGOTIATION OF THE TIME HORIZON

In any scenario planning process there comes a point when it is necessary to determine the relevant time horizon for building the scenarios. This is achieved through a process of negotiation among the participating learners rather than being derived on the basis of analysis alone. The time horizon takes into account the purpose and use of the scenario planning intervention, the position and profession of the learners, the business, its industry, and political cycles and top leadership mandates. Of course, the time horizon also takes into account the resources and time devoted to the scenario planning intervention.

As we saw in Chapter 1, Normann (2001)[11] offered a framework to aid in determining the time horizon for a set of scenarios in relation to a mental space which he called "the conceptual future." This "conceptualization" rests on the actual meaning of "the future," according to the OED.[12] In the English language, the dictionary informs, a future event is considered to be a "time to come." The future, in other words, is not something we go into, but something that comes at us. (This also implies that the future is different from the long term, which always happens later.) Moreover, in English what will happen in the future is considered a "condition in time to come *different from the present*." So there is a difference inherently built into "the future" that differentiates it from "the present." Finally, attending to the future entails what the dictionary calls "the prospective condition (of a person, country, etc.)." The future in English is thus also an inherent, even inevitable, aspect of the present (see Box 2.4).

The conceptual future in the OSPA is thus considered a mental space that allows the mind to be freed from the framings it has inhabited, used, and been limited by in the present and in the past. Its role is to help free the imagination and to bring forth tacit knowledge and intuition, yet be of service in the present. The conceptual future varies in different industries—decades in the oil industry, months in mobile telephony.

BOX 2.4 FUTURE, ADJ. AND N.

B. n. (noun)

†1. *pl.* Future events. *Obs.*
2. the future.
    a. *Time to come*; future time. Phr. *for the future*: in all future time.
    b. What will happen in the future.
3. a. A condition in time to come *different* (esp. in a favorable sense) *from the present.*
3. b. *The prospective condition* (of a person, country, etc.); *spec.* a prospective condition of success, prosperity, etc.; *(there is) no future in (something)*: there is no prospect of success or advancement in (it).

Adapted from the OED (accessed online November 2014).

THE OSPA'S THREE ARROWS OF TIME

Over a decade ago, the management consulting company McKinsey[13] introduced a framework for growth that considered three different time horizons. More recently, our good friend and colleague, Bill Sharpe (2014), has illustrated how working with multiple time horizons is relevant to scenario planning.

In a quite different way, the OSPA works with three arrows of time, only one of which is coincident with the arrow of time—the flow from past, through present, to future—that is the mainstay of predictive science.

To clarify the conceptions of future time available to strategists and in decision-making processes, we have developed a heuristic called the "three arrows of time," depicted in Figure 2.2:

- The *White Arrow* represents the future embodied in our action planning. It is the future dependent on our will. It is manifested in processes such as schedules, roadmaps with milestones, budget plans, and goals with detailed targets and action plans. Management by objectives and most kinds of plans (strategic, tactical, operational) are familiar examples of this stance on the future. The White Arrow is informed by our sense of the gap between our current situation and the vision to which we aspire. For example, a company aiming to quadruple profits in three years will allocate relevant targets for achieving this goal to different parts of the organization. Similarly, a government aiming to double the number of jobs available to 18–25-year-olds will translate this aspiration into relevant goals and targets for individual ministries. This White Arrow can hide deeper assumptions about the way the world should work, such as a deeply held narrative or myth of progress.

- The *Black Arrow* timeline depicts the momentum of the past, the things that have already happened and that are expected to continue to have impact

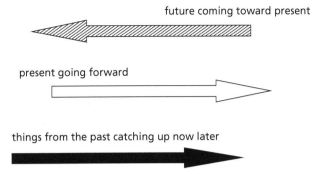

future coming toward present

present going forward

things from the past catching up now later

Figure 2.2. The OSPA's three arrows of time

on one's situation in the future. The Black Arrow is informed by horizon scanning, forecast-based planning, and trend/mega-trend impact analysis. For example, governments rely on demographic forecasting to anticipate how many children are going to be born and need to be educated, or to calculate when pensions will need to be paid out and for how long. Such analysis, in turn, informs the White Arrow timeline and the targets for maternity facilities and school building programs.

- The *Shaded Arrow* depicts future developments that are coming toward us independent of our will. The Shaded Arrow is informed by redirecting attention to novel developments, emerging issues, weak signals, disruptive changes, etc. Imagination plays a large role here. For example, no one could have predicted the rise of the digital economy over the past ten years using the evidence base that was available in the Black Arrow timeline in 2000. An instance of this is that, in the September 2014 weekend when the iPhone 6 was released in the US, more computing power was made available to its users than the entire world had in 1995.[14] Indeed, peer-to-peer businesses, such as Uber and Airbnb, did not even exist in 2000, except perhaps in someone's imagination.

In the OSPA scenarios are built as plausible contexts within which the activities in the White Arrow planning are expected to occur. These plausible future contexts are constructed from the interaction of the yet-to-unfold certainties identified by the Black Arrow and the uncertainty of less familiar and novel developments introduced by the Shaded Arrow. The resulting scenarios (combining Black Arrow and Shaded Arrow conceptions of the future) can then help users to assess priorities and options for action, that is, the White Arrow (strategies or intentions). Which aspects of these Shaded Arrow and Black Arrow futures are used and highlighted depends on the purpose of the scenario planning process and its intended uses.

TIMELINESS IN THE RHYTHMS OF ORGANIZATIONAL ROUTINES AND PROCESSES

In the OSPA we position scenario planning interventions and processes as means to some other end, that is, the *use(s)* that learners will make of them. It is important to think about when these uses will occur at the start of the scenario planning process to ensure it can deliver relevant insights, at the right time, to the right people. Any scenario planning intervention may be premature or inopportune, given the state of uncertainties in a potential user's environment (see Hodgkinson and Wright 2002). It might also occur too late, where the key strategy it was supposed to inform has already left port.

Wilkinson and Kupers (2014, 60) suggest that "the scenario 'magic' is not in the quality of the scenarios as a product" but in the ability of the organization effectively to make use of the scenarios by linking the scenario planning process with other organizational processes. By implication, the matching of organizational rhythms and routines with the scenario planning process needs careful consideration.

Sensemaking in the safe space: plausibility, memorability, and consistency

In this section we explain how the social processes in scenario planning move between different ways of "knowing the future."

THE CO-PRODUCTION OF PLAUSIBILITY

In the OSPA there are two logical ways of articulating the imagined (or "intuited") future context. One way is to describe it in terms of a system of causally linked variables—a system map. The other is to tell a story, with a start, middle, and end of what happened and how, which links the future to the present. The plausibility of the scenario is developed by the iteration between these two logical descriptions until coherence is achieved. It is this coherence between storyline and system map that is key to co-developing, testing, and assessing plausibility.[15] Plausibility is also co-produced in the sense of being developed, tested, and refined by people coming together and jointly establishing system maps and storylines. The iteration between these different logical descriptions contributes to further understanding and to greater clarity about the deeper underlying structure of the problematic situation.

The iteration between system mapping and storytelling helps to reveal feedback loops that determine the stability of the scenario. This system map (state-domain) is developed in a social process of model building (Vennix 1996). Learners can start by producing a logical frame for each scenario, and progressively refining and clarifying this logic through rounds of storytelling—or vice versa. Chapter 4 overviews different methods.

MEMORABILITY ENABLED WITH STORYTELLING

A story describes a series of events and how these are linked in time and related to different actors, that is, the characters of the story. A story is told through time; every story has a start, middle, and end. If a storyline is too complicated it will not be easy to recall. In the OSPA, the storytelling is not aimed at developing magnificent novels: the scenarios are powerful and memorable "story frames" rather than fully fleshed out and completed novels such as Tolstoy's *War and Peace*. Developing sufficiently memorable and yet still-open stories enables the scenario learners to immerse themselves in the new and different future contexts. It also helps them to develop their sense of future as well as to explore the scenarios for themselves to get to the level of detail they need.

Storytelling is also good at eliciting tacit knowledge and helping people respect different perspectives and imagine new possibilities. In the OSPA, the telling of stories by the scenario learners is also important in helping to forge shared understanding. It involves multiple rounds—creating, telling, refining, retelling—and cycles with the system mapping to ensure plausibility.

A story is not the same as a position, so no one has to be for or against it. The power of stories to shape reality is seldom acknowledged in technocratic professional cultures, where professional training is embedded in a positivist epistemology that believes in objective facts independent of the observer. Yet every person is always embedded in many stories—those of one's family, the institutions one affiliates with, one's religion and culture, one's locale, one's professional development.

Van der Heijden (2005, 114) observed that scenarios are "expressed as internally consistent and challenging narrative descriptions of possible futures in this external world." Wilkinson and Kupers (2014, 95) noted the storytelling power of scenarios in their history of the fifty years of Shell scenario practices, *The Essence of Scenarios*:

Perhaps the greatest power of scenarios, as distinct from forecasts, is that they provoke rather than suppress conversation and, in turn, enable new common ground to be forged in a process of sequential consensus building that uses the efficient mechanism of storytelling to forge more shared and systemic understanding. Strategic conversation lies at the heart of the adaptive capacity of any organization—and scenarios help make this kind of conversation possible.

Memories of the future

The storytelling process is critical to memorability because, as the neurobiologist David Ingvar noted, the part of the brain where memory is stored is also the one where imagination operates. The human brain, both consciously and subconsciously, processes signals from the environment and rehearses possible actions and options, not in a narrow sense of predicting what will happen but in terms of having "time paths," or what Ingvar called "meaningful memories of the future" (Ingvar 1985).

Scenarios are not intended to be entertaining, but instead to provide a stage setting where the listeners or readers of the story can conjure up images of a plausible setting where they can imagine themselves acting, living, and working, as actors would do on a theater stage. In this memorable setting of the future, participants can safely rehearse its possibilities (its promises and challenges) before it happens, as one does in the transitional spaces we mentioned earlier.

Good fiction contributes to clarity in people's minds

Effective scenario narratives, like good literature, are "open stories" that help their readers to generate meaning when they use them:

I believe effective scenarios need to be like good literature—they need to be read by users in ways that help their minds render futures "more real than real." By this I mean more real *imagined* futures than an actually real, existing present so that the futures are clarified in the mind in order to ensure that we attend to them (Ocasio 1997). (Ramírez 2008, 189)

Effective scenario stories have other properties.[16] In her *Dreaming by the Book*, Elaine Scarry (2001), a Harvard University professor in English and aesthetics, explored how poets and writers help readers in constructing clear images in their minds. She suggested that in reading literature, people form mental images that are not only "vivid" but actually "radiant." As radiance is made possible by powerful light, she proposed readers become enlightened in reading this work, creating images that in their minds become alive—perhaps more alive in the minds, she suggested, than the images of live persons in the readers' immediate surroundings with whom they actually relate. If Scarry is correct, effective scenarios will be like well-written fiction, inciting listeners or readers to imagine more clearly about their subjects than they usually think about the immediate reality around them.

Knowledge in literature is co-produced between writer and reader; they engage with each other in a form of conversation (van der Heijden 2005). This is also the case between the two roles of the scenario learners—both as the producer and consumer of the scenario system maps and storylines. Scenarios in this sense play the same role as novels. As Carlos Fuentes (1993, 28), a major Mexican literary critic, put it: "What then is a novel, other than telling that which cannot be told otherwise? A novel is a verbal search of that which awaits being written" ("búsqueda verbal de lo que espera ser escrito").

The novel, like the scenario, enables conversational relations between readers and the writer in reading and rereading: "never again should we have only one voice or reading. Imagination is real and its languages multiple" ("Nunca mas debe haber una sola voz o una sola lectura. La imaginación es real y sus lenguajes son multiples") (Fuentes 1993, 21).

Scenarios as novels can thus be understood as scans or searches, often expressed in writing as stories of that which is yet to be imagined. These fictions are relations between the writer (the scenario planning facilitator and the scenario builders), and the reader (the learner or user of the scenarios). In these relations the writer enables the reader to imagine, that is, to form the clear, enlightening, even radiant mental images of what might happen, so that these clearly imaged futures take on a "realistic" position in the attentive mind of the user.

Social benefits of scenario planning

In the OSPA, a scenario planning process aims to enable people to understand the strategic frame they have been using and to consider alternative frames. This, in turn, improves the quality of strategic conversations within the organization (van der Heijden 2005). Here we consider broader benefits of the process.

As we have noted, effective conversation requires a shared vocabulary. Scenario planning processes are often triggered by situations that people find difficult to describe and which might benefit from new concepts and terms. An example of this can be found in the history of Shell's scenarios work. In the 1980s, the Shell executives initiated a scenario planning process to better understand the meaning and implications of "sustainable development" for the oil and gas business (Wilkinson and Kupers 2014). Another example occurred in the Risk-World scenario planning case study (Appendix F), where the concept of "malicious systemic risk" emerged in the course of developing the scenarios. This kind of risk was perceived to be different from innocently motivated hacking by computer whiz kids keen to demonstrate their prowess to their peers and the concerns about technological incumbency that had driven the hype about a Y2K crisis in the run-up to end of the twentieth century. Instead the term appeared to some of those involved in the scenario planning process to indicate the vulnerability of large global systems to new social movements. In turn, this newly understood sense of the term malicious systemic risk enabled more mainstream attention to and discussion of the implications of future possibilities that were at that time, at best, only being discussed in the margins of the field of risk.

According to Lang (2012), scenario planning can also be undertaken with the specific purpose of enabling accelerated social capital development.[17] (See also Chapter 5.) *Social capital* is a term used in management studies and related disciplines to denote how many people any one person or group can access, how that person or group is able to mobilize the knowledge and capabilities of those network contacts, and the qualities of that network (see Adler and Kwon 2002). Lang found empirical evidence that two rounds of scenario planning work done in the innovative British higher education institution, the Open University, and one round in the EPO (Appendix E) provided the learners with a renewed and richer network of collaborators. Lang found that the social capital produced by the scenario planning process was guided first by the new, shared cognitive framework that the scenario planning reframing produced, which in turn enhanced the structure and quality of relations in the expanded network. This was remarkable because research on the formation of social capital up to then had indicated only an alternative route, namely, where adding to the stock of one's relations (such as by building up one's LinkedIn connections, adding "friends" on Facebook, attending the World Economic Forum in Davos, or adding business cards to one's Rolodex) is what leads to better quality relations; and the number and quality of relations then (eventually) help the network participant to produce new shared frames of understanding with others in the network. Her empirical findings reinforce the important role that scenario planning as a social process can have in enhancing one's social network and social capital. That enhanced social capital can then in turn help users to forge common ground.

Lang thus empirically showed that the scenario planning process fosters the forging of common ground. Emery and Trist (1965), cited earlier, suggested that this is exactly what turbulent contexts call for (Ramírez et al. 2008b). In the OSPA, the social process of scenario planning forges new common ground by acknowledging and airing different viewpoints. It allows these to be compared in the "transitional" safety of the future conceptual space, often providing an upframed assessment of the strategic situation.

Ethics and governance in scenario planning

Tuomi (2013) proposed that there are limits to anticipating the future in an era of unpredictable uncertainty and social complexity. We suggest that in TUNA conditions, the contribution of scenario planning can and must be considered in terms of its potential to support wider engagement. Through a more participatory process of learning with futures rather than about the future, scenario planning contributes new options to and more flexibility in strategic processes. The possibility for this in an information-intensive world with highly distributed computing (and thus analytic) power is becoming more relevant and widespread. This diffusion of power in a more connected world, in turn, means all types of large organization—whether central government, multinational corporation, or international institution—are well advised to engage with a more diverse set of wider stakeholders and their interests to ensure, renew, or even reinvent their license to operate.

In helping people in groups and organizations to develop their own sense of future it is important to pay attention to power and governance. We believe that because of its attention to social processes, the scenario planning processes we have developed in Oxford can help learners to avoid what might be considered the "colonization of the future" by dominant powers or vested interests. Such colonization can occur when "the strategic agenda" is imposed from the outside or unilaterally by the powerful, for example by multinational companies seeking to secure the global supply chains for bananas in Central America (Koeppel 2008), or by top executives pushing their pet projects within an organization.

We cannot underline strongly enough that to remain effective scenario planning must continue to be critically attentive to issues of power in social processes. In our experience, all too often, when imagining, articulating, or creating a possible future with scenario planning, questions of ethics are unfortunately left implicit and unaddressed (see Box 2.5).

Ethical issues relevant to scenario planning have been examined in the field of what is called "critical futures," from which we in the OSPA have learned important lessons for scenario planning. For example, Causal Layered Analysis (Inayatullah 1998) provides the scenario learner and process facilitator with tools for unearthing the dominant and alternative strategic narratives and

---

BOX 2.5 ETHICAL AND POWER-ORIENTED QUESTIONS IN SCENARIO PLANNING SOCIAL PROCESSES

- In whose interests are the scenarios being built—and *against* whose interests?
- Who finances scenario planning initiatives and with what strings attached?
- Is the scenario planning *process* itself, not only the result, going to be considered ethical, particularly by stakeholders who will inevitably be excluded or feel marginalized?
- How well has the scenario process and design been documented, for it to be tested and contested critically?
- Who gets involved and how? Who gets excluded and why? Who might be impacted and how? Who convenes meetings and with what mandate?
- Who is attempting to shape a future with the scenarios, and what alternative futures are being excluded by the way this set of scenarios are built and designed?

their deeper mythological foundations. Such tools can be useful in scenario building processes that need to avoid capture by powerful, vested interests. Such tools can help to analyze and assess "critical" questions, that is, questions concerning established roles and power structures.

Ethical considerations are implied in making careful and well-informed choices about the nature and mode of participation in the scenario definition and building process. This was particularly evident in the AiA case study (Appendix D). In that scenario planning process, the selection of participants (the scenario process learners) took three months and involved a wide-ranging search for suitable candidates. In addition, oversight of the project budget was separated from the steering of the content and process and the building of the scenarios, which were co-produced by the large stakeholder groups participating in each workshop. Funders were, in effect, not able to decide which scenarios were developed.

Attention to the different roles and modes of participation is a useful starting point for those aiming to facilitate OSPA scenario planning processes (Zurek and Henrichs 2007; see also Elahi 2008). In Chapter 4 we discuss the pivotal role of the scenario learner in the OSPA, and in Chapter 5 we discuss the role of scenario process facilitator and the methods s/he can use to support the learners in building scenarios.

Conclusion

As we have explained in this chapter, scenario planning is inherently a social process, or more accurately it comprises a series of interacting social processes centered on a reframing-reperception learning loop.

The more explicit and flexible sense of future generated in this process supports and is manifested in accepting multiple frames. Being able to contrast these in a safe space enables new, more numerous, and often more distinctive strategic options to be considered by the scenario learner.

By enabling multiple future contexts to be respected and compared, the scenario planning process opens up a safe space for disagreement among experts and non-experts to be aired and examined, be they senior corporate executives, erudite scholars, strong-minded thought leaders, or anyone that wants to question, support, or oppose the dominant or official view.

The capacity of scenario planning to host opposing views within its transitional safe spaces can help participants to avoid the extremes of groupthink and fragmentation, thereby increasing the chances for effective group learning, organizational development, and change management.

Not attending to the human, social, and cultural qualities of the scenario planning process can be very costly. They can result in the delivery of a set of "stranded assets," that is, a set of vivid stories of the future that no one knows what to do with, or perhaps even more wasteful, a set of scenarios that advocate for the "official future."

The main conclusions of this chapter are that the success of scenario planning depends on the quality of interaction of social and cognitive processes and, in turn, on how well these are made to fit into and support other social processes in and beyond the organization undertaking scenario planning.

▓ NOTES

1. This also happens at the macro level socially as cultural patterns, and at the individual level as learned knowledge schemas (Cornelissen and Werner 2014).
2. Uncomfortable knowledge can be constructed and imposed either "intentionally" or as a "by-product of some social process" (Smithson 2008, 214). An obvious example of intentionality here is the use of power to silence certain voices, such as an authoritarian government closing down access to the Internet in that country. An example of a by-product is the solidarities and the discrete perceptions of reality they shape and channel, for example, the 2014 Maidan Square demonstrations in Kiev (Thompson 2008).
3. We are aware that others, like Hirschhorn (2012), have used the term "backcasting" to depict an action plan derived from an ideal future.
4. One might even extend this to the macro level, where the sensemaking process would involve much larger groups (comprising "social fields", as we see later) including entire societies, as was done by South Africans in the transition from Apartheid (see Kahane 2012).
5. Perrow concluded that that nearly catastrophic event was what he called a "normal accident," that is, a result that should be expected to occur normally when highly complex systems are designed with such highly interdependent technologies that human operators cannot fathom all of the possible connections and failure modes.
6. We recognize that such an independent perspective is not possible.
7. They also manifest and sustain power, as Foucault's research demonstrated.
8. In system dynamics terms these errors arise through positive feedback loops; interventions such as scenario planning can prevent them from going "too far" by introducing "balancing" processes. We thank Kees van der Heijden for suggesting this.
9. This is brilliantly explained by Jerry B. Harvey (1988) in *The Abilene Paradox and Other Meditations on Management*.
10. We acknowledge that other senses of future may not be disabled by short-termism.
11. Ramírez worked with Normann from 1985 until Normann's passing away in 2001. Van der Heijden worked with them from 1986.
12. The actual dictionary definition is given in Chapter 3, in the subsection on "Knowledge of the future is not the same as long term thinking."
13. See the McKinsey book *The Alchemy of Growth: Practical Insights for Building the Enduring Enterprise* by Baghai et al. (2000). *Horizon one* represents those core businesses most readily identified with the company name and those that provide the greatest profits and cash flow. Here the focus is on improving performance to maximize the remaining value. *Horizon two* encompasses emerging opportunities, including rising entrepreneurial ventures likely to

generate substantial profits in the future but that could require considerable investment. *Horizon three* contains ideas for profitable growth down the road; for instance, small ventures such as research projects, pilot programs, or minority stakes in new businesses.

14. *The Economist* (2015).
15. Kees van der Heijden (personal communication) has suggested that these work in relation to each other as a Laplace transformation: enabling the description of a system to be translated from structural characteristics into temporal development and vice versa.
16. Much of this section is drawn from Ramírez (2008).
17. We believe this specific purpose for conducting scenario planning has never been studied before.

3 Scenario planning as a knowledge acquisition and generation process

Introduction

In Chapter 2, we made the case that scenario planning is inescapably a set of social processes. In this chapter we direct attention to how those processes contribute to the acquisition and generation of new knowledge. We highlight how scenarios can serve as "memories of the future," which connect prospective reframing with retrospective sensemaking. We consider what forms of knowledge are usable, what knowledge aspirations are not compatible with the OSPA, how the truthfulness of such knowledge can be established and verified, and how all these matters relate to scenario planning. We explain how knowledge of the future is not the same thing as long-range analysis (for example, conditional projections that produce "baseline" scenarios with "what if" high/medium/low variations). We also discuss knowledge about the future extensively, while acknowledging that such a notion may appear to be paradoxical. Throughout the chapter we repeatedly remind the reader that knowledge concerning the future is always tentative and partial, and involves scanning, search, and research.

As we saw in Chapters 1 and 2, knowledge acquisition, generation, and joint assessment in the OSPA pivot on the reframing-reperception cycle. Scenario planning redirects the learners' attention to knowledge of the context of their situation. Box 3.1 lists some of these factors.

We do not engage in an ontological debate of what might be "unknowable"; we have learned that such a debate is not helpful. Instead, we limit ourselves to the consideration of that which is not *now* known, in the sense of "not known in the here and now" by the scenario planning learners.[1] If something is taken, in the here and now, to be "unthinkable" it might nevertheless be *imaginable*. This is useful in situations where available procedures to know something "factually," on the basis of statistical repetition, are inapplicable or indeed contribute to failure (Ramírez and Ravetz 2011).

We argue that the aim of scenario planning in the OSPA is *not* to undertake a comprehensive survey of all future possibilities. Instead, it is to clarify a meaningful variety of possible future contexts and to assess which future elements might be predetermined in a given time, that is, common across a

---

BOX 3.1 TYPES OF FACTORS HIGHLIGHTED BY SCENARIO PLANNING KNOWLEDGE PROCESSES

Factors which:

- have been taken for granted—for example, in the EPO case (Appendix E), that growth in a "knowledge economy" would inevitably involve more patenting;
- have been "known" tacitly but never labeled or made explicit—for example, in the UEG case (Appendix C) the unsustainability of the economics of post-World War II European medicine;
- are still emerging, novel, and have been felt (perhaps in a gut feeling, hope, anxiety, misgiving, doubt, or intuition) but not articulated, shared, or tested; or the initial and tentatively labeled concept is ambiguous in the context of novel technological developments, as the Risk-World case (Appendix F) explores;
- have remained out of the frame of attention, away from the central focus, in the periphery of perception—as had been China's role in shipping in the first round of scenario planning done by Wärtsilä's Ship Power division (Appendix A);
- no one in the organization or system owns, because they lie between organizational silos, or across sectoral or disciplinary boundaries—as are various parts of policy in the AiA case (Appendix D);
- have socially messy, complex, or wicked characteristics but have been dealt with piecemeal rather than holistically—as are the links between energy and society explored in the Shell 2001 case (Appendix B); and/or
- are "blind spots," that is, are known by others in other organizations or wider fields of expertise—as was the case for some stakeholders in the AiA case, as well as the EPO case regarding the role society might have on the future shape of IP and its legitimacy.

---

set of plausible alternatives. These plausible alternatives are manufactured through storytelling and system mapping, rather than calculated and selected. This is discussed further in Chapter 5.[2]

We assess scenario planning as a research methodology to carry out interesting, usable, and rigorous inquiry that generates insights through interdisciplinary reframing. We conclude the chapter with reflections on how the social process insights from Chapter 2 impact the role of scenario planning in accessing and generating knowledge. In so doing we situate the OSPA as part of the movements toward "post-normal" science and "design rationality" within the tradition of engaged scholarship and action research.

What is knowledge?

As Einstein noted, information is not knowledge. He thought the only sources of knowledge were experience and expertise, and that humans could not solve their problems with the same thinking used in creating them. Another Nobel Prize laureate (in economics), Herbert Simon, said in his Nobel Lecture (1978):

The flowering of mathematical economics and econometrics has provided two generations of economic theorists with a vast garden of formal and technical problems that have absorbed their energies and postponed encounters with the inelegancies of the real world.

Real-world actors, as we explained in Chapter 2, are engaged in ongoing sensemaking. They imagine the future as well as model it—or imagine it *as* they model it—and decide if what they and others imagine makes sense. In a TUNA context they also need to avoid the traps of linear thinking to "look around the corner." They suffer simultaneously from an excess of information that might be relevant and massive uncertainty about which aspects of it to attend to. Questions nag: what information should be treated as reliable? How should information be assessed, regarding whether it's likely to be useful and relevant to the task? How can one work out how things done now will evolve in the future?

Acquiring "new" knowable and previously "unknown" knowledge is often about surfacing *tacit* knowledge—the type of knowledge Polanyi (1966) referred to when he proposed that "we can know more than we can tell." As we explore in Chapter 6, this involves a process of learning that directs attention to error—the things one thinks one knows but upon critical examination finds one does not. Knowledge can be made explicit or remain tacit, and scenario planning can help make the implicit explicit.

KNOWLEDGE AS "TRUTH SEEKING"

Knowledge relates to truth; knowing something manifests and makes available those parts of that thing which we take as the truth we know about it.

The branch of philosophy that studies how people know and know truthfully is *epistemology*. Epistemology matters in any field of expertise and professional practice because a given epistemological stance underpins the methodological approach used in a process of inquiry—including scenario planning. Every methodological approach in turn comes with a set of methods, techniques, and tools. Those are deployed to approximate the ideal of truth which the epistemology and methodology seek to obtain. (A related branch of philosophy is *ontology*, which concerns the very nature of being and reality.)

There is a long tradition in Western philosophy of thinkers who have proposed different epistemological positions that help establish whether a given proposition is true, and thus counts as knowledge. This tradition was helpfully explored by C. West Churchman in *The Design of Inquiring Systems* (1971), and what follows is adapted from that book. We have used his account of these views on truth in teaching scenario planning with advanced learners, and found them to be tremendously helpful.

As Churchman put it, John Locke proposed that truthfulness arises from an *inductive* process of inquiry where the inquirer looks at what she sees and builds up associations and generalizations about the world. Locke's ultimate arbiter of something being "true" was whether there is consensus among a "community of inquirers." This view is still very much alive today. It is the basis of peer review in scholarly journals, with the community of scholars represented by the reviewers determining if a manuscript can be published so as to become the latest version of what is known to be true in that field of inquiry. Based on this Lockean ideal of truth, in the OSPA we strongly recommend having various rounds of peer review of draft scenario sets and then more polished versions.

Gottfried Leibniz put forth the idea that truth resides in innate ideas and is manifested in axioms arrived at through a *deductive* process. Here the inquirer emphasizes the production of theoretical hypotheses and the use of logic. Hypotheses for Leibniz are to be produced and tested against axioms, and those which are consistent with axioms are to be regarded as "true" because they are internally consistent. In Leibnizean epistemology, true outcomes are added to the truth system as part of a growing fact net, and knowledge generation expects these fact nets to converge and form an optimal net explaining everything. The Singularity University project is a current example of this hope.

The insistence of positivist epistemologies on quantification and "confidence levels" to manifest knowledge as statistically probable aligns with this Leibnizean tradition of truthful knowledge. In scenario planning as understood in the OSPA, fact nets are important. They are built up while scenarios are being created, in that imagined future factual relations are nets which help to ascertain whether a scenario is plausible. This fact net logic of truth is what systems diagrams seek to obtain as a plausible truth in the future. Such diagrams connect future contextual factors into internally consistent stories, and we discuss them later in this chapter. As we see in Chapters 2 and 5, the construction of future plausible fact nets is a social process, and plausibility is co-constructed in conversing about alternative possible future fact nets (Ramírez and Wilkinson 2009a; Ramírez and Selin 2014).

Immanuel Kant combined the preceding two epistemological stances and sought a productive and iterative synthesis of theory and data. Kant's view of truth was thus more open; it involved generating hypotheses from the inputs, with the resulting hypothesis in turn generating alternative models, so that an input could be subjected to different interpretations. These interpretive models were also to be constructed by the inquirer as fact nets, and "truth" was to be obtained through the hypotheses which best fit the data and model. Models not producing satisfactory results could be "turned off." This way of producing knowledge is manifested in grounded theory, with iterations of gathering data, theorizing from the data, further data gathering, etc. This is very much how a set of scenarios produce (tentative) knowledge in the

OSPA. The initial set is then compared with the scenario planning learning, and—as required by the purpose and agreed intended use—the scenarios are then accepted, updated, or revised (Ramírez et al. 2013).

Friedrich Hegel's epistemological contribution was a more explicit and developed version of the Kantian system of inquiry. Here the inquirer constructs a strongly felt "case" to defend a first thesis (let's say, "thesis A"); then a first observer wonders what it would be like to feel and believe equally strongly an antithesis and proposes this (let's say, "antithesis B"). This antithesis depends on feeling and belief more than on Kantian logic. A second observer (the Hegelian "bigger mind") builds a new world view where the conflict between thesis A and antithesis B is used to make new sense, manifested as a synthesis (let's say, "synthesis C"). For Hegelian inquirers this form of establishing truth through A-B-C iterations suggests that wisdom results from a conflict of ideas, and truth depends on one's belief about the debate's effectiveness. Contemporary examples of Hegelian pathways to truth are double-blind reviews in academic journals, parliamentary debates before determining government policy, and also in scenario planning. In the OSPA, Hegelian truth is manifested in seeking a set of scenarios that are strongly felt as being in disagreement with each other about what the future might hold, as well as in disagreement with whatever strongly felt sense the intended learner may have of that future in the here and now.

Churchman (who was one of Ramírez's doctoral supervisors) proposed another epistemological perspective on truthful knowledge in the twentieth century, which he attributed to his teacher E.A. Singer, Jr.[3] Churchman built on the debate of the Hegelian inquirer, and accepted the helpful and perhaps inevitable role of multiple data sources, of hosting multiple interpretations of reality, and thus of considering the possibility of multiple truths. He proposed that these multiple truths would be found by continually challenging system knowledge from multiple points of view. In Singerian epistemology, truth is temporary and context dependent, and it is based on two premises. The first involves a system of measures outlining how disagreements are to be resolved among a group. The second involves a strategy of agreement which encourages those inquirers seeking to produce truth(s) to attack the prevailing paradigm of that which is considered truthful at a given point in time. This means seeking truth is necessarily a subversive process, which seeks to unseat prior views of truth. However, this subversion is constructive, a bit like Schumpeter's (1994) well-known view of innovation as "creative destruction." In the OSPA this constructive view of subversion is what reframing through scenario planning seeks to obtain. It is also why we cannot agree with Sardar's critical depiction of scenario planning discussed later in this chapter (see Table 3.1).

Ever since the philosopher of science Karl Popper (1959) proposed that truth is only at best tentative and the latest as-of-yet non-falsified version of knowledge, it has become widely accepted that theories in science can only be

Table 3.1 Comparison of three major knowledge traditions used in scenario planning

	Positivism	Constructivism	Critical constructivism (OSPA)
View of reality	Objective reality, i.e. reality independent of the observer	Socially constructed reality	To be useful, knowledge of reality has to be acceptable and depends on human perceptions and relationships. Any one version is tentative, and expects to benefit from being critiqued.
View of future	The future as "real"	Any story of the future is as real as the next one	The future is first and always a plural fiction but not every story counts; those that count need to be useful in learning.
Effectiveness criteria	Calculability, falsifiability, reproducibility, consistency	Imaginative, intuitive, plausibility, communicability	Meeting three criteria together: plausibility, relevance, challenge

the tentative manifestations of truth, and remain truthful until disproven. Disciplined imagination methods such as scenario planning are of help in developing new hypotheses and even full-blown theories, through what Chermack (2007) called "theorizing."[4] A theory is a particular view (a well-described view) from which and with which one can see something, like a modern set of spectacles or looking glasses.

With this rich history of how we think about how we think and know, it is not surprising that at the beginning of the twenty-first century various epistemologies exist in the social sciences, drawing on those "inquiring systems" described earlier. As it is well beyond the scope of this book to discuss them in detail, we focus on three which bear most directly on scenario planning as understood in the OSPA (see Table 3.1). The social sciences are important in a book about the OSPA because most research on scenario planning emanates from the social sciences.

The epistemology most used by social science has been adapted from the "natural" sciences (physics, chemistry, etc.), namely, *positivism*. Positivists, grounded in Leibnizean thinking, assume that an external reality exists independent of the knower, and the knower's task is to discover it and establish knowledge about it "objectively." In the OSPA we respect this stance and use it in aspects of scenario planning interventions, for example, to establish as a fact what is known by the intended learners of scenario planning in the here and now. But it is not the primary epistemology used, because knowledge of the future challenges some basic positivist tenets, as we discuss in what follows.

In the second half of the twentieth century, a critique of positivist epistemology called *constructivism* arose, made popular by the book *The Social Construction of Reality* (Berger and Luckmann 1966). In constructivist epistemology, everything (including facts) is assumed to be socially constructed, for it is people who relate to their environment and construct the knowledge they have of it. Much of the OSPA epistemology is constructivist, but not all of it.

A third important epistemology, which also arose within twentieth-century social science, is *critical theory*. It suggests that the proper role of the researcher is to critique what is assumed to be known, paying particular attention to power structures and relations, and their influence on what is known.[5] Van der Heijden (2005) noted the value of scenario planning lies in developing alternative future contexts to test and challenge the status quo framing that underpins the "official future." Scenario planning as understood in the OSPA helps learners to take a critical stance, and rejects attempts to impose positivist metrics of effectiveness on scenario planning work. The OSPA instead situates scenario planning epistemologically as a pragmatic perspective that emphasizes improved strategy making as the outcome of inquiry rather than testable knowledge production (Walton 2008).

One articulation of the critical-constructivist epistemology of the OSPA was proposed by Wilkinson and Eidinow (2008). They distinguished "problem-focused" from "actor-centric" scenario planning, and suggested a third type, which they called RIMA—*reflexive interventionist or multi-agent* based. They emphasized the importance of involving different epistemologies in a scenario-based process of action learning in the public interest. They suggested that by combining the problem- and actor-based epistemologies, the RIMA approach can create a more effective bridge between longer-term thinking and more immediate actions. This also situates scenario planning as a method-ology of what Funtowicz and Ravetz (1995) call "post-normal" science, where scientific inquiry sweeps in value contestations and disputations of facts.

Positivism is limited in OSPA mostly because knowledge of the future is not suited to the three conditions for establishing truth which positivist scientific knowledge operates on, namely, falsifiability, reproducibility, and consistency. These conditions require facts (to help falsify); and "other things being equal" (*ceteris paribus*) laboratory conditions that leave out context (to enable reproducibility of procedure and consistency of outcomes). But as we have explained already, facts are in the present and of the past; and scenario planning explicitly brings in the context. In addition, scenario planning is done in the here and now for a specific learner in particular circumstances with a given purpose. This makes consistency among cases to enable com-parison nearly impossible to obtain. Importantly, this means that the know-ledge scenario planning proposes about the future cannot be "objective"; instead it is ("only") a plausible hypothesis (Dufva and Ahlqvist 2015). This matters because the scenario planning intervention will be designed and implemented to clarify the "hypothetically factual" knowledge base (that is, conventional wisdom), and to contest this with new knowledge developed from using alternative conceptual frames and concomitant, well-reasoned logic.

One other important aspect of knowledge for scenario planning work is that while knowledge is manufactured with machines, metaphors, and models (Fox

Keller 2002; see also Lakoff and Johnson 2008), it is manifested, captured, and shared by means of symbols.[6, 7] Symbols help minds to share knowledge in the forms of ideas, theories, or hypotheses—as well as in-form-ation. So attending to symbol making is an important part of ensuring that scenario planning is actually used, as we outline in Chapters 4 and 5.

Knowledge of the future?

In the OSPA, the assumption is that the future has not yet come. It has not yet taken place in the present; it is an emerging story that is not factually real— yet.[8] The conundrum introduced earlier about how non-facts could possibly be known (actually known, known "for a fact"), and how that non-factual knowledge can sit alongside factual knowledge, has given rise to a wide-ranging debate about knowledge of the future in the journal *Futures*. The journal's then editor, Z. Sardar, put it this way in a 2010 paper:

Foresights do...not really exist...[P]lurality is indicated whenever future is used, with the exception of futurology...[T]he label we use to describe explorations of the future...can point...practitioners towards multiple possibilities and open the mind of the layman to pluralistic potentials of the study of the future...

On the whole, there seems to be constant tension between futures studies, seen as pluralistic, multicivilisational, and challenging the basic axioms of the dominant system, and all the other terms we use to appear normal, objective, strategic and business like. (2010, 180–2)

In the same paper, Sardar expressed deep misgivings about scenario planning:

A great deal of foresight work is concerned with "scenario planning", which, in my opinion, is devouring futures studies.

Within some businesses, corporations and government institutions scenarios are seen as the only way of exploring the future.

Futures studies thus becomes synonymous with "strategic foresight" or "scenario planning" with a clear emphasis on winning over others, instead of exploring and developing creative, novel and inclusive solutions. Indeed, it is turned into a "management tool" as we can see in Michel Godet's extensive work. (2010, 180)

As we see in this book, and specifically in this chapter, we do not agree with Sardar's view of scenario planning. In the OSPA we *do* think that the reframing at the heart of scenario planning helps individuals and groups in "exploring and developing creative, novel" perspectives (Ramírez and Wilkinson 2009b). And rather than being focused on what he called "winning over others," good scenario planning as understood in the OSPA allows learners to explore, appreciate, and even empathize with perspectives that disagree with theirs—often for profound reasons.

BOX 3.2 SARDAR'S FOUR CHARACTERISTICS OF KNOWLEDGE OF THE FUTURE

- *Wickedness*—It would not be an understatement to say that futures studies deals almost exclusively with wicked problems. But futures studies are . . . also wicked in the sense that they are playfully open ended . . . and quite happy to borrow ideas and tools, whatever is needed, from any and all disciplines and discourses . . . it is not just multi- and trans-disciplinary, it is unashamedly un-disciplinary: that is, it consciously rejects the status and state of a discipline while being a fully fledged systematic mode of critical inquiry;
- involves *mutually assured diversity*;
- *Skepticism*—Futures studies need to be skeptical of simple, one dimensional solutions to wicked problems as well as of dominant ideas, projections, predictions, forecasts, and notions of truth to ensure that the future is not foreclosed and colonized by a single culture; and
- *Futureless*—Futures studies are "futureless" in a technical, specific sense: since we can have no true knowledge of the future, the impact of all futures explorations can only be meaningfully assessed in the present.

Sardar (2010, 183–4)

Sardar went on to suggest that the knowledge that futures studies engages with manifests the four characteristics in Box 3.2. We in the OSPA believe these characteristics helpfully qualify the knowledge involved in scenario planning. Nonetheless, some tricky issues that pertain specifically to scenario planning remain to be explored, such as: what is the nature of knowledge regarding that which does not yet factually exist? How might such knowledge about non-facts be generated, and by whom? How is such knowledge used?

KNOWLEDGE OF THE FUTURE IS NOT THE SAME AS LONG-TERM THINKING

The future is always an aspect of the present. The future has not "taken place," but the present always "holds" the future, and holds it as potential. Indeed, the future is never "later," it is always (experienced, imagined) "now." Fred Emery captured this point of view nicely in the title of his book *Futures We Are In* (1977). Similarly, Scharmer (2007) proposed that the future emerges and that these emerging futures are already in the present, lying latent. David Bohm (1980) coined the term "implicate order," which is an ordering of reality inherent in the present as potential, and as time arrives this implicit order unfolds and becomes "explicate" reality (see Box 3.3).

In the OSPA we agree with these views that the long term and the future are not the same thing. The long term is always located later. As Canadian science fiction writer William Gibson put it, "the future is already here, it's just not very evenly distributed."[9] As we explained in Chapter 2, the future is an aspect

---

BOX 3.3 DAVID BOHM: ORDERS AND UNFOLDINGS

In his 1980 book, *Wholeness and the Implicate Order*, physicist David Bohm noted two different frameworks for understanding reality. In the *explicate order*, space and time are dominant factors for determining relationships of dependency. This is the reality we experience every day.

In the *implicate order*, he suggested, "space and time are no longer the dominant factors determining the relationships of dependence or independence of different elements." He suggested instead that these are derived from a deeper, less visible, interconnected order which he called the "implicate" or "enfolded" order.

In later books, *Unfolding Meaning* (1985) and *On Dialogue* (1996), Bohm claimed that understanding the implicate order requires "deeper listening and more open communication to cope with the complex problems." He proposed creative dialogue, and a sharing of assumptions and understanding, as a means by which the individual and society as a whole can learn more about themselves and others, and achieve a renewed sense of purpose.

---

of our present, and when we attend to this aspect "prospectively" we expect that something will come to us, something different from the present.

There is a growing body of work on how and where knowledge of the future is embodied. Scientists have found that the parts of our central nervous system (including but not restricted to our "brain") which house our imaginations of possible futures are also the places which house memories of the past. This is why scenarios have been referred to as "memories of the future" (Ingvar 1985; see also Schacter et al. 2007). This feature of our innate information management apparatus has some disadvantages. It is in memory that we store the heuristics (or rules of thumb) that have served us well and which we routinely depend upon to reach decisions in situations that conform to some pattern we have experienced before. Such heuristics feature as pre-judgments or preconceptions, as well as biases in decision making, which as we saw in Chapter 2 "anchor" expectations and perspectives. Yet, in a study of eighty failed strategies, Finkelstein et al. (2013) found that 82 percent of the failures were related to "misleading pre-judgments."

In a highly cited paper, Schoemaker (1993) suggested that scenario planning can be used to counteract such biases. Indeed, in helping learners to develop alternative frames for cognition, scenario planning seeks to make preconceptions explicit and visible to the learners, and to render them discussable in a productive and constructive way. Schlag (2002) and Damasio (2000) have suggested that in cognitive psychology terms, such preconceptions are underpinned by aesthetic (attractive/repulsive, or beautiful/ugly) forms which inform our thinking; these operate even before more explicit considerations such as ethics (good/bad) come to influence our decision-taking. This means that the reframing sought by scenario planning must operate at a deep level of consciousness, tapping into information stored in non-word forms.[10] Much work remains to be done on the cognitive psychology and neurology of how this clarity operates.

SCENARIO PLANNING PROVIDES NEW KNOWLEDGE THAT REFRAMES THE SITUATION, WITH PERSPECTIVES FROM THE FUTURE

The future possible contexts imagined with scenario planning are therefore most importantly knowledge about the present situation, helped by a better understanding of how this context might unfold in different futures. Such knowledge often has been previously unseen (that is, remained "tacit") or underappreciated by the learner, or it may be novel or newly created.

This attending to one's knowledge of the context is something that people do routinely, but without explicitly realizing they do it. Just like yoga helps one to attend to the breathing one always is doing (is the breathing deep or shallow? is it fast or slow?), so too scenario planning helps people to direct attention to the context, and to focus on the futures in the present. Pierre Wack found such mindfulness essential—he was preoccupied with how best to bring Oriental mindfulness to Occidental board rooms. He called it "intuition": the looking into the "micro" world in one's mind with the help of the "macro" world in one's context, then testing in iterations the insights of intuition with empirical realities as seen anew with the reframed mind.

As seen already in earlier chapters, *reframing* involves the newly shaped understanding of their situation that scenario learners create with the help of the imagined future contexts. Thus the 9/11 attacks in New York and Washington have been understood very differently depending on whether one attended to them with Shell's Business Class scenario or the Prism scenario (see Appendix B). As we saw in Chapter 1, if learners holding one frame consider the alternative reframings, our experience suggests they will better *reperceive* their situation because of the comparison they have made. Put differently, scenario learners want to be better prepared for whichever future unfolds. In order to understand the opportunities and challenges that a shift in future context holds for them, they are well advised to see the context from contrasting perspectives (scenarios) that can help them consider an alternative way of framing their understanding. See Box 3.4 for a beautiful example of how this works.

This reframing of knowledge often produces new, shared strategic vocabulary through the social processes of sensemaking discussed in Chapter 2. For example, the term *Silicon Age*, the name of one of the UEG scenarios in Appendix C, connotes a specific set of possibilities for the medical doctors that are using the UEG scenarios to direct R&D spending and policy.

BOX 3.4 REFRAMING *13 DAYS*

In the film *13 Days* on the Cuban missile crisis, President Kennedy—JFK—is given a scenario of how the crisis will unfold by his military colleagues. Unfortunately, this will unleash World War III. JFK asks his brother, Attorney-General Bobby Kennedy, to manufacture an alternative scenario. Bobby and those he consults think that a blockade of Cuba is better than bombing the nuclear missiles—*if* this scenario is accepted by the Soviets. But a "blockade," they discover, is also an act of war. To prevent war, JFK relabels the Bobby scenario and calls it an "embargo," which is not an act of war. They try it out. Relabeling opens up a new reality. They then realize that the reframing of the crisis as an embargo might help Khrushchev to tell his generals that another scenario than the war scenario (which positioning the missiles in Cuba was meant to develop) is possible. Bobby meets the Soviet ambassador secretly to test if this message is also plausible in the Kremlin. They agree on a secret deal to remove US missiles from Turkey to make it plausible. And so World War III is averted.

A similar reframing was performed more recently, when the originally named Hurricane Sandy was relabeled as Tropical Storm Sandy. The relabeling changed what insurance money could be paid out to affected New Jersey and New York residents.[11]

KNOWLEDGE ABOUT THE FUTURE IS PARTIAL, TENTATIVE, AND HYPOTHETICAL

Because the future is both "not yet in" and also "an inherent part of" the present, knowledge about it can at best be only partial, hypothetical, and tentative. Scenario planners have dealt with this in a number of ways. Pierre Wack (1985a) suggested that an important role of scenario planning in strategy was to separate out what he called "predetermined elements"—that is, sticky tendencies which would continue in all scenarios of a given set—from those parts of the future that remained scenario-dependent, that is, the "critical uncertainties."

New insights are created with scenario planning through identifying, researching, and, most importantly, combining the critical uncertainties. This also produces new questions, which in many scenario engagements leads to further research. This is very much like the way social science research produces grounded theory,[12] as we discuss in Chapter 5.

Knowledge in scenario planning therefore typically involves learners explicitly addressing knowable, known, and (for them) unknown aspects of the future contexts they might be in. For any individual learner the scenario intervention is an exploration of the limits of what is known. It follows that doing scenario planning expands what the individual learners can talk about, know, and collectively appreciate.[13]

KNOWLEDGE OF THE FUTURE WITH SCENARIO PLANNING ENGAGES UNCERTAINTY

We saw in Chapter 1 that in TUNA conditions the applicability of probability is limited, so learners would be well advised to avoid seeking accurate predictions in situations where it is illogical to expect these. "In an equivocal, postmodern world, infused with the politics of interpretation and conflicting interests and inhabited by people with multiple shifting identities, an obsession with accuracy seems fruitless, and not of much practical help, either" (Weick 1995, 61).

Scenario planning helps people to imagine possible futures and to converse about new developments. Scenario planning seeks to help learners in TUNA conditions productively to engage otherwise unintelligible puzzles or conundrums, and to appreciate better the implications of the ambiguities they face. These ambiguities may appear as incompatible certainties that without a scenario planning intervention could lead to fragmentation, but with scenario planning can help produce interesting insights for the different learners involved, as illustrated in the AiA scenario planning case study in Appendix D.

Scenario planning also helps learners to clarify what they feel they ought to understand better: phenomena such as hunches, doubts, ill-defined and awkwardly labeled issues. In addition, emerging, almost imperceptible trends which can raise uncomfortable questions in people's minds can be "put on the table," debated, and redefined to be further researched. People are sometimes acutely aware, but sometimes only vaguely or implicitly, that they do not understand these ephemera very well, particularly in terms of what they mean or how they might play out. This pertains to tacit knowledge as well as questions that have remained unarticulated. Richard Normann, as we saw in Chapter 1, suggested that upframing helps such matters to be examined more productively (see Box 3.5).

Situations of risk are different from situations of uncertainty (Knight 1921). Ramírez and Ravetz (2011) underlined the dangers of applying risk-management tools designed for dealing with stable and predictable situations, to novel or ambiguous challenges often characterized by the deep uncertainty (referred to as Knightian uncertainty) of TUNA conditions. For instance, probabilistic risk assessment tools assume a normal statistical distribution of data collected in the past, and expected to remain relevant in supporting decisions about future situations. That is, the underlying causal structure—the "system conditions"—does not change. In these situations the so-called "bell curve" (the "normal" or Gaussian distribution) provides an accurate guide to the distribution of future events. For example, in the insurance industry, the underwriters of policies assume that demography is destiny. Insurance premiums are based on the statistically derived risk profile of a population, and premiums are adjusted from year to year as new data are collected. High-impact but low-probability risks are usually excluded from

---

BOX 3.5 RECONSIDERING CERTAINTIES AT WÄRTSILÄ

A scenario planning workshop on possible futures for shipping was conducted with members of the management team of Wärtsilä's ship engine division and a small number of invited experts of related fields (such as marine insurance, financing, regulation, logistics, and so on). Several "upframed"—that is, contextual—uncertainties regarding global shipping were identified, as well as sixteen contextual factors that the fifteen participants unanimously agreed would certainly remain or would have happened by the end of the agreed scenario time horizon.

After the uncertainties had been related to each other and combined into a small set of plausible and contrasting scenarios, the workshop participants revisited those factors they had all been certain about prior to exploring the plausible combination of uncertain factors as scenarios. Only a fraction remained.

Following this first iteration of scenario planning work, the substantial decrease in the number of factors in the context of global shipping which were believed would remain certain meant that the appreciation of what had been "known" before the workshop had been transformed in the space of a few hours of reflection.

New opportunities and new challenges had been identified.

For more detail about the Wärtsilä scenario planning processes, see Appendix A.

---

general insurance cover or carry an additional cost (e.g. cover for extreme sports such as paragliding or off-piste skiing).

However, when a novel event occurs, by definition it falls outside the range of any statistical probability assessment. For example, who could have predicted that the fastest rise in sexually transmitted diseases in the UK would occur in the over-sixty population? Experts have speculated that this may be linked to the availability of the drug Viagra, which itself was discovered through the treatment of heart disease. Similarly, the 2008 financial crisis illustrated the foolhardiness of using probabilistic assessment to estimate the potential for catastrophe of a novel situation. In this case a globalized financial system had been made much more complex by the widespread use of new financial products, automated trading, and long, opaque chains of banking sector intermediaries operating between lenders and borrowers.

Scenario planning helps individuals to engage with deep uncertainty—and that is why probability is unhelpful in assessing which scenario might unfold (Ramírez and Selin 2014). We elaborate on these ideas in the next section.

Engaging the unknown and the uncertain: scenario planning as research methodology in the OSPA

Research is an activity through which learners engage that which they do not know and/or are uncertain about. Scenario planning has been the object of social science research for many years, but as we see it in the OSPA, scenario planning is itself a research methodology, not just a management practice.

Researching social phenomena with scenarios in TUNA conditions focuses on the boundary between the contextual and transactional environments (see Chapter 1, especially Figure 1.2), setting the stage for what strategists or other learners might need to do interactively within different future transactional environments. Scenario planning learners researching such conditions are well advised to use methodologies that are open to multiple points of view. A thirty-year-old book provides excellent guidance.

BEYOND METHOD

The diversity of available methods with which to carry out social science research was explored by Gareth Morgan in his remarkable 1983 edited volume *Beyond Method: Strategies for Social Research*. He and his colleagues reviewed twenty-one different approaches with which to research social phenomena. In Morgan's own words, such "diversity ... is clearly overwhelming" (1983, 368). But is this overwhelming diversity a problem, or a treasure trove that offers a rich palette of possible ways of knowing?

Morgan's response to this question was clear: no research method among the twenty-one presented is clearly superior to all the others because no meta-criteria exist to make this judgment.[14] Thus, while acknowledging the whole history of epistemology has hinged on stabilizing what is meant by knowledge (1983, 372), he concluded no one of the twenty-one existing social science methods is capable of explaining the other twenty. His efforts to bring together, deeply analyze, and compare all those research methods led him to work within a more limited goal, namely, "exploring and understanding [the] significance" of each of them (1983, 373).

Morgan found that "it becomes clear from reading [the twenty-one approaches in] this volume that social scientists, like other generators of knowledge, deal in possibilities ... [and] ... are concerned with the realization of *possible knowledge* ..." (1983, 369, italics in original). His stance was that a "reflective social science" would need to replace "the notion that assumptions and knowledge can be certain, authoritative, and unambiguously 'true' (except under limited, controlled circumstances) with the idea that uncertainty is a defining feature" (1983, 383).

For us in the OSPA, Morgan's views mean that scenario planners have to be both methodologically open and also very clear about the assumptions they as learners make in deploying this or that method of inquiry. It is in this sense that we consider scenario planning to be a research methodology. That is, scenario planning as understood in the OSPA can be seen as research that produces knowledge through action (Morgan 1983, 399)—or more precisely, through interaction, as we saw in Chapter 2. We in the OSPA are aligned with Morgan in considering scenario planning as "an approach to research that is substantially rational in the sense that its practitioners develop a capacity to observe and question what they are doing and to take responsibility for making intelligent choices about the means they adopt and the ends these serve." Like Morgan's researchers, good OSPA scenario planners "actively examine the choices that are open to realize the many potential types of knowledge waiting to be engaged, with active anticipation of the consequences of such engagement" (1983, 406).

THE "INTUITIVE LOGICS" SCENARIO PLANNING METHODOLOGY

Some influential scenario planning scholars (Wack 1985a, 1985b; Bradfield et al. 2005) have claimed that the scenario planning which engages the unknown involves "intuitive logics." We here examine this choice of label. As we noted earlier, intuition was very important for Pierre Wack; he in fact thought that what he called "intuition" was the central point in scenario planning. Wack was intent on helping highly paid experts in organizations to train intuition, rather than ignoring it, as an essential quality of the entrepreneurial business leader. Van der Heijden et al.'s (2002) book *The Sixth Sense* explored this aspect of scenario method.

Yet what does "intuition" really mean? It may mean what in East Asian cultures (where Wack traveled and studied extensively) would be called "mindfulness." Or, as Kahneman and Klein (2009, 515) argue, it could mean a form of accessing knowledge derived from judgments made vis-à-vis the predictability of the environment in which the intuition is exercised.[15]

In scenario situations, where there is precious little *predictability* of the environment, Kahneman and Klein's description of "intuition" is unhelpful. However, Wack's notion of intuition as a "felt sense" (what is colloquially called "gut feeling") can be helpful in uncertain conditions.[16]

Thus, in OSPA methodology "intuition" holds an important role in the iterative process of disciplined imagination which opens up new, critical, and different future possibilities in the present and contributes to developing new shared vocabulary. Intuition enables "upframed" learning and shared understanding about a "whole" situation, that is, in articulating the bigger picture of the known and of the as yet unknown. Intuition is also important in the OSPA iterative search and research process, where plausibility rather than probability is used to guide attention to what needs to be researched further. Moreover, rather than being independent of the inquirer, plausibility is co-created with other learners, iterating between story and system maps, followed by creative dialogue and critical reasoning. This iterative articulation process of what is intuited involves "disciplined imagination" that engages the mental models of others, without individuals having to agree with each other. As we saw in Chapter 2, the conversations engage shared sensemaking via structured and open-space dialogues designed and managed as safe transitional spaces, typically held in workshops. These processes are in turn supported by analytical research, modeling, and peer reviewed refinement of successive drafts of the scenarios between workshops. We discuss the role of models and modeling in scenario planning later in this chapter.

The type of insight that the imagination of scenario learners produces can also be called "intuition." Insight about the role of uncertain contextual factors can be cultivated using a variety of scenario building methods which we discuss in Chapter 5. It is important to recall that the aim is to appreciate how connections in the future among uncertain contextual factors can shift the understanding of the present situation. So an understanding of how the "system" describing how these uncertain contextual factors might be connected in the future is fabricated by the scenario planners. It is then tested for plausibility with the learners over several iterations. With each iteration new questions tend to be discovered and researched; the set of scenarios is expanded or reduced; and the storylines are further refined. In theory, this cycle might go on forever. In practice the number of iterations will typically reach what social scientists call *saturation*, the point beyond which an extra iteration adds very little extra knowledge. The iterations can also be limited by the available time and resources, or by the rhythm of other organizational processes for which the scenario planning outputs are often inputs for decision making, such as strategic planning cycles or risk-management requirements.

SCENARIO ITERATIONS AS A METHODOLOGY TO PRODUCE "INTERESTING" RESEARCH

Ramírez et al. (2015) proposed that developing and revising scenarios, when considered as a methodology of scholarly inquiry, is a good way to produce *interesting* research. The notion of interesting research had been taken up in the Academy of Management, the premier association of management scholars in the world (Bartunek et al. 2006). For them interesting research:

- develops theory;
- is more likely to produce learning, to be read, understood, and remembered;
- disconfirms some, but not all, of the assumptions held by those who read it; and
- is counter-intuitive in the sense that it challenges established theory and/or creates an "aha" moment.

These are all qualities present in scenario planning, particularly given the OSPA's role as a methodology for reframing.

Alvesson and Sandberg blamed the lack of interesting research on "the almost total dominance of incremental gap-spotting research within management studies" (2013, 129). They proposed that gap-spotting research makes it difficult "to ask more fundamental and skeptical questions that may encourage some significant rethinking of the subject matter in question" (2013, 134).[17] In other words, the type of inquiry that scenario planning—as understood in the OSPA—excels in is not undertaken enough, and so not enough interesting research is being produced.

Instead, Alvesson and Sandberg advocated the pursuit of "more genuine and scholarly values and qualities like being intellectually broad-minded, independent, imaginative, willing to take risks, enthusiastic about intellectual adventures, and frequently provocative." What is needed, they believed, is researchers "with a broader outlook, curious, reflective, willing and able to question their own frameworks and to consider alternative positions, and eager to produce new insights" (2013, 143). They called for "methodologies that more directly stimulate new and challenging ideas and contributions" (2013, 144). Such scholarship, they proposed, would set or upset paths, challenge consensus, span theoretical frameworks, and bend frames (2013, 148).

Ramírez et al. (2015) pointed out that this is exactly the type of research that scenario iterations as understood in the OSPA can help inquirers to produce. They compared three research studies which used scenarios as the core scholarly methodology to create new lines of inquiry—on the way retailing formats are unfolding in India, on Mediterranean migration patterns, and on local adaptation options to climate change in the tourism industry in the Mexican Caribbean. Their analyses demonstrated that scenario planning as a research methodology can help to produce new "interesting" research lines of inquiry, as well as research that is both usable and rigorous.

Eliciting and accessing knowledge

At the time Pierre Wack was working on scenario planning, from the 1960s to the 1980s, knowledge was less easy to access than it is today. Wilkinson and Kupers (2014) reported that in that era, before the days of personal computing, the scenario team in Shell comprised twenty-five persons, the majority of them analysts, and two experienced businessmen.

Data, information, and knowledge are all being fundamentally transformed as we write this in 2015. Recent studies have found that over 80 percent of all data in the world have been produced in the last two years, and that a single issue of the *New York Times* contains more information than was accessible in a whole lifetime a few centuries ago. The wide availability of digital storage, with online access, semi-automatic translations, and powerful search engines, means that accessing knowledge may have at least partially overcome the challenges posed by growing knowledge accumulation.

Nonetheless, significant costs are incurred in accessing, marshaling, analyzing, and combining existing knowledge to produce a set of scenarios. Why might this be the case? Perhaps such costs arise because these activities are not (or not yet!) amenable to direct translation from the powerful search engines (or "big data") to actionable stories for specific learners. Emerging approaches such as crowdsourcing, open source, and networked foresight may cut costs and/or accelerate the production stages, but far more careful design of the inquiring system and the truth values sought will be required than has been the case in the past.

ACCESSING INNOVATIVE KNOWLEDGE

There is a huge literature, well beyond the scope of this book, on the "knowledge economy" and how sharing knowledge fuels innovation. This phenomenon is behind the huge growth in patenting and was explored by the EPO using scenario planning (see Appendix E).

Knowledge that is situated in a specific setting often involves understanding that cannot be easily transposed from one set of circumstances and actors to others. Knowledge sharing is key to making tacit knowledge explicit and to generating new and shared insights.

Yet, as we saw earlier, knowledge of the present developed from future perspectives cannot be "disciplined" in the positivist sense of empirical, predictive science. Furthermore, new knowledge is interesting but also challenging—if, that is, it undermines established power structures. So not all new, and in this sense innovative, knowledge is readily accepted. This is well documented in the history of scientific progress: as Kuhn noted, science proceeds one death at a time. Indeed, despite rhetoric on the need for more interdisciplinary understanding, academic disciplines represent silos of power and authority which all too often keep interdisciplinary work as an exception. So how can new knowledge generated by learning with futures in a scenario planning process avoid these challenges and be put to use? According to Alvesson and Sandberg, not by producing gap-filling incremental research. Instead, the usability of the new insights generated with scenario planning can be facilitated by engaging directly with the experts who work in silos. This is evident in the AiA, Risk-World, EPO, and UEG cases in the Appendices.

As elaborated in Chapter 4, processes of accessing knowledge can also be helped by other interactive processes, such as reaching out to remarkable individuals, organizing learning journeys to settings with emergent versions of a plausible future, and eliciting tacit knowledge through drawings.

Remarkable people

Pierre Wack got the idea of "remarkable" people from his mentor George Gurdjieff, a Sufi-trained mystic.[18] Wack saw these remarkable people as intellectual entrepreneurs who opened up new frames of reference that tempted curiosity—early detectors of a new, still emergent future possibility or of an already emerging order. He discovered these people through his regular travels to the East, where he sought to gain different perspectives from his Western-trained way of thinking.[19]

Some now seem to think of remarkable people as the powerbrokers who are "setting the agenda," not necessarily the pre-sensors as Wack thought of them. Others today think people are "remarkable" if they are at the top of their field—best-selling authors, Nobel Prize winners, top achievers in the world of sport or entertainment, etc. While they are clearly successful, such people are not necessarily remarkable in Wack's sense. Given the increasing numbers of "thought leaders" invited to big events to offer keynote addresses, or whose TED talks are available online for all to be edified, the cult of celebrity poses a stiff challenge to Wack's notion of remarkable people. As one of our former Shell scenario colleagues once glibly commented, "I have now met several so-called remarkable people, and found them to be rather unremarkable." Scenarists working in the OSPA tradition keep the original notion of remarkable in the sense of perspectives that help to expose, challenge, and reframe conventionally accepted wisdom. See Box 3.6 for a brief example from our practice.

Remarkable people are not necessarily people one has never met, but can also include people whose remarkable views one has never accessed because the settings in which one meets them does not allow this. Recall that generating and accessing knowledge with scenario planning involves searching for better questions, and avoiding defaulting too quickly—and too early—to problem-solving approaches. This can be achieved in several iterations of the scenario planning cycle. The UEG case (Appendix C) shows how interesting research is enabled with the OSPA. In that case, some twenty-five

---

BOX 3.6 JUST CREDIBLE ENOUGH

Just after the collapse of the Berlin Wall, Ramírez and Richard Normann were working on what Finland's economy might be after the collapse of the USSR (which was a very considerable percent of Finnish business customers) with a very high-profile Finnish investing group. The consultants brought in Dr. Noriko Hama—a Japanese economist then working in London—to speak with the board of this company, as she had recently written a book on the future of Europe called *Disintegrating Europe* (1996). Her views contravened the prevailing mindset at the time. Her analysis was just credible enough to spark a conversation to explore its plausibility, and it became a central feature in one of the scenarios that were then developed.

experts invested large amounts of their time voluntarily because they found the exchanges so fruitful and interesting. Disagreements between disciplines, such as radiology or surgery, provoked them to surface and test the assumptions they were making, such as whether antibiotics might cease to be effective. This brought forth new understanding for them as learners.

Learning journeys

Learning journeys involve attending to Gibson's observation that we mentioned earlier, that "the future is already here, it's just not very evenly distributed." If a group of scenario learners in the Belgian banking sector wanted to better understand how a widely available, very high-speed broadband Internet service might affect banking and retailing, they could travel to South Korea, where that situation has been unfolding for some time. If they wanted to consider how mobile phone retailing might transform the financial services sector, they could look at the rapid uptake of M-Pesa in Kenya. If their scenario planning included attention to "garage innovation" and how venture capital might transform new business start-ups, Silicon Valley would be a good place to visit. Ideally, these learning journeys would involve gathering different perspectives by meeting with different stakeholders and as many remarkable people as possible in their own settings in the emerging ecosystem.

Accessing innovative knowledge within ubiquitous information contexts

In today's fast-paced world of social media enabled connection and community, there are many ways to both connect with, and feel overwhelmed by, the numerous and diverse cutting edges of multifaceted modern societies. With ubiquitous instant global news, myriad online descriptions of local events, and 24/7/365 streaming of trivia (dancing cats!), information and misinformation can spread more widely and quickly, and can have more unexpected impacts, than ever before.

As opposed to discovering "new" knowledge, we can become flooded with information signals of the present: "the latest" news. The challenge for scenario planners is to try to find a higher logical perspective and assemble logical insights about key developments that are relevant and challenging to the scenario planning learner's perspectives, *focusing on the wider context*. Daniel Dennett (1995) called such a perspective a sky hook, SRI a helicopter view, and Richard Normann (2001) a crane.

Revealing and adopting alternative frames is not easy. Two common challenges are: (1) avoiding stereotypes to instead develop new frames as archetypes; and (2) producing requisite variety. The examples in Box 3.7 may help to convey these challenges.

BOX 3.7 VARIETY AND STEREOTYPE ISSUES IN DEVELOPING A SCENARIO

Ensuring requisite variety. According to scenario writer Betty Sue Flowers (2007), Emeritus Professor of English, University of Houston, old myths do not get replaced by new myths and in modern societies different myths—heroic, religious, scientific, and economic—coexist. She suggests a new "ecological myth" is beginning to emerge which points to a new model of progress, in which capitalism contributes to the regeneration of natural capital. For example, in the early years of its work using scenarios, the Intergovernmental Panel on Climate Change (IPCC)'s scenario framework consisted of a 2 × 2 matrix in which one of the axes juxtaposed "economy" versus "environment." By implication, this axis can reflect only two of the four perspectives of "nature" described by the "myths of nature in cultural theory," developed by Schwarz and Thompson (1990). In this typology of myths, both the egalitarian perspective, which assumes nature is more fragile than the economy, and the individualist perspective, which assumes the market is more fragile than nature, in effect support the view of the trade-off of more economy or more environment, albeit for different reasons. Similarly, in the three scenarios in the Risk-World scenario planning case study (Appendix F), three active perspectives are reflected—the individualist, the egalitarian, and the hierarchical. In modern societies, according to Marchais-Roubelat and Roubelat (2008), scenarios can help navigate different myths. Working with myths in a way that enables scenario learners to listen for the story that is emerging is, we believe, fundamental to the framing and reframing potential enabled in the scenario planning process.

Avoiding stereotype. The so-called "blue-greens story" recounted by some now retired scenario planners in Shell, dealt with the Brent Spar incident. In 1995, Shell was planning to sink the Brent Spar oil storage platform and tanker loading buoy, which had reached the end of its economic life, on site in the North Sea. As the story has been told, the Shell senior managers at the time reportedly thought that all environmentalists were blue-greens—or BGs. BGs at that time were people who sat on the boards of high-profile established NGOs like the WWF, were members of the right (typically gentlemen's) clubs, and then went on shoots together in Africa or Northern Canada. Unexpectedly, Greenpeace activists occupied the buoy and staged a highly effective international media campaign against the planned sinking, claiming it was full of toxic waste. As Elkington and Trisoglio (1996) proposed in their critique of Shell's handling of this incident, Shell's reaction to Greenpeace's occupation of the buoy, and its inability to imagine that possibility in advance, was captured by what according to the story was its single "BG" perspective of what "greens" were. The story these managers told themselves was the story that BGs told each other. Alternative stories, where environmentalists might be "red" (left wing radicals turned environmentalists) or "green" (deep ecologists concerned about the planet's sustainability) were either ignored, unknown, or dismissed. That Greenpeace would act according to a red or green framing, and not the (implicit, unquestioned) blue one, was unexpected. The lesson? The stories that bind people can blind them to their deeper underpinning mythology.

Thus, scenario planning can be thought of as a methodology that constructively brings a requisite variety of alternative perspectives to bear on a situation. Often one of these perspectives reflects the prevailing conventional wisdom, and the others give voice to alternative perspectives that are suppressed either by the absence of any real strategic conversation, by ignorance, by organizational power dynamics, or by professional cultural pressures favoring conformity and consensus.

The roles of modeling in scenario planning

Modeling provides a way to develop new knowledge that is useful for intervening more effectively in a given situation. It involves developing a deeper level of logic (that is, more systemic understanding) of a given situation, and looking beyond events and trends to render explicit the underlying causal structure of a situation. There are many different ways to model, including visual models (e.g. drawing rich pictures in Soft Systems Methodology, architectural drawings); computing-based and/or mathematical (or "formal") models; and physical models, such as design prototypes. There are also many different purposes for developing models, such as prediction, simulation, and communication.

Moreover, any model is parsimonious: it reduces complex realities and manifests these in a salient and comprehensible form. In scenario planning, it is important to avoid "model lock-in" (which prevents alternative framings) and to remember that a model designed to "work" to some specific purpose, set of learners, and situation might not be useful for others.

In the OSPA, a scenario is a flexible and disposable *descriptive* model, that is, it provides a description of a future context in a way that is considered to be plausible, challenging, and useful for the intended purpose and user it was designed for.

As we explained in Chapter 2, in the OSPA we do not use the term "scenario" to describe the range of possible outcomes of a formal model, or set of coupled formal models, as has been done for example by scientists in the Intergovernmental Panel on Climate Change (IPCC).[20] Instead, we suggest scenario planning can help avoid models locking into the present, as discussed by Mangalagiu et al. (2011).

In the OSPA we maintain scenarios as bespoke, usable, and disposable models, and carefully attend to the sequencing of qualitative and quantitative modeling in order to enable conceptual reframing and avoid default to the official future.[21]

In the OSPA we also respect that quantification is essential in scenario planning interventions in cultures (national or professional) in which numbers are used to consider options and inform decisions. But note that even in this application, quantification is indicative rather than predictive. So quantitative modeling within scenarios—such as projecting the demographic profile of a country, estimating the remaining supply of an industry's key resource, or forecasting global GDP, can have several uses. They can enable a check of the internal logic of each scenario, and they can also offer examples and numerical illustrations that enhance the plausibility of each scenario (Wilkinson and Kupers 2014). And while quantification is a welcome aspect in the OSPA, assigning probability to the scenarios is not.

Scenarios can be translated into one or more formal models to enable them to be contrasted with each other using quantitative metrics; essentially this means forecasting *within* each of the scenario contexts. The Shell 2001 global scenarios in Appendix B illustrate this value of quantification. It suggests the trajectory that can be expected within a scenario. In some cases, it may be possible to use the same quantitative model to illustrate all the scenarios in a set.[22] In other cases, it may be more helpful to the learner to select different models to illustrate and/or check the internal consistency of the storyline and/or system map.

Thus, the OSPA is incompatible with scenario approaches that seek to model situations by providing comprehensive inventories of all contextual factors, calculating the outcomes of all possible combinations, and using some form of (typically probabilistic) analysis to reduce the combinations to the most "likely" set—and pretending this can be done "objectively" (Lloyd and Schweizer 2014).

COMPARING QUANTITATIVE AND QUALITATIVE MODELS

In the OSPA we recognize the limits of linear thinking, as we work with more complex, emergent situations and embrace systems thinking. We consider the future to be fictional and useful rather than factual and truthful; so it is these fictions that need to be modeled, not "reality."

There are many different kinds of models and modeling approaches that can be used at different stages in a scenario planning process. In what follows we review the three main models.

Quantitative models. As Harvard professor Clayton Christensen has remarked, the invention of the spreadsheet has spawned a modeling industry of ratios which has invaded and colonized the administrative world. Recently graduated MBAs with no industry knowledge working in rating agencies now tell deeply experienced CEOs of sophisticated technology companies what to change in their debt or return-on-capital ratios so that their financing is rated favorably. Professional institutionalization has contributed to ossify these modeling procedures, making them difficult to avoid, even as what is modeled becomes ever more divorced from the realities of the real economy. This "managing by ratios" financial modeling trend not only renders the exercise of experience-based knowledge and judgment less common, but assumes there will be no new field-level constraints or disruptions, which is a naïve assumption under TUNA conditions. Scenario planners have to determine where and how to situate their practices in such administrative contexts where the strategic imperative is gaining or sustaining the dominant position within the industry (i.e. sectoral competitiveness).

Given that learners participating in a scenario development process are looking to inform new and better coping options that might work under multiple futures, mathematical models can be both useful and problematic in scenario planning. There are two important challenges.

First, the scenario planner can usually only insert quantifiable facts into the models that have been derived using data about the past. Some of what used to be important may also remain important in the future, but looking only to past quantifiable facts precludes novel developments. These include social and institutional innovation and the unprecedented dynamics of more connected societies and globally interdependent markets, not to mention the potential of game-changing technologies and the impacts of anthropogenic global environmental changes. For example, measures of productivity and national industrial production systems that were important for economic growth in the 1950s are irrelevant to the measurement of networked, platform-dependent professional services in today's global value chains. Many of today's socially and economically important phenomena—whether global environmental change, the food-energy-water stress nexus, rising and structural inequality, or even tweeting—look like anomalies in established formal models.

Second, as discussed above, any model can only partially represent that which it seeks to present. Typically it leaves in assumptions which may have held and still have strong historical support and legitimacy but may not remain valid over the future time horizon of the scenario planning intervention.

Qualitative systems modeling. There is a considerable literature on system dynamics that is relevant here, and reviewing it thoroughly is well beyond the scope of this book.[23] In Chapter 2 we showed how, in addition to the storyline, scenarios are described using system maps that visually manifest the causal logic of the future context of the learner's situation. Such maps link factors to each other through causal loop diagrams. These are representations, or qualitative models, of a system. They describe the key variables that produce the system and the positive ("reinforcing") and negative ("balancing") connections between those variables. Some of the connections form feedback loops, which can be thought of as subsystems that either amplify[24] or dampen the dynamics of the larger system. In scenario planning, the emphasis on feedback loops helps the scenario learner to clarify the stability (or instability) of the scenario. For example, in a system characterized by multiple dampening loops the causal dynamic is self-sustaining, meaning that if the scenario came to be, the system it represents would likely be stable and endure for a long time. As qualitative system dynamics models visually manifest the underlying structure of phenomena supporting and even determining behavior in and of a system,[25] they are sympathetic with soft systems thinking. However, Checkland's

Soft Systems Methodology has been found difficult to implement in practice (Lang and Allen 2008), and to our knowledge it has been used in only a few scenario planning interventions.

Design prototyping. In the OSPA, scenarios are used to test, develop, and rehearse new and different options for action to intervene in the present situation. In effect, each option is a form of design prototype—a so-called clay model, which takes a physical form. This was explored in depth in the Fourth Oxford Futures Forum held in 2014; the report is available online,[26] and a special issue based on that Forum is being prepared for the journal *Futures*. We explain in more detail in Chapter 5 how the scenarios are linked to strategic management systems to generate and test options.

MODEL BUILDING IN GROUPS

As mentioned in Chapter 2, scenario building is a social process which iterates between the development of system maps and the use of storytelling to provide clearer and more logical descriptions of each alternative future context. We noted that the system maps are developed in a process of group model building. Sometimes it is possible to describe all the scenarios using the same causal loop diagram, with a different emphasis given to the feedback loops of various subsystems. In other circumstances, this is neither possible nor effective in terms of enabling reframing to serve the purpose of the scenario learner. In our teaching we have found Senge's (1990) and Vennix's (1996) guidance on the issues relating to model building to be an effective mechanism for team-based learning.

SOME USES OF MODELING IN THE SCENARIO PROCESS

Modeling takes place at various points in the scenario planning process. Key moments are listed here.

Opening up causal logics. Similar to the surfacing of myths in storytelling, qualitative models can help to reflect and open up the causal logics that are being assumed in the conventional framing of a strategic situation. As we have discussed, it is important for every learner in a scenario planning process to articulate their own views and compare them with others. Modeling offers a structured way of eliciting the knowledge that may have been taken for granted and explicitly organizing it as a model, or set of models, of the future situation.

When ambiguity arises in understanding a frame offered by a participant in a group for other group members, or when contrarian and incompatible certitudes are present, flexible modeling can help avoid personalization of who is right and who is wrong. Instead it can redirect attention to why different perspectives arise in terms of the framing and associated uncertainties assumed by each perspective, helping all involved to adequately describe the underlying causal logics. This frees the inquirers' minds to become more open because the conversation moves from the person to the group's different model(s). The models, in turn, become "actors" in the group, and the substance of the matter as modeled is distanced from the proponent or the attacker (Ramírez and Drevon 2005). Qualitative models can thus help the scenario planners to make space to accommodate conflict, and help each individual to help others in the group to clarify what factors in the context they have taken as unchanging (that is, predetermined elements) and what factors are critical uncertainties. As we saw in Chapter 2, modeling can thus convert what would otherwise remain a zero-sum strategic framing contest into a learning dialogue. For instance, scenario planning in the Risk-World project (Appendix F) allowed incompatible ways of framing the shifting landscape of risk to be jointly considered.

Building new and shared knowledge. Soft Systems Methodology (also covered in Chapter 5) was designed by Peter Checkland and his colleagues to integrate systems ideas, dialogue, and action-orientation into a coherent modeling approach. It takes differences among the worldviews of people affected by a situation explicitly into account, seeking to help them agree about what actions are desirable and feasible to improve that situation, however modestly. Soft Systems Methodology assumes upfront that clashing worldviews are always present in human affairs, and takes the disagreement as a source of insight, energy, and creative tension (see Checkland and Poulter 2008). Another comparable method that has been used in scenario planning is fuzzy logic (see Chapter 5, note 2).

Decision support and analyzing options. In any scenario planning intervention, it is possible to test existing strategic options or illustrate the economic and financial implications of new options implied in each scenario (or generated using the whole set) through quantification. An example is the different rates and patterns of economic growth that are plausible in each of the Shell global scenarios (see Appendix B). The quantification of the scenarios can also be useful for reviewing the costs of options and the level and timing of finance needed to maintain an option as a real choice. In our experience, this "wind-tunneling" work supports redesigning the options rather than enabling an accurate and precise calculation of decision outcomes as a guide to rational choice.

Rehearsing the future and visualizing scenario implications. This combination of qualitative-quantitative modeling helps in designing and prototyping the kinds of actions that will be successful in the context of the differing interactions implied in each scenario storyline. It supports a form of immersive learning, such as policy gaming, role-playing simulations (both competitive and collaborative), and 3D rendering of what new possibility spaces might look like.[27] In the Wärtsilä scenario planning case (Appendix A), the shipping division developed prototypes of the kind of ship that would be successful for the company to build in each of the three scenarios. This helped to render and clarify strategic choices that were being taken by different actors across the company.[28]

Engagement and communication. The outputs of group model building, such as causal loop diagrams or system maps, and the quantitative illustration of scenario stories using graphs to represent a forecast within the scenario, do two things: they help to visualize and communicate the frame suggested by each scenario storyline, and also help in comparing the scenarios in the set with each other. This in turn contributes to manifesting meaningful differences and to the memorability and communicability of the scenario set within and between different professional constituencies, as seen in the EPO scenarios described in Appendix E. As the saying goes, "a picture says a thousand words," and so a forecast-based graph always assumes a scenario, but rarely makes the scenario it assumes explicit.

The roles of research in scenario planning

In the OSPA, three types of research support scenario planning. Each contributes a different kind of knowledge for designing, manufacturing, and contrasting an effective set of scenarios.

First, there is *research to look back*. In order to be used, scenario planning has to be usable. To be usable, scenario planning needs to find a home in the minds of the learners it serves and supports, who work in some organized setting. In an established organization, that home—a distributed, intricate set of tasks, roles, relationships, routines, norms, and myths—has been built up for years. So the scenario planner needs to research not only the nature of that home as it now exists, but also how and why it came about, its developmental trajectory, and key events or inflection points. Particularly for organizations that had not used scenarios in the past (see the UEG, Wärtsilä, and AiA cases in the Appendices), this "homemaking" is important to prevent scenario planning being rejected outright before it has had a chance to prove its worthiness. We return to the notion of "homemaking" in Chapter 4.

Moreover, the futures that scenario planning brings to the learners in an organization will also need to have a home not only in the present but also in the past (Heckscher et al. 2003). This is because the past is the source of an organization's (or a profession's or culture's) identity; and the present is where current goals, interests, and power are played out. If a set of scenarios cannot be accommodated within the organization's identity, they will not be accepted as relevant in the present. Investigating how scenario planning might have

---

BOX 3.8 CLEAR REASONS TO DOUBT

When one of us (Ramírez) visited BMW's Mini car manufacturing facility in Oxford with a group of utility managers, one of the German plant managers—let's call him Franz—told us the following story. One day after a couple of years in the UK, Franz was looking forward to announcing great news to the workers: HQ in Munich had determined that a new car model would be built in the plant. He expected this news to be received with great joy, as in his experience in Bavaria such announcements are taken by the workers as both recognition for work well done and as ensuring more secure employment for years to come. Franz told us he was most surprised that the news did not result in cheers and joy. He asked his British colleagues why this would be the case.

He was told that although they liked him quite a lot, he was the third or fourth manager to give such news to the same workers, in the same plant. Before him, some manager from Rover had given similar news, and the new car never saw the light of day. (BMW had bought Rover, and with it the Rover plant that it redeployed to manufacture the new Mini.) Before the Rover executive, someone working with Honda had given similar news, and that car never saw the light of day either. (There had been some sort of joint-venture agreement between Rover and Honda whereby Honda-designed Rovers had been built in the plant by these workers.) And before that, someone working for British Leyland had announced a new car to these same workers, and that car also was never produced. In other words, the workers were carrying with them three or four futures that had not happened when Franz announced a new (possible) future to them.

The workers had clear reasons to doubt whether Franz' announced future would come about. Whereas in Franz' automotive manufacturing experience announced futures always did come about, in the experience of these workers they often had not.

---

been accepted in yesterday's present(s) helps to ascertain how it will work when brought into the present setting. See the example in Box 3.8.

To ascertain what trends in the present context are unsustainable, the astute scenario planner will research the past contexts that have led up to the present context.[29]

Next, there is *research to look forward*. As we discussed in Chapter 2 and earlier in this chapter, looking forward is not simply a matter of a linear extension of the usual decision-making time horizon. In the OSPA it entails working with an upframed 360-degree scan of the environment, and activating the future-to-present arrow of time (the shaded arrow in Figure 2.2) that redirects the scenario learner's attention to developments waiting to be discovered in the present.

In the OSPA, we thus differentiate between two very different modes of looking forward to enable scenario learners to redirect attention to new, less familiar, sometimes ambiguous, still emerging signals of contextual change, namely, searching and scanning.

In *searching* the focus is on aspects of the future that learners have already decided are interesting before attempting to retrieve new information. As seen earlier, several challenges may arise in this mode: digesting large volumes of data and information, perhaps structured in trends and shifts; filtering out noise to identify the most relevant signals, and developing agreed criteria for doing this (such as little-understood, high-impact, perhaps awkward to examine, high-uncertainty, and/or game-changing developments); and deciding what to do about surfaced issues that are uncomfortable or awkward.

In *scanning*, learners ideally remain open and curious, and direct more attention, to consider less familiar, sometimes difficult to express, still emerging factors of change in the contextual environment (so-called "weak signals"). They scan before attempting to decide if and how they fit with existing domains, established categories of expert inquiry, or even organized power structures. Weak signals can include signals that do not fit the schema of established approaches, or which lie beyond the accepted or official future of the organization or system undertaking the scanning. Scanning is about actively looking for what one has not yet searched for—like going to see what titles are offered in a bookstore section that one rarely visits. It also involves connecting the new signals and ideas to the (or one's own) existing knowledge base, and processing it accordingly. Scanning promotes attention to weak signals and blind spots. Ramírez and Ravetz (2011) called the stance of "letting go of the familiar" to help the mind to reperceive, "Zen-like" and "aesthetic." Getting oneself into such a stance, as we saw in Chapter 2, is sometimes assisted by the form of storytelling which helps to investigate and create new meaning and new interpretive frames. In other words, scanning can enable new units of analysis ("points") to be seen and to be connected with established points in novel and interesting ways.

The concept of *horizon scanning* has gained popularity in recent years in some governments (for example, Singapore and the UK). Also called environmental scanning or forward scanning, horizon scanning is a multidisciplinary approach to systematically looking forward. According to the OECD:[30]

Horizon scanning is a technique for detecting early signs of potentially important developments through a systematic examination of potential threats and opportunities, with emphasis on new technology and its effects on the issue at hand. The method calls for determining what is constant, what changes, and what constantly changes. It explores novel and unexpected issues as well as persistent problems and trends, including matters at the margins of current thinking that challenge past assumptions.

Horizon scanning concepts also utilize methods such as Delphi searches (Robert et al. 1998) to compare and build on expert views; and megatrends analyses,[31] often utilizing decadal timeframes to consider multiple trends with uneven impacts. However, the direction of scanning is past to future only (see van der Heijden 2005, 227–8).

In the OSPA, forward scanning not only stretches the time horizon that is considered, but also seeks to support broader or "out-of-the-box" thinking to better appreciate the possibility of disruptive change in the wider context. Forward scanning seeks to populate the contextual environment of the scenario learner's situation with illustrative story snippets developed using trend-crashing and trend-bending, rather than trend impact analyses. The combination of looking-back and looking-forward research structures the inputs for developing the scenarios. In Chapter 5 we offer details on the different scenario building methods.

Finally, there is *research to enrich and clarify the scenario set.* This mode of scenario-focused research is often a form of peer review; it builds on, tests, and refines the initial framework for structuring the scenario set as well as the initial drafts of each scenario. This research clarifies the story elements and underlying system mapping of each scenario, and contributes to structuring the uncertainties represented in the set of scenarios. This mode of research can also include prototyping as well as quantification to verify consistency. The output is a rendering of a deeper, shared understanding for the learners of framing and reframing offered by the individual scenarios and the scenario set, in the form of story maps and system maps (see Chapter 5), as well as coherent, contrasting, relevant, and radiant narratives.

Conclusion

Issues associated with knowledge acquisition, production, generation, and deployment in scenario planning work are always socially complex and intellectually challenging. They involve analytical, critical, and creative thinking, and forms of scanning that do not fit the search-based knowledge acquisition routines used in everyday problem solving.

The OSPA does not seek comprehensive knowledge of the future, recognizing this is neither possible nor useful. Instead, truth and usefulness when TUNA conditions prevail have to be contended in other ways, which we have analyzed in this chapter. We offer a summary of the differences between conventional forecasting and OSPA scenario planning in Table 3.2.

The OSPA ascribes to a critical-constructivist epistemology that underpins a pragmatic methodology well suited to strategy and policy as social learning processes. These in the OSPA provide a potent source of enhanced adaptive capacity in TUNA conditions.

The implications of the OSPA knowledge aquisition and generation process are reflected in Chapters 4–6, first in terms of scenario learners (Chapter 4), then in the concrete practices of scenario planning that facilitators and the learners they support are advised to consider (Chapter 5), and finally in the pedagogy of learning with and learning about scenario planning (Chapter 6).

Table 3.2 Forecasting versus OSPA scenario planning

	Forecasting	OSPA scenario planning
Future as...	Distant from the present, which will happen later—something one "goes into"	Paradoxical; in the present, already here, but not having taken place yet and not factual
	Continuity of the past	Different from the present; something that is "to come"
	Projection of today's trends, fact-based	A conceptual space in the here and now, always a fiction
		Open but not empty, attentive to its being a playing field of power
Ontology and epistemology	Positivist epistemology: the future as real and knowable in advance	Ontology: future is paradoxical, an aspect of the present but not yet having taken place
	Measurable and calculable (as in risk), predictable	Critical-constructivist epistemology: knowledge of the future is partial, ambiguous, involves the senses and feelings and invokes curiosity
	Probability is a useful guide to future outcomes	Turbulence, unpredictable uncertainty, novelty, and ambiguity (TUNA) conditions present an opportunity, not just a problem
		Plausibility is co-constructed and co-established socially as well as conceptually. Activating it redirects attention to signals of the future in the present that could not otherwise be seen
Emphasis on use/users	Is for "anyone," can be produced by individuals	Based in phenomenology—individual free will and intentions matter
	Separation of producer and user is valuable for objectivity	Has to be for someone—learner(s)—for some purpose, for something(s)
		Requires co-production and iteration
	Universally relevant	Designed to be disposed; accepts limited shelf life
	Reproducible, analytical outputs	Recycle with care
		Outputs always to be considered as inputs
		Is inherently a social and research process that involves the users/learners
Functions and forms	Trend analysis and projections	Pre-decision and post-decision interpretive frames and reframing in TUNA conditions
	Baseline and sensitivity analyses	Transitional space (see Chapter 2) in Singerian inquiry
	Enables collaboration on basis of (required) consensus	Supports collaboration without consensus; makes disagreement a constructive asset
Scenario planning as...	Stories that are derivatives of models, i.e. uncertainties are "in" the model	Reframing what is perceived in terms of "do-ability" and enabling new actionable possibilities to be considered
	Models as truth machines: hard systems thinking, formal models, trend analysis	Uncertainties surveyed are "of" or "about" the model (and its assumptions)
	Context of model typically ignored	Qualitative models (e.g. causal loop diagrams) can be illustrated using quantitative modeling: every model-based forecast assumes a scenario

▓ NOTES

1. This qualification also refers to Herman Kahn's (1962) famous phrase, "thinking about the unthinkable," which is catchy but an oxymoron.

2. The scenarios in the OSPA are *not*, as some authors (e.g. Lloyd and Schweizer 2014; Schweizer and Kriegler 2012) have suggested, "selected" "subjectively" from a supposedly "objective" and finite (even if considerably sized) set of possible combinations of factors.

3. Singer was a student of William James, who was one of the three key builders of pragmatist philosophy. We believe the epistemological innovation here was really Churchman's, not Singer's.

4. The etymology of the word "theory," from the Ancient Greek *theoros*, is closely related to "theater."

5. For an accessible summary, see Craig Calhoun (1995).

6. Philosophers Ernst Cassirer (1964) and Suzanne Langer (1942) distinguished symbol systems that have a one-to-one symbol-symbolized meaning architecture, such as languages and their dictionaries, from symbol systems that do not have that, such as music, painting, and sculpture.

7. In the 2014 Oxford Futures Forum, designers who make sense of and create possible futures with the help of these non-discursive symbol forms were brought together to compare their sensemaking and future design knowledge creation with forms of knowledge creation, capture, and sharing more traditionally associated with scenario work. See Fourth Oxford Futures Forum Report, May 2014: <http://www.sbs.ox.ac.uk/sites/default/files/corporate-events/oxford-futures-forum/docs-2014/OFF2014-report-design-and-scenarios-v2.pdf> (accessed January 2015). See also a forthcoming special issue of *Futures* on this topic.

8. Remember that all facts are in the past—facts *are* past act-s, and action-s, and inter-act-ions.

9. Gibson is reported to have first said this in an interview on *Fresh Air*, National Public Radio (August 31, 1993) (unverified), he repeated it, prefacing it with "As I've said many times," in "The Science in Science Fiction," *Talk of the Nation*, NPR (November 30, 1999, timecode 11:55). <http://en.wikiquote.org/wiki/William_Gibson> (accessed January 2015).

10. For a fuller argument, see Ramírez (2008).

11. <http://www.climatecentral.org/news/senator-urges-noaa-not-to-change-sandy-classification-15236> (accessed September 2015).

12. Care has to be taken when using "grounded theory," which some influential scholars have argued is an often-used excuse to do bad research. See Suddaby (2006).

13. Scenario planning often produces new questions, perhaps more than new answers. Attending to these questions (perhaps before others do, or articulated in a novel manner) can contribute to the crafting of a distinctive and eventually winning strategy.

14. Morgan explained: "As Godet has shown in relation to mathematics, there is a fallacy in the idea that the propositions of a system of thought can be proved, disproved, or evaluated on the basis of axioms within that system...(so) it is not possible to judge the validity or contribution of different research perspectives in terms of the ground assumptions of any one set of those perspectives, since the process is self-justifying. Hence the attempts...to judge the utility of different research strategies in terms of universal criteria based on the importance of generalizability, predictability and control, explanation of variance, meaningful understanding, or whatever are inevitably flawed" (1983, 15).

15. As Kahneman and Klein (2009, 515) put it: "[S]tarting from the obvious fact that professional intuition is sometimes marvellous and sometimes flawed, . . . [we attempted] to map the boundary conditions that separate true intuitive skill from overconfident and biased impressions . . . , [and concluded that] evaluating the likely quality of an intuitive judgment requires an assessment of the predictability of the environment in which the judgment is made and of the individual's opportunity to learn the regularities of that environment. [We found] that subjective experience is not a reliable indicator of judgment accuracy".

16. Modern neuroscience would support this form of cognition. There are three clusters of neurons in the human body—the heart sac, the gut, and the brain. There are more neurons in the gut than in the brain, and this discovery would suggest that our mind is made up from these multiple "brains."

17. See also Alvesson and Sandberg (2011).

18. Wack had become a disciple of Gurdjieff after the latter took the young, near starving Wack under his wing in Paris during World War II.

19. Wack always kept a list of twelve or so remarkable people on him. We do not know all of the people listed, but we do know that one of them was Richard Normann. His name had been on Wack's list when van der Heijden worked with Wack. Richard Normann, together with Ramírez, influenced his creation of the "business idea" as a way of grounding scenario work.

20. Nor do we use the term "scenario" to mean a counterfactual possibility—for which there is little supporting data—within a model; as is done, for example, in liquidity assessments by treasurers (see Wilkinson and Ramírez 2010).

21. In the OSPA, scenario planning helps to grapple with and model uncertainty, that is, determining which models can best describe and understand what is going on. This contrasts with the term "scenario" as it is used in formal, quantitative modeling, where the scenarios reflect uncertainties "within" the model. See Wilkinson and Ramírez (2010).

22. Quantitative modeling in scenario planning work can also involve "anticipatory" systems (Rosen 1985; Köhler et al. 2015).

23. Arguably, the "father" of the field of system dynamics is MIT Professor Jay Forrester, and his classic *Industrial Dynamics* (1961). See his voluminous body of work, as well as that of John Morecroft, John Sterman (creator of "The Beer Game"), Peter Senge of *The Fifth Discipline* (1990) fame, Jac Vennix (mentioned in Chapter 2 and later in this section), and many others.

24. Example of an *amplifying loop*: the level of population determines the demand for food, more population increases the demand, and more food tends to increase population, so the interrelation between the variables is "positive." Example of a *dampening loop*: an increase in the price of oil reduces economic output, but reduced output tends to lower the price of oil, so the interrelation between the variables is "negative." See Senge (1990).

25. This is also a step in some quantitative modeling that uses a theory to determine a model structure; see Senge (1990) and Peter Checkland's Soft Systems Methodology.

26. <http://www.sbs.ox.ac.uk/school/events-0/oxford-futures-forum-2014> (accessed September 2015).

27. Examples of the latter include landscape visualization that provides a sense of what the future situation might look like in the scenario; the mock-ups used by architects when presenting future buildings to urban planners and community stakeholders; and the 3D computer simulations that industrial designers use to manifest a new product.

28. The Fourth Oxford Futures Forum in 2014 focused on the interface between scenarios and design.

29. At the time of this writing, in 2015, both authors are members of the World Economic Forum's global strategic foresight community. In its opening session in New York in December 2014, the members drew a collective map of the forces and events that have produced the world they inhabited. This can be found at <http://reports.weforum.org/global-strategic-foresight-community/activities-of-the-community/> (accessed September 2015).

30. <http://www.oecd.org/site/schoolingfortomorrowknowledgebase/futuresthinking/overview ofmethodologies.htm> (accessed September 2015).

31. Megatrends are "deep-set trajectories of change that will reshape the landscape for government, business and society over the coming 20 years" <http://theconversation.com/the-seventh-megatrend-why-australia-must-embrace-innovation-41232> (accessed September 2015). The term was coined by John Naisbitt in his blockbuster book *Megatrends: Ten New Directions Transforming Our Lives* (1984).

4 Working with scenario planning learners

Introduction

This chapter describes the OSPA approach to engaging learners effectively in the scenario planning process.

As we noted in Chapters 2 and 3, the social and cognitive aspects of the scenario planning process enable people critically to assess the mental framework they have been using to perceive their situation; and to shift attention to the wider context to enable alternative frames in a safe space. We have also explained that scenario planning is best understood as part of a wider intervention and can be an iterative process. The purpose of any intervention that includes building and using scenarios ultimately has to be established with the learner or learners: scenario planning is for learners, and ideally it is done *with* them. In much of the literature learners are referred to as the scenario planning "user" or "client."

In the OSPA, the essential role of scenario planning is supporting learners to reframe how they understand their present situation. Yet learner groups and their purposes may vary considerably, so a set of scenarios developed for one set of actors for some purpose is likely to fail to enable reframing if used by another set of actors for another purpose. This tailoring for one specified learner (or small set of them) and their given purpose distinguishes the OSPA from other ways of deploying scenario planning, such as for assessments or forecasts, which are for everyone or anyone.

In our experience, failure to clarify who the intended scenario learner(s) are, and when and how their reframed understanding is going to be used, are the main sources of reported failure in scenario-based interventions. However, in some situations beset by TUNA conditions the learners and uses can be only loosely identified prior to starting an intervention, and a scenario planning learning community must be assembled and organized. This often presents in the "wicked" public policy settings that we first described in Chapter 1.

This chapter is organized in five sections. In the first section, we explain what we mean by the "scenario learner," and clarify different uses of scenario planning. We highlight some principles that can help to avoid failures. In the second one we describe how, in some circumstances, the scenario learner community needs to be assembled or organized.[1] We discuss different approaches that may be used to relate the learning generated in scenario planning to something that the learners seek to reframe and reperceive, including Normann's and van der Heijden's business idea, Vickers' triangle of judgments, and Checkland's Soft Systems Methodology. We emphasize the usefulness of scenario planning in helping the learner to know their "self" and their business context better by reframing how they appreciate their wider contexts.

In the third section we explain how scenario planning helps to redirect the scenario learner's attention and thus support them in asking better strategic questions. It is here that the question of fitness becomes relevant, that is, the fit between core capabilities and the imagined (plausible, challenging) future context. In the fourth section we consider practical matters and some of the better-known available techniques that can be used to engage learners effectively. These include techniques to stimulate deeper inquiry and active listening to overcome what we call attention and connection deficits. We also touch upon certain timing matters not addressed in Chapter 2. In the final section we reflect on engaging the learner to ensure use and usefulness in scenario work.

Starting with learners, purposes, and intended uses

People, both as individuals and in groups, are generally neither mindless nor insensitive to changes in their surrounding contexts. And each person and each group has some more or less well defined—and often complicated—views of the future.

As we understand it in the OSPA, scenario planning is not about "feeding" people's minds with new facts they did not have before, nor about crossing a data "gap," nor about "filling" an information "void." Instead, scenario planning is about how perceptual and conceptual frames in someone's mind at a particular point in time can be usefully challenged. As Wack (1984) said, scenario planning is designed to help people's minds gently consider alternative perceptions and conceptions about their contexts.

As we explained in Chapter 2, individually and collectively we each hold views—of ourselves, of our contexts, of the future—that are particular to our own self, culture, and situation, including our mood (e.g. calm, shocked, safe, threatened). We hold these views in the present and regarding our future.

Some aspects of futures appear to us to be certain, such as concerning our inevitable passing away or our expectation that the laws of gravity will remain unchanged until you finish reading this book. Other aspects are felt instead to be *uncertain*. For instance, we cannot be sure whether another epidemic disease will break out, or when a banking scandal or terrorist attack will occur next. We deal with both in our minds. The expressions "making up" or "changing" one's mind hide complex and subtle processes. Minds are not like clothing: much of what is in the mind remains intangible, and it is not easy to take off what one has been minding and put that—or indeed, something else—back on. Scenario planning is designed to help learners in TUNA conditions to surface, guide, and make productive such changes of their minds.

SCENARIO PLANNERS AS "MINDFUL" LEARNERS, NOT MINDLESS AGENTS

Wack recognized the challenge of connecting the inquiry on alternative plausible external contexts (which he called the "macrocosm") with the mindset of the scenario learner or decision maker (which he called the "microcosm"). He considered the top managers' perception of their business environment to be as important as investment in infrastructure. His reasoning was that strategy comes from this perception. He explained:

Our real target was the microcosms of our decision makers: unless we influenced the mental image, the picture of reality held by critical decision makers, our scenarios would be like water on a stone. This was a different and much more demanding task than producing a relevant scenario package. (Wack 1985a, 85)

Finkelstein et al. (2013) have given empirical support to Wack's views. As we noted in Chapter 3, in a study of eighty failed strategies they found that "misleading pre-judgments" characterized 82 percent of these failures, while "misleading experiences" related to 64 percent of them, and "inappropriate attachments" to 43 percent. Senior managers in organizations appear all too often to be ill prepared to consider alternative judgments and to use them to identify, interpret, and assess unexpected possibilities. In the same vein, a recent study of over 300 global senior executives found that 80 percent of the respondents felt their organizations had less capacity for peripheral vision than needed. In another study two-thirds of corporate strategists admitted their organizations had been surprised by up to three high-impact events in the last five years; and 97 percent said their companies lacked an early warning system to prevent such surprises in the future (Schoemaker et al. 2013). No wonder then that Sutcliffe and Weber (2003, 80) concluded that:

The task of leaders is to manage ambiguity and to mobilize action, not to store highly accurate knowledge about their environment. The more effective way to improve the performance of a company is to invest in how leaders shape their interpretive outlooks.

Thus, the OSPA sees reframing itself as a process of *learning with* plausible alternative future contextual environments to help minds reperceive. This learning then supports other activities and processes, and this support also needs to be designed into the scenario planning intervention. For instance, the members of the UEG's Future Trends Committee that produced the scenario set (described in Appendix C) for the 22,000 medical doctors and forty associations in their federation, learned that they had been too inattentive to how forces in the wider context could bend certain unsustainable trends (e.g. public sector finances in the EU) upon which their profession and its development had been built. The Committee members concluded that henceforth they themselves needed to bring more of their limited time and attention to bear on these factors. Also, as we saw in Chapter 3 in the Wärtsilä case, the first Ship Power scenarios reframed the amount of risk—and opportunity—that had been held within the board members' minds (see Box 3.5 and Appendix A).

USEFULNESS IMPLIES A LEARNER

It may appear banal and self-evident, but for reasons we outline below this is often forgotten: *for scenario planning to be useful, it must have a learner and a use.* Lack of clarity about the learner and how and when the scenarios will be used is a common cause of failure.

As we noted in Chapter 2, the learner does not exist in a vacuum. Scenario planning learners, whether as individuals or members of groups or teams, always work and learn with others, support and serve others, depend on others' work, and make up their minds in the context of others doing the same thing.

Sometimes the learner is self-evident: the strategy director who wants the strategy's assumptions checked, or the policymaker who wants to prepare for alternative future conditions. But as mentioned earlier, in some scenario planning situations the learner community or group needs to be identified, assembled, and organized. Such situations often exist in interorganizational or public policy settings, or when attention needs to be redirected to an "orphan issue," that is, an issue that falls between the cracks of established silos of issue owners. In such situations a joint "horizontal" initiative, creative coalition, or cross-sectoral partnership may come together and constitute a learner group to address a still emerging but highly puzzling and disturbing situation with the help of scenario planning. The AIDS epidemic in Africa is an example, where participatory scenario building among different organizations enabled collaborative strategy, which in turn led to a reframing of the role of poverty in the epidemic (see Appendix D). Another example of an effort to create a learner group is the World Economic Forum's "metal and mining" scenarios of 2010. That project manufactured a client group made up of CEOs of big private firms, the heads of NGOs such as Transparency International and Greenpeace, and ministers from countries such as Chile and South Africa. In these kinds of situations the primary learner group would not have existed without the scenario planning intervention. In effect, in these situations the scenario planning process becomes a form of temporary institution.

Actually, the assembling and sustaining of the learner group, and the people the learners must serve so that the purpose is met, must be deliberately considered throughout the scenario planning process—from before the beginning to after the end. One of us once visited a government ministry in an Asian country in which a group of intelligent, young, keen, capable scenario planners commented that their "excellent" scenarios work was not being taken up by the policymakers for whom they were developed. Upon asking the scenario planners in what way they expected the policymakers to learn with and to use "their" scenarios in their (policymakers') work, the young scenario planners were perplexed. Surely this "use" issue was not within their remit, but within that of the policymakers?

From teaching and working with many experienced scenario planners and process facilitators, we have found that neglecting to attend to this important aspect of "recontracting" with the learners and their purpose can contribute to failure. This may extend to changing the learner group's composition during the process, such as in one of the learning cycles.

USES OF THE LEARNING VARY SIGNIFICANTLY

The usefulness of scenario planning in strategy and policymaking extends both ways beyond the point of decision making, that is, to the pre- and post-decision arenas that accompany any decision-making process, as we describe next.

Pre-decision, scenario interventions can help reset and recontextualize the strategic agenda. They can help review whether a specific decision or strategic issue has been too narrowly defined. For example, the scenario planning project carried out by UEG[2] was designed in part to reassess the broader issues affecting how its curriculum decisions might be made (see Appendix C).

Post-decision, scenario planning can help in testing and prototyping possible ways of manifesting the decision prior to committing expensive resources. It can help to avoid confirmation bias in the monitoring and assessment of impact, and keep this process alive with the help of early warning or tracking systems geared to the broader context to attend to possible shifts that might affect the validity of the decision. For instance, Nokia and Statoil directed their competitive intelligence units to devise early warning systems (EWSs) to alert senior management as to whether the newly framed understandings based on their company-wide scenarios were beginning to unfold as expected. The companies then used the signals collected and analyzed by this EWS to refresh and update their scenario sets. Our research showed that they did this iteratively, each time a new set of scenarios was produced by their scenario planning interventions (Ramírez et al. 2013).

Thus, an essential component of the OSPA is that every intervention involving scenario planning must have worked out an explicit idea of the learner and the usefulness in its own specific situation. This explicit emphasis on specific, intended use is also a way to distinguish forecasts, which tend to be for anyone, from scenario planning, which has to be for a specific learner (a "someone"), for a purpose, and for a use.

Sometimes settling this purpose for and with scenario planning learners takes a lot of effort. In the AiA initiative (Appendix D) it took several months to achieve a workable purpose. It involved the formation of the Advisory Group, over one hundred expert and stakeholder interviews, and the first large-scale, five-day scenario orientation workshop.

FAILURES TO USE THE LEARNING

The costs of an unused or poorly utilized scenario planning intervention can be considerable and can extend beyond the obvious: many person-days and other resources—goodwill, curiosity, attention, intuition, trust—could all be wasted. In addition, there can be substantial opportunity costs for the organization sponsoring the initiative. However, the bigger risk of a poor experience with scenario planning is that failure to meet expectations can be used by critics to deny the value of scenarios in any future strategy exercise, and thus deny the opportunity to reveal and challenge the implicit and dominant frame.

Ignoring the actual learner is what we can call a "production" stance toward scenario planning; that is, in research and policy settings experts produce a set of scenarios and then "hand them over" to the decision makers. We have also encountered this production stance in many corporate situations. For example, when the planners in one well-known global corporation visited one of us over a decade ago, the planners told us that in their company scenarios "hit the air, not the road." In the same way a senior executive of a German company who participated in one of our Oxford programs told us that in his previous company, what he termed "excellent" scenario planning work had in his view "unfortunately not been taken up"; he considered this was "particularly unfortunate as what the scenarios had considered might happen actually did happen." We pointed out that what he was talking about was good (or possibly, lucky) analysis and prediction and poor scenario planning work. Why? Because purportedly "excellent" analysis that is not taken up for reframing and reperception (learning) is useless.

So in the OSPA we would rate as "good" scenario planning work that which is effective in supporting the learner to reframe and reperceive their understanding of their present situation and to bring forth new action, even if what the learner imagined never comes to be.

Working with the scenario planning learner

CLARIFYING THE LEARNERS AND THEIR PURPOSES

A key principle in the OSPA is that it is the responsibility of the scenario planner (the facilitator) to identify and "contract" with the intended learner(s). This contracting involves several things: working with the intended learners to ascertain the exact purpose(s) the scenario planning work is meant to accomplish; ensuring that the learners fully appreciate what the scenario planning work can and cannot do; and specifying when and where the reframing and reperception obtained via the scenario planning work will actually be used. An example is the contracting process that one of the authors undertook with the incoming president of the UEG, Prof. Michael Farthing (Appendix C). Together they went through his agenda and examined every meeting, speech, and other relevant items already booked in, to ascertain in which of these his organization's newly reframed appreciations stimulated by the scenario planning project would play a role, and how. How might these (still to be developed) new understandings reshape upcoming meetings with the funders and regulators? How might the newly obtained insights be included in the agenda of a meeting on possible changes in the profession's teaching curriculum? How might new and challenging views on the profession's future context attract the right people to a high-level policy meeting he was convening?

In our experience, this clarification and specification of learners, purpose, and use sometimes takes *more* time, resources, effort, and attention than researching, designing, and building the scenario set itself. But at the risk of repetition, the opportunity costs of not doing this are so substantial that the investment is worthwhile. This is echoed in the literature; in fact, Schoemaker (1998) identified it as the first item on his list of the twenty common traps and pitfalls to be avoided in conducting scenario planning.

A good historical example comes from the early years of Shell scenario practices. Top executives refused time and time again to pay attention to the scenarios that were being put on the table by Wack and Newland. The reasons given varied, but what the scenario builders soon came to understand was that the plausibility of the scenarios they were offering was different from the future seen in the minds of the executives. To address this issue, they devised a set of scenarios, later referred to as "ghost" or "phantom" scenarios (Wack 1985a), that started with the future the executives were already expecting. They used rhetoric to encourage the executives to reflect more deeply on the wider assumptions that needed to be made in order for the expected future to come about. The executives considered these wider assumptions built into their own implicit framing of the situation to be so miraculous that they were able to free up their minds to consider alternative scenarios.[3]

THE PROBLEMATIC "FOCAL QUESTION" ISSUE

Many scenario planning "training" programs and guidebooks claim that the starting point of scenarios work should be defining, clearly and in advance of any scenario building, what they term the "focal question" for the scenarios to address, followed by conducting a comprehensive scan of the external environment around that question. In our experience this approach can distract the scenario planner from the hard work of identifying the learner, clarifying purpose, and specifying use. Furthermore, this question can constrain the actual learning generated in the scenario building. It may be an urgent or "burning" question, to which the learner (or his superiors) needs an immediate answer. But in the OSPA it is the learner, not the question, that will benefit from the scenario planning. As our editor, John Selsky, put it, in the OSPA scenario planning practitioners do not answer questions, they question learners—or they question answers that learners have assumed before.

So in the OSPA we suggest that scenario planning work should start with the scenario planner (an internal staffer or an external consultant) exploring the world as understood in the intended learners' minds, rather than the planner starting with general assessments for anyone of the world "out there," independent of the intended learner's own understanding of it. That is, the scenario planning inquiry should begin with understanding how the minds of those who will learn from and with the scenario set today frame and map what they perceive. Much scenario planning involves engaging what for the users appears to be the puzzling situation they are facing and its context. This is essential if scenario planning work is to contribute to the learners' reperceiving in the present, rather than simply contributing yet another bit of impersonal or generic analysis about what the future might look like.

In the OSPA, we use a rule of thumb that no more than one-third of the resources to be invested in scenario planning should be devoted to designing and producing the scenarios. The other two-thirds should go to defining and developing who the learners are, and doing the necessary research.[4] In many situations, this may involve assembling and organizing the learner group, as discussed earlier. The two-thirds also involves ensuring the learners' expectations are realistic, and ascertaining that they have carefully considered how exactly their reframing and reperception will work as an input that actually enhances or supports their value creation activity. Some scenario planning efforts reportedly go even further than we suggest in terms of such investments. According to anecdotal evidence, one pan-European initiative by the Climate Change Consortium aimed at encouraging cost-effective action on climate change actually invested €2 million on building scenarios and €20 million on marketing the fuel standard policy option that emerged from them! In the EPO case in Appendix E, the scenario planners ensured that the scenario work was actually used in mapping the patenting journey of the future in workshops. This helped the Office to think of renewing the strategy of the organization and its stakeholders, which was a foreign concept given that the mandate up to then had been understood as defined by the international treaty underpinning the EPO, not its own strategy.

There is an exception to the 1/3–2/3 guideline, and it occurs in interorganizational scenario work. In such projects we have found that a more realistic guideline is approximately 1/5–4/5. The World Economic Forum (WEF) has, for example, invested considerable effort in convening a diverse set of stakeholders (and payers, sponsors, and consulting partners) in its "sector" scenarios, such as the futures of financial architecture, or the metals and mining industry scenarios. This has enabled the WEF to ensure that enough support for the scenarios will translate into usefulness, for example, enabling the community of mining and metals CEOs to keep coming together to discuss relevant and difficult issues. Similarly, a three-month search and selection process was necessary to identify the relevant stakeholders that would become the scenario builders for the AiA project (see Appendix D). In that case the first large-scale workshop was devoted to clarifying what the scenario planning would be used for and what they needed to focus on.

The political sensitivity of the challenges and need for full transparency in conducting such a scenario planning project—under the full gaze of public scrutiny—can raise ethical questions about who decides and when, which scenarios are developed, and for use by whom and for what purposes. This in turn can provoke the need to clarify the governance process and mode of engagement in the scenario building process from the outset. (This is strongly related to the contracting issues discussed in the previous section.) This working with and for the learner does not happen only before the scenario design and production work. It also happens during and even after that work; helping people think for themselves during the process is far better than "outsourcing" thinking because the learners tend to feel committed to what they have created themselves.

Similar to the thriving industry of megatrends, so-called "generic" scenarios are available, often for a fee, from specialized providers in different sectors (e.g. pulp and paper, energy) or geographies (e.g. countries). But these are essentially trend analyses or generic assessments, not learner-tailored scenarios. While such assessments have their uses, they cannot replace the working through of reframing options for oneself in highly social learning processes, as we discussed in Chapter 2. "Generic" scenarios published for anyone will be at best of very limited value for any particular learner. They may pique interest like a provocative newspaper editorial, but that is all. Thus, they are a lamentable and ineffective attempt to shortcut the patient work of identifying the learner and the purpose.

GROUNDING THE UNDERSTANDING OF THE LEARNER SITUATION: THE BUSINESS IDEA

In his best-selling book *Scenarios: The Art of Strategic Conversation*, van der Heijden (2005) introduced the concept of "the business idea," which arose when collaborating with Normann and Ramírez in the 1980s on the future of refining technical services in Shell International. The business idea "depicts what is fundamental for success in specific terms in one holistic representation" (van der Heijden 2005, 63). Appreciating and mapping the business idea and how the learner understands it is the starting point for any scenario planning effort.

In the OSPA the business idea is basically about how an organization creates value. The value that is created need not necessarily be profit or shareholder wealth; it may also be the enhancement of the public good, the fulfillment of an interest group's increased capacity, better art, or other increase or improvement in some value. So business ideas can and do exist in NGOs, intergovernmental bodies, government agencies, community groups, municipalities, professional associations, research groups, and so on.

It may take some effort to determine the business idea of an interorganizational arrangement seeking to use a set of scenarios produced by its members, perhaps more effort than the straightforward business idea of a consumer products corporation. In addition, multiple or multi-level business ideas are possible in these kinds of situations, one at the level of the interorganizational collective and one for each party. In such situations a two-step process is advisable: scenarios are developed first for the larger entity, then they are adapted, transplanted, refocused, and adopted by each learner or learner group in its own context. A useful rule of thumb is that wherever there is a management team, there is a business idea (van der Heijden, personal communication).

The "business idea" approach helps the scenario planners (whether they are internal staffers or external consultants) to engage with the minds of the intended learners and jointly ascertain what "business," or value creation activity, they currently understand they are in, and what they consider has made them successful. Because scenarios are always about what the possible future contexts of this value creating activity might be, ascertaining the learners' understanding of the business idea and the assumptions they make with that idea of the context is helpful. It helps to clarify how effective the scenario learner thinks his/her organization is at creating value and why, and focuses attention on how plausible contextual changes could alter this effectiveness.

HOMEMAKING

One of the authors some years ago went for a set of job interviews in a well-known higher education institution. In each meeting this person asked the interviewer (faculty member, administrator) to draw a map of their department and their institution, where they placed themselves in it, and what place the candidate being interviewed would have if hired. The fact that most of the interviewers put the candidate in the center and themselves in the periphery of each of their maps said a lot about what was going on in that organization at that time; there was a lot of unacknowledged disagreement on mandate, roles, and relations. Scenarios too will be "candidates" hosted in a learning setting, and need to find a place in it.

Appreciating the scenario learner's sense of his/her business idea is just the beginning of how the scenario planner helps the learner. As discussed in Chapter 3, a home for scenarios has to be made within the learner's value creating system; as we shall see, a set of scenarios often require transplanting from the greenhouse where they are first developed to the garden in which they will actually help to change minds and create value. Both the scenarios that challenge the prevailing framing for doing business, and the new business idea that the scenario planning process informs, will have to find accommodation with the other extant processes informing the learner, such as strategic planning, business development, risk management, human capital planning, forecasting, modeling, visioning, and so on. If not, the new species (scenario planning) in the (decision-supporting) ecosystem of processes may be rejected and unable to survive.[5]

The learners will not only use the scenario planning process to reconsider and possibly change their own individual mind, they will want to share the reframing insights with others. To do so they will typically use two-dimensional media: paper, reports, PowerPoint slides on screens, etc. This presents a challenge: the learner sometimes finds it difficult to convey to other people the multidimensional insights stimulated by the scenarios. In teaching scenarios we characterize the scenario planner as a hare, and the learner as a professional or manager working in an office or a cubicle. Somehow the hare must share these insights with the manager who works, with colleagues, in the limited two dimensions afforded by paper and presentations on screens. We revisit these issues in Chapter 5.

Up to this point we have discussed several aspects of the interface between the scenario planner and the learner's mind: ensuring that the intended learner and those she works with understand *what* scenario planning is and the potential value it offers to reframe their understanding; eliciting the learners' understanding of their business idea and *how* the scenario planning process will contribute to transforming their definition of that business idea; and ascertaining *where* the scenarios will sit in the organization whose mindful learners intend to use them. Beyond these activities the scenario planner needs to consider exactly *why* the scenarios are going to be used and for what ends and purposes, so that they can be useful. We explore such topics next.

WHAT KINDS OF LEARNER JUDGMENTS WILL THE SCENARIOS SUPPORT? VICKERS' TRIANGLE

Sir Geoffrey Vickers was remarkable in many ways. Among the positions he held was secretary to Churchill's War Cabinet and head of the National Coal Board of the United Kingdom when coal was the number one fuel for the country's economy. His ideas on judgment in decision making strongly influence the OSPA.[6]

One of Vickers' (1965) main ideas was to define what in his experience contributed to making a "good" decision. He suggested that a good decision is one based on good judgment in three distinct but interrelated areas—reality, values, and instrumental capacity (see Figure 4.1):

- A sense or appreciation to judge or even reappraise *where* the decision is taking place, that is, a "reality check: what is going on" in its context in Figure 4.1.
- A set of *values* to assess or judge if the decision is being made according to relevant appropriate (or good) metrics, and which will help the learner's mind to determine if the decision is effective or not in terms of "values: what it means to us" in Figure 4.1, where "us" is specific to the decision maker's situation.
- Judging whether the *strategy* (what Vickers called the direction of travel) that the decision directs or supports is right; this is the "instrumental: what can we do" judgment in Figure 4.1.

Vickers suggested these three elements—appreciating the *context*, assessing the pertinence of the *values*, and understanding the *strategy*—are present in

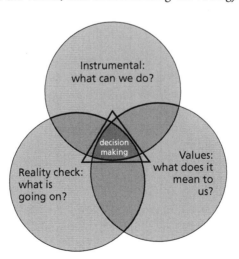

Figure 4.1. Vickers' "three judgments"

Vickers (1965, 40)

the minds of all decision makers in all their decisions and decision situations, whether implicitly or explicitly. He considered how these elements might be related to each other in the decision makers' understanding, how one element may be prominent at any given point in time, and how the three might best be balanced. Making a wrong judgment in any of these three areas leads to a "bad" decision overall.

By offering a way to assess "good/bad or indifferent" in relation to a decision, Vickers' judgment framework provides an important reference point for evaluating the effectiveness of the reframing and reperception function of scenario planning in the OSPA. The quality of a decision does not depend on the accuracy of its outcome, which cannot be judged in advance, but on the quality of the judgments involved in decision making. And it is possible to assess whether the scenario planning intervention has improved such judgment capacities.

We have found this framework useful in ascertaining which of these three elements the scenario planning process is most effective in supporting decisions by the learner (see Burt and van der Heijden 2008). For example, a scenarios engagement done on the future of Turkey in its context for a major energy company in that country was driven by the context ("reality check") element of Vickers' triangle; the project helped the senior managers to reappreciate a changing and turbulent context. The UEG scenario planning intervention described in Appendix C was driven by the strategy direction ("instrumental") element; it explored which strategy might best help the leaders of the profession to reframe their views on how they and their colleagues could create value in three different future contexts. The AiA scenario planning process (Appendix D) attempted to navigate an embattled strategic framing contest that reflected differences of perspective on all three bases of judgment, and likely grounded in value differences; this manifested the "values" element in the triangle. For example, reality as framed by Western medical experts differed significantly from the reality framed by African government officials: the former were pushing for large-scale deployment of antiretroviral drug treatments; whereas the latter were keen to avoid becoming dependent on foreign medical assistance, and their populations could not afford to deploy such drugs at scale due to widespread poverty, lack of infrastructure, and other development challenges. Only by enabling more shared and systemic understanding of the multiple drivers and impacts of the epidemic was it possible to identify more and better intervention options that could avoid such extreme polarizations and help to forge new common ground by aligning shared values.

How does Vickers' framework relate to our core reframing and reperception concerns? The scenario planner may consider periodically which of the judgments is best supported by the scenario planning project, asking questions as in Box 4.1.

BOX 4.1 QUESTIONS POSED BY VICKERS' TRIANGLE

Will the scenarios contribute most to:

- Reframing the views of what is going on in the context? In so doing, will they help senior managers to make more sense of this, and upon reperceiving give a new sense to those they manage? This was clearly the case in the Wärtsilä project described in Appendix A, where, for example, more attention was directed to China in the first Ship Power intervention.
- Reframing the views of the direction of travel or strategic intent the organization (or set of organizations) is embarking on? In so doing, will they help senior managers to make more sense of this direction/intent? This was evident in the Wärtsilä and EPO examples found in Appendices A and E.
- Reframing the values that are being used to assess whether something is right or wrong, good or bad, attractive or repulsive? In so doing, will they help senior managers to revisit the valuations they make? This clearly occurred in the AiA and Risk-World examples found in Appendices D and F.

Considering these questions helps to ensure the scenarios are useful in reframing the learner's understanding of a situation. These considerations will first work for the immediate scenario learner's reperception, but will come into their own when s/he interacts with counterparts to create value. For instance, in Wärtsilä the scenarios changed the conversation that top management had with customers. In the EPO the scenarios helped them to reach out to fast-growing patenting offices, transforming what had been a club of three (EPO, JPO, and USPTO) into a club of five (including Korea's and China's patenting offices) in a first meeting in Hawaii. In the UEG the leadership took their scenarios to funders and authorities, changing the association's R&D policy priorities.

GETTING TO KNOW THE LEARNERS AND HELPING THEM TO REPERCEIVE THEIR "SELF" AND THEIR WIDER CONTEXTS

In the OSPA it is very important for the scenario planner to get to know the mindset and milieu of the learner for two related reasons. First, it provides insight about the framed constraints on his/her images of the future. Scenario planning learners are often deeply embedded in organizational cultures. Cultures, especially strong ones, are grounded in often unexamined ways of viewing the world, and those ways of viewing get reinforced by formal performance systems, informal sanctions (both positive and negative), routines, norms, planning rhythms, and myths. Second, keeping a critical distance from the learner's existing views helps the scenario planner to begin to imagine alternative framings that might be useful for the purpose at hand. The seven open-ended interview questions developed by van der Heijden

---

BOX 4.2 NON-THREATENING WAYS TO ACCOMMODATE SCENARIO PLANNING

- Work from what influential minds within the organization consider its "official future" to be, as discussed in Chapter 1, instead of challenging the established practice of forecasting by attempting to replace it with scenario planning. This might be done as a pilot project to appreciate scenarios, using "phantom scenarios" (recall from earlier in this chapter that these are implied but not yet rendered explicit scenarios being used already).
- Present scenario planning as a complement, rather than an alternative, to forecasting. Here one broadens, not replaces, the arsenal of approaches to engage how uncertainty is experienced and conceptualized.
- Present scenario planning as a tool to improve the scope and efficacy of forecasting. Invite forecasters to render their assumptions explicit, to seek out trend bends, and to include potential new trends in their models.
- Invite learners in the organization to reflect on situations in their everyday lives in which it has been the plausible, rather than the probable, that has been helpful. Then demonstrate that scenarios can work with their understanding and their mindfulness in much the same way in their work settings.
- Invite people to see how judgment relies on stories rather than numbers in many situations.*
Note: these techniques are not always acting as Trojan horses!

* See John Kay's (2013) *Financial Times* column on the 2008 financial crisis for an example of this point.

(2005, 176–7) help the scenario planner to ascertain from intended learners what needs to be established, what needs to be constructively questioned, and which cultural blinders need to be opened up.

Introducing scenario planning into organizations with the types of strong professional cultures which support forecast-based planning can be challenging, even if a powerful insider is supporting a scenarios-based planning approach. Scenario planning can be accommodated in such organizations in several non-threatening ways, as described in Box 4.2.

Helping to redirect the learner's attention

As we have said repeatedly, scenarios enable reframing; they signal what will be attended to ("in the frame") and what will not be focused on ("outside the frame"). This in turn supports reperception.

For example, in research on scenario planning work in Statoil and Nokia mentioned earlier in this chapter, Ramírez et al. (2013) demonstrated how the "early warning signals" that the companies' competitive intelligence teams paid attention to were redefined by new framings of their situations, brought about by the companies' successive scenario planning rounds; the teams changed what they ought to look out for. As a result, the cycle between reframing and reperception contributed to the importance Statoil's senior managers gave to climate change.

We may explain early warning signals by means of what we call "canaries in the mind." This is the title of a paper by two of us (Wilkinson and Ramírez 2010), in which we recalled that canaries were used in coal mines because they stopped singing and died when there was a build-up of toxic gases, giving miners underground a clear warning of imminent life-threatening danger and the time to escape. Using this as a metaphor, we suggested that the financial and economic crises that started unfolding in the mid-2000s were like "canaries in the mind" in providing early warnings about how people—financial analysts, policymakers, and other industry stakeholders—understand and enact foresight. We suggested that the lessons learned from the 2008 financial crisis could avert continued misuse of scenario planning in many domains, not only finance. We proposed that the canary that has stopped singing is signaling that it is not only *what* those stakeholders think about the future that is problematic, but also that failures to reconsider *how* they think about *and with* the future may be perilous for people facing TUNA conditions. That is, the crisis revealed something faulty in the way that foresight and scenarios have been used (or not used, as the case may be), for example by the now defunct Financial Services Authority regulator in the UK.

Despite attempts by the scenarios community for nearly sixty years to embrace non-linear, non-deterministic thinking, the effectiveness of foresight interventions using scenario planning remains unclear. In many policy arenas too many "late lessons" are gained from early warnings—lessons that help solve yesterday's problems.[7] And while the prospect of gaining "early lessons" from early warnings is appealing, empirical research of what people actually learn from crises and unique events has found underwhelming results, as we saw in Chapter 2. (Recall that managers perceived organizational failures as unique events that had little learning value.) If learning from crises and failures is rare—and rarely considered worthwhile or useful—then it will be difficult for people to gain usable insights from them, other things being equal.

In helping scenario planning learners to reframe, it is also important to examine the use of language and the far from neutral way it directs attention. The renowned work of sociologist Michel Foucault has considered how language reflects and supports power. So the particular selection of terms used to frame any particular situation will manifest power in some way: are a group of fighting men considered "freedom fighters" or "terrorists"? Is a wage increase a "cost of production" or an "employee benefit"? Depending on which conceptual frame is considered and then adopted, the options for action that will be enacted—policies, strategies, even "solutions"—may vary considerably.

It is not only the different "what" choices offered by multiple framings, but also the quality of the framing that scenario planning produces that matters.

For example, in the archetype scenarios deployed within the influential Inter-governmental Panel on Climate Change (IPCC 2007), the vertical axis depicts possibilities as "*either* economic or ecologic." This has reinforced rather than dampened the environment–economy trade-off in key policy conversations, and we expect this perceived polarization of values will last for quite some time. The "successful" influence of the framing produced by those archetype scenarios may in the end be counterproductive, because in the IPCC case it precluded certain options from being seriously considered for some time, especially those that would be *both* ecologic *and* economic.

What is the pay-off from directing scenario learners' attention effectively? Sometimes understanding one's future context as a new environment, or in any case as an environment that has become reframed, can also lead one to understand oneself differently; one reperceives oneself in context perhaps as having more or fewer options than one had originally thought, or holding different roles, or with changed relationships with others. In such cases, rather than simply supporting a conventional linear planning process, the critical reflection in scenario planning learning can provoke discussion about the need to develop new capabilities or new strategic initiatives. Such discussion may result in strategic renewal or even a shift in the organization's identity. This was explored both in the UEG and the EPO scenario projects (see Appendixes C and E). Alternatively, scenario planning can help learners to conclude that the future context is unfolding as expected or desired, and there is no need for new capabilities or strategic renewal.

Matters of technique to engage learners effectively

FACILITATION OF THE SCENARIO PLANNING PROCESS: ACTIVE LISTENING AND DEEPER INQUIRY

Often scenario planning learners work with internal or external facilitators. There is an enormous literature on facilitation which informs this role, which is well beyond the scope of this book to analyze. Our approach is consistent with the "process consultation" approach developed by Edgar Schein (see Schein 1999, 2013). In this section we highlight aspects of this practice which we have found significantly contribute to obtaining the expected out-comes of scenario planning as we understand it in the OSPA. While scenario planning is becoming better known, in many situations people who wish to consider using it—internal staff as well as external consultants—are unfamiliar with the mode of thinking that this entails. They need to "learn the ropes" as to what scenario planning can and cannot do. In addition, they need to under-stand whether the scenario planning approach fits (or can be made to fit) the situation they are facing, whether it's within an organization or in multi-organizational situations. So both active listening and a deeper form of interrogating the situation (more on this below) are important.

Developing an understanding of the scenario planning process in the OSPA involves deploying techniques and processes that encourage self-reflection by the learner (who ideally is also involved in building the scenario set) as well as by the scenario process facilitator(s). In getting to know the scenario learners, and working with them to define the scenario purpose and intended use, the facilitator is well advised to remain open minded and avoid rushing to conclusions. Facilitators need to be aware of their own preferences and should mindfully practice active listening to avoid injecting their own interests or biases on to the scenario's purpose. It is the learner's purpose that matters.

In our experience, scenario planning learners are often unaware of what they don't know. Similarly, one often finds that scenario learners are blind regarding what they *do* know; that knowledge is either forgotten or not foregrounded. For example, two of us working on the future of Scotch whiskey found that what the scenarios work actually did was simply to bring to the foreground of the company's executives something they knew and had forgotten, namely, that the way risk had been priced into the bottle by suppliers and retailers alike was detrimental to their own business. In helping the learner carry out deeper inquiry the facilitator wants to make the learner the inquirer (see Chapter 3), so that s/he can confidently and critically re-examine what has been taken for granted.

We recommend that the facilitator conduct lengthy (90–120 minute) confidential interviews with every relevant individual learner (plus key stakeholders the learner will have to work with in using the scenario planning). This ensures that the facilitator can understand and empathize with the current framing, and that the learner and facilitator agree on why it is necessary to challenge it with plausible alternatives, and how the reperceiving so obtained might be helpful.

The aggregate findings produced in conducting these interviews should be anonymized if necessary and reported by theme, rather than by interviewee, as a "chorus of voices." The findings should then be presented to the entire set of relevant individuals. Finally, the facilitator should manage structured dialogues where the learners can step back from their immediate day-to-day responsibilities and become aware of the multiplicity of views already in place (in the room or in the organization). In the OSPA this three-step process should already begin to design and utilize the future as a safe transitional space (see Chapter 2) to consider, discuss, and compare what is known with what is suspected to remain unknown but researchable.

Given that no one knows today what we don't know (yet), the scenario facilitators and the learners they work with would be well advised to extend the initial inquiry beyond the direct learners, to reach a wider set of colleagues and experts that, typically, access knowledge which the direct learners normally would not access. For example, in the EPO scenario planning project (Appendix E) the original set of thirty external interviews was extended to cover 110 individuals. We discussed these matters in Chapter 3.

THE CONNECTION AND THE ATTENTION DEFICITS

The emphasis on learners and reframing is also important in the roles scenario planning can play in overcoming what we term *connection deficits* and *attention deficits*. Both of these can occur in any large organization due to the structuring of authority, the richness of specialisms, and the pressure for short-term results.

A *connection deficit* occurs when specialized functions become more important than the organization as a whole, and each of those functions pursues its own interests, not the interests of the organization.[8] The result is that communities of experts become separated from each other. Someone is in one "silo" of the organization reporting to his boss, and another person whose knowledge might be of help is in another silo, reporting to her boss. This is often not simply a communication challenge but also a power struggle, as bosses vie for limited resources and thus don't cooperate on "neutral" terms but on their own partisan terms. Divisions in organizations really do divide!

The silo mentality motivates those divided organizationally to protect their particular silos, not to help others in different parts of the organization. It also motivates them to hide failures and, perhaps paradoxically, also successes—so as to avoid more powerful division bosses, or even HQ, from stealing the key people responsible for those successes. This can suppress "best" practice (Arvidsson 1999), with what is bandied around as "best" really being only the "best promoted" (or shouted about the loudest).

We are not making the unitarist assumption (which critical organizational theorists would decry) that all members of an organization naturally collaborate with each other to help the overall organization do well. Instead, we in the OSPA seek to use scenario planning to create bridges across internal divisions which bring forth zero-sum games and political infighting, and thus suppress the potential for *positive*-sum games, that is, collaborations in what could be common ground.

An example of the traps of silos of expertise is evident in the Ministerial structure of most central governments. Treasury officials and ministers of finance tend to be senior to their colleagues in environmental, labor, or (in some countries) agricultural ministries, in status if not in actual rank order. As a result, the design of policies that address the challenges of low growth, climate risk, and rising inequality can be overlooked as each minister seeks to implement the most cost-effective actions in his/her respective empire. The

UK Foresight Program offers several examples of how scenarios have been developed on an interministerial and interdisciplinary basis to successfully overcome the connection deficit in bureaucratic organization and appreciate emerging challenges that would otherwise fall between the cracks of different ministries.

An *attention deficit* occurs when there is a relative deficit of attention among key decision makers dedicated to matters which may be important but which have been building up over the longer term (such as demographics or climate change) and could have sudden and unexpected effects (such as suddenly recognizing that pension liabilities are due). With 24/7 monitoring and ubiquitous information, managers are pressed for short-term results and may be too busy dealing with urgent matters—playing the zero-sum game, perhaps—to take the time to consider important issues that may well change the game altogether. When operating in this all-too-common "urgent" mode, reacting may be more expedient than investing in an "away day" (away from the urgent) to think things through carefully.

Scenario planning can help to counterbalance this short-term reactive focus. As discussed earlier, scenario planning can be a powerful process for overcoming attention deficits, thereby shaping and redirecting what learners attend to. Recall the shifts in "early warning" attention at Statoil and Nokia, mentioned earlier, on account of the scenarios work undertaken. In those projects, scenarios were used to redirect attention, framing and reframing what the firms' top managers attended to.

TIMING MATTERS IN THE USEFULNESS OF REFRAMING

In Chapter 3, we clarified two time matters in the OSPA: the difference between time horizon and temporal orientation, and the use of three arrows of time in creating a set of scenarios. An additional time matter that we mentioned only in passing, and dwell upon here, concerns organizational rhythms. In designing a scenario planning engagement, the facilitator has to take into account the cycle of annual activities and the routine pace of work of the organization(s) with which the scenario planning will have to connect.

Every organization develops its own peculiar rhythm of activities, such as the annual budget, the two-year plan, or the five-year vision. For scenario planning interventions to be useful and used, it is important to appreciate these rhythms and understand how they direct the attention of the intended learners toward or away from how the plausible futures operate in the work setting here and now.

It is therefore very important to consider when is the right time to intervene in, or perhaps even disrupt, these activities and cycles. For example, it may be advantageous or politic to interrupt the usual rhythm of the strategic planning systems and decision-making cycles of the organization. So it is crucial to have a thorough appreciation of what is being interrupted—or disrupted—and to what effect.

It is also important to clarify any "past futures" of the group, organization, or situation that may currently exist. Examples might be a hoped-for merger that did not happen, or a division cherished by some managers that had been expected to prosper and was then sold instead. These are futures that did not happen. Recall the story of the new car announcement at the Mini factory in Chapter 3. New future framings that the scenario planning process will consider will have to fit the pattern of both futures that did come about and those that never materialized. So the scenarios have to find a home not only in the organization's present but also in the organization's past.[9]

TRANSPLANTING AND TEST DRIVING

Our colleague Trudi Lang adapted Barbara Czarniawska's research[10] on how ideas are "transplanted," to propose that a set of scenarios needs to have the "ground prepared" by the organization in which they will be used in order for them to survive, thrive, and serve the people in it effectively. Lang (2012) suggested the idea of transplanting a set of scenarios from the greenhouse in which they were produced to the garden they will inhabit. We use this idea to reidentify who the key learner is if the scenarios that are developed, e.g. for headquarters, are then to be used in a particular function, country division, or business unit. The original scenarios cannot be used in the new setting unchanged; they have to be recalibrated or translated for the new learner now at the center (e.g. the head of the receiving function, country, or business unit). The idea of transplanting reinforces the view discussed earlier in this chapter that scenarios are always for some*one*, and not for *anyone*.

We also use the idea of "test driving" in two senses. The scenarios themselves will be "driven" along a test road, with different groups of people exposed to them (in the car, so to speak; or perhaps watching the car from outside) in order to debug them and correct possible faults.

In addition, the insights about decisions and actions that the scenario framings yield need to be test driven. For instance, in a recent corporate scenarios project, one of the authors and three colleagues held a two-day session in which the learners road tested what it would feel like to live in each of the two scenario worlds they had considered, and to assess how two existing competitors and a possible new one would behave if these contrasting worlds were to unfold. This was done by allocating roles to executives and simulating how it felt to "drive" their firm (as well as the competitors' firms) in the competitive landscape that each scenario created. This prepared the firm for new competitive moves which logically could take place in those future contexts. As it happened, within three months of the test drive, one of the futures unfolded roughly as the scenarios had suggested might be the case, although it arrived in a fraction of the time expected, which was years away. Moreover, the firm's competitors reacted roughly as the test drive had suggested they might, though far earlier than had been imagined. The test driving exercise enabled the company to be better prepared, not to panic, and to respond in a well thought out manner.

In the same way, a Harvard Business School case published in 2002 explained how Morgan Stanley's scenarios rounds on the future of Japan conducted in 1997, 1998, 1999, and 2000 led to ten action items each time; and each time 75 percent of them were then implemented. In one of the rounds, "[t]he key insight was that things would get a lot worse before they got better. Accordingly we stayed away from investing in retail, at a time when Merrill went ahead in a big way. We also identified opportunities in an increasingly distressed economy, and invested appropriately, rather than divesting and withdrawing."[11] Again, test driving scenarios was enormously beneficial to the company.

LITERATURE, STORIES, AND REFRAMING IN THE LEARNER'S MIND

Recall our discussion in Chapter 2 of the role of literature and stories in stimulating reframing. We said effective scenario stories create a relationship between the writer (what in this chapter we have called the scenario planning facilitator) and the reader (in this chapter, the learner), whereby the writer enables the reader to imagine what might happen in alternative framings of the future context. How then does the learner's mind grasp the scenarios? Wack suggested that scenarios enabled "gentle" reperceptions.[12] How does the learner's mind "gently" relate new frames (imagined or perceived) to existing preconceptions, that is, to help change his/her mind? And how does the mind then guide the eye (or ear or skin or nose) to perceive anew?

We saw in Chapter 2 that the neuroscientist David Ingvar became well known for coining the term "memories of the future" (Ingvar 1985), when he found that the part of the brain which imagines the future is also the part that stores memory. And so scenario planners strive to create "memorable futures," that is, images which will be remembered in use and attended to. As our Oxford colleague Trudi Lang (2012, 335) put it in her DPhil dissertation:

More recently, neuroscientists have found that the same part of the brain that is responsible for creating memories of the past also creates memories of the future (Schacter et al. 2007). The importance of these "memories" is that they provide common conceptual "hooks" for what is noticed and attended to by multiple actors. These memories or hooks enable self-organization among actors along coherent lines—a form of holography where the whole is present in the parts...Thus, in the same way that values, mission, and vision statements can cohere actors, scenarios can too.

These memories or images held in the mind can be mapped using a technique called *cognitive mapping* (Eden 1988; 2004).[13]

[C]ognitive mapping...describe[s] the task of mapping how a person is thinking about a problem or issue. The maps are a network of nodes and arrows as links...[They are] a particular type of directed graph...where the direction of the arrow implies believed causality. Cognitive maps are not simply...word and arrow...diagrams, or influence diagrams...or a mind-map/brain-map...Mapping processes often lead to the later development of influence diagrams as a lead in to system dynamics simulation modelling...Cognitive mapping is a formal modelling technique with rules for its development. (Eden 2004, 673)

Cognitive mapping can be used in scenario planning with groups of perhaps six to ten people, not just with individuals. They are constructed iteratively between a facilitator and a group of learners, first to make sense, then to develop options and find common ground, namely, the consensus map that mirrors their collective sense of future. Doing so renders the images and "memories of the future" explicit and possible to share and learn from. The objective is to:

guide careful problem construction whereby each member of the team can gently "change their mind" and do so creatively. By seeing others' concepts in the context of their own concepts the meaning of them changes; this process coupled with sensitively managed social dynamics leads to new insights (team elaboration) created by the synergy stimulated by the team map. (Eden 1988, 8)

The consensus map often includes causal loops, which we discussed in Chapter 3 in terms of system maps. Eden (2004, 685) found that:

the discovery of loops usually arises from the aggregation of beliefs from a number of participants in the process and thus represents synergy from the synthesis of individual wisdom....[L]oops can become a significant focus of group effort...to identify other concepts that impinge on the loop and which may (change) loops from vicious...into virtuous circles and so move to a strategy for changing a problematic situation.

The system maps (discussed in Chapter 3) that are used in the OSPA in developing and refining individual scenarios can be related to these cognitive maps, though they are made up of far fewer elements and are meant to capture the essence of each scenario's logic as well as the differences that contrast one scenario from another in a given scenario set. Whether the detail Eden's approach offers is to be used or not depends on the purpose of the scenario planning intervention agreed with the learners.

Conclusion: engaging the learner's mind actively

In this chapter we have explained the emphasis in the OSPA on the scenario "learner." In our experience the learner is actually a group of people—learners assembled from different business units and teams within a single large organization. In some cases, they are drawn together by a common purpose from different organizations. We also explained that the new knowledge and insights (learning) enabled in the reframing-reperception process, and carried out by this group of learners, needs careful translating and transplanting to different functions, levels, and geographies. In effect, this means paying attention to simulating the learning journey for others who have not been directly involved, rather than simply presenting a new "truth" and assuming it will be accepted.

In Chapter 1, we introduced the reframing-reperception loop enabled in the scenario planning process. We saw that scenario learners frame and reframe their appreciation of how the world works at a higher logical level (upframing) and then engage in a process of immersive learning (downframing) to design and rehearse new and better options, which in turn can result in the reperception of their situation and self.

We have alerted reflective practitioners to issues they should attend to so they can achieve this more effectively. Table 4.1 illustrates the reframing that each of the six case studies in the Appendices offered for the learners involved.

Table 4.1 Summary of cases and scenario project impacts

Purposes / Cases	Wind-tunneling existing strategy	Make sense of turbulent context	Invent or create new options	Open up conversations and enable collaborative strategy	Reframe	What was reframed
Wärtsilä Ship	x	x	x	x	x	The role of China; what kind of ships might be built, what kind of shipping and ship-building business models might prevail
Wärtsilä Power		x	x	x	x	Role in relation to customers
Shell	x	x		x	x	The key actors that are deciding the rules of the global energy game are not governments and energy companies
UEG		x	x		x	European healthcare and professional roles
Aids in Africa		x		x	x	The role of poverty as only one of many drivers of the spread of the epidemic
EPO	x	x		x	x	IP legitimacy and role
Risk-World		x	x	x	x	Need for governance of emerging socio-technological regime shifts rather than technology assessment and risk management

Given that reframing and reperception involve actively engaging the learner's mindset and sense of future, it is important to recall that in the OSPA, scenario planning is both an intellectual as well as a social process which uses a mix of critical, creative, and analytical thinking. Neither reframing nor reperception results directly or automatically from the existence of a set of scenarios but rather occurs in the *use* of the scenarios. As we discussed in Chapter 3, scenario planning enables an immersive learning experience. Effective scenario learners are not passive readers of a scenarios product (book, booklet, film); instead they insert themselves into each frame and story, thereby developing a felt sense of each plausible future context. Rehearsing existing and new actions in each scenario enables the learners to reperceive their interactions, roles, and self in the present. As we have discussed in this chapter, this is an actor-centric experience that prioritizes the scenario learners and their needs, and their perceptions of their situation and wider context, before attending to the other methodological choices in scenario planning.

■ NOTES

1. One can even say that in some cases, the learner community needs to be "manufactured."
2. <http://www.ueg.eu/research/gi2040/> (accessed November 2014).
3. In Shell's culture this is referred to as the "story of the three miracles." See Wack (1985a).
4. This does not mean that it is a linear process; in the OSPA we treat it as a cyclic process. But it does mean that substantial attention and resources have to be devoted to setting expectations and embedding the learning in practical terms.
5. Claudio Ciborra's (1996) pioneering work on how new ICT systems are taken in ("hosted") within an organization replete with legacy ICT systems that will not be shut down is good reading for handling such conundrums.
6. Vickers wrote several delightful books on how big policy and strategy decisions are taken, and how such decisions sit within and contribute to complex democratic societies. He was a master in crafting good titles too: *The Art of Judgment: A Study of Policy Making* (1965); *Freedom in a Rocking Boat: Changing Values in an Unstable Society* (1972); and *Human Systems Are Different* (1984). His work has been immensely influential and is being analyzed by our colleague Peter Checkland in a forthcoming book. He also contributed the foreword to a book entitled *Towards A Social Ecology: Contextual Appreciations of the Future in the Present* by Emery and Trist (1973), whose thinking has played an important role in developing the OSPA.
7. Our suggestion was supported by research carried out by the European Environment Agency and published in 2002.
8. In organization studies this is called *suboptimization*.
9. This has been extensively analyzed in Heckscher et al. (2003).
10. <http://www.gri.gu.se/english/contact-us/staff/barbara_czarniawska/> (accessed November 2014).

11. <https://hbr.org/product/Morgan-Stanley-Japan-200/an/702458-PDF-ENG> (accessed November 2014).
12. One wonders about the alternative. Would a "brutal" reperception be obtained through electroshocks, or brain surgery?
13. As Eden (2004, 674) put it: "Usually cognitive maps of problem situations are reasonably large—over 100 nodes on the map, as compared to 12–20 nodes discussed in some of the research literature. Group maps are often developed by merging several cognitive maps derived from each member of a problem-solving team. They are inevitably much larger—often over 800 nodes. Thus, the ability to conduct formal analyses, that are meaningful to the client group, becomes of greater importance."

5 How scenario planning is done

The OSPA in action

Introduction

In this chapter we highlight how the choice of methods, techniques, and tools within the OSPA methodology depends on several elements that scenario planners need to take into account. We must note at the outset that this is not a "how to" chapter. We do not offer recipes, nor do we attempt to list all of the scenario planning methods we are aware of. Instead, we seek to clarify how choices about scenario planning intervention design and methods (now the topic of a growing literature) can best be informed by considering a broader set of design considerations and intervention logics that underpin scenario planning engagements. These wider considerations are all too often overlooked by scenario planners, and are not consistently dealt with in available articles and reports. So instead of recipes, the chapter is more like what an art critic would say about artful mastery. It is more a commentary than a set of instructions, a commentary on the choices that the artist makes and on the considerations behind those choices.

Such choices depend on the characteristics of the scenario learner, which we discussed extensively in Chapter 4, and on the learner's intended use and purpose. They also depend on the kind of situation faced, including what we may call the "authorizing environment," that is, whether the learners are solely within one organization (as in the Wärtsilä and Shell cases in Appendices A and B); in multiple sponsoring organizations (as in the Risk-World scenarios in Appendix F); in multiple stakeholder organizations (as in the AiA case in Appendix D); or in what Ahrne and Brunsson (2005) called a "meta-organization" (as in the UEG case in Appendix C).

Methodological choices also depend on other things. In the OSPA we have found it useful to think of a scenario planning intervention in terms of an engagement space designed with and for the learner. In this space different techniques and tools are brought together as one method, and manifest the intervention design (this is covered in detail later in the chapter, particularly in relation to Figure 5.1).

In this chapter we discuss each of these elements in this OSPA framework in some detail, and we discuss how and when to evaluate a scenario planning intervention, as well as the set of scenarios it generates. As this book's authors, we also offer reflections on the current roles of scenario planning, and point to some new directions on effectiveness and evaluation being offered within the literature, based on our decades of combined practice-based experience.

Methodology

In Chapter 3, we outlined our views on methods for reframing and reperception, explaining that methods are chosen because they articulate and reflect a methodology, which in turn manifests the epistemological stance of how scenario planning supports the scenario learner. This methodology plays an important role in making knowledge generation and knowledge acquisition work, in terms of the desired rigor and usefulness.

Various typologies have been proposed to classify scenario planning methods. For instance, van Notten et al. (2003) differentiated methods according to purpose (exploratory, decision support, etc.), and Wilkinson and Eidinow (2008) classified methods according to their epistemological assumptions and learning purpose. Ramírez and Selin (2014) proposed a three-dimensional typology, consisting of a $2 \times 2 \times 2$ matrix in which the axes reflect: (1) whether quantitative or qualitative techniques are favored; (2) whether plausibility or probability is used to guide the assessment of the scenarios; and (3) whether there is a stronger preference for scientific or artistic methods. Others have suggested that such either/or distinctions are false or can be bridged; for example, "quantitative–qualitative" divides can be bridged by explicitly relating scenario narratives with model-based simulations and quantification (Alcamo and Henrichs 2008; Wilkinson and Kupers 2014). Volkery and Ribeiro (2009) noted the importance of attending to the culture (e.g. national, professional) of the scenario learners. All typologies seek to ascertain which methods work well.

WHAT DO WE MEAN BY "WORK WELL"?

In clinical medicine, the effectiveness of a method is assessed using randomized, controlled trials that inform a meta-assessment of different treatments. There is no such thing in scenario planning to determine objectively that one particular method is best.

Instead, lots of viable methods are available, all of which have been reported (usually by their proponents) to have "worked well" in this or that kind or number of settings. However, in many such reports, "working well" meant that something that was imagined in the scenarios actually took place. In other words, the scenario set was evaluated as if it worked as a prediction. We think that prediction is *not* a good criterion to determine if scenario planning worked well; if prediction were possible, scenario planning has no relevance and is not needed, as was discussed in Chapter 1. Instead, in the OSPA a set of scenarios operate as framing and reframing devices and contribute to reperception, which are not easy to measure or evaluate in terms of direct impact on decision outcomes. However, scenario planning can be assessed and evaluated in terms of intermediate impacts that support the wider purpose of the intervention; for example, contributing new options for strategic planning (as in the Wärtsilä and EPO cases in Appendices A and E), or forging new common ground in situations characterized by values in conflict (as in the AiA case in Appendix D), or contributing shared understanding of a new, still emerging phenomenon (as in the Risk-World case in Appendix F).

Moreover, in most of these purported assessments there is no reference to how the claim of "working well" was substantiated or how it met the wider purpose served by the scenario planning intervention, largely because this key step of purpose-setting is often neglected, as we indicated in Chapter 4.

HOW MANY STEPS IN A SCENARIO PLANNING INTERVENTION OR CYCLE?

Many books and articles by respected, experienced scenario planning practitioners (henceforth "scenario planners") describe their scenario method as a series of steps, but all too often without first clarifying the intervention design logic (see Box 5.1).

We believe there is no such thing as *the* correct number of steps. How many steps one takes depends on many factors. They include the availability of resources and time; the depth and breadth of engagement required to ensure legitimacy and serve the purpose;[1] and the cultures of those involved. Other factors include: the number of workshops where face-to-face activity can take place; the volume of work to be done asynchronically at a distance before,

---

BOX 5.1 SOME EXAMPLES OF STEP-BASED SCENARIO PLANNING

- Orru and Relan's (2013) thirteen-step process.
- Schoemaker's (1993) ten-step process.
- Gugan's (2008) six-step method.
- Kahane's (2012) four-step process, based on his work in community conflict settings in South Africa.
- The Shell (Royal Dutch Shell 2003) scenario planners' four-stage process.

In addition, some of our colleagues in the WEF have opted for an eight-step process.

after, and in between workshops; the investment in learning journeys; the quality of peer review that the purpose requires; the scenarios literacy and skill of the learners; and the competence of the facilitator.

Typically, a OSPA scenario planning intervention includes determining the learners and the purpose of the intervention; then defining, developing, verifying, and refining a set of contrasting strategic frames; then using these to reframe the current situation (upframing). This is followed by immersive learning and rehearsing of new ideas and options, which contributes to the learners' reperceiving their position in the present situation (downframing). In the OSPA we believe that rather than assuming a linear learning process (for example, reframing enables reperception), iterating between reframing and reperception through the several cycles of scenario building is needed to avoid the extremes of groupthink and fragmentation common in social learning processes. (Refer back to Figure 1.4.)

Therefore, rather than thinking in terms of the number of steps, the OSPA's emphasis is on the number of cycles that might be needed to revisit different methodological choices; for example, revising the time horizon used or the choice of axes in the deductive method (see below), or expanding the group of learners for whom the scenario planning has been designed. More importantly, in the OSPA the emphasis is also on the number of iterations of building and using needed to support the reframing-reperception learning loop, so that the learners can find new and better ways of dealing with their current situation, which we discussed in Chapter 1. Documenting the learning in each step and iteration can help identify whether another iteration is required, or whether the iterations have reached saturation point by delivering diminishing learning returns.

ROLE OF THE FACILITATOR

At this point it is useful to note the facilitator role, which in the OSPA is broadly compatible with Schein's (1999) views on effective process consultation. Our treatment is succinct because the literature on effective facilitation is too large to do justice to here; and in any case this book is written both for the facilitator and for the learners that work with the facilitator. Sometimes the intervention design and facilitation of the scenario planning process is undertaken entirely by those who seek to benefit from it, particularly if these learners are already effective scenario planners. In such circumstances they might rotate the role of a lead facilitator. In many other situations, an external facilitator is engaged to design and facilitate the intervention. An important task throughout the intervention is to document what is being learned (whether this is done by the learners or the facilitator can be determined in each case). Documenting not only enables the learning journey to be fully appreciated in retrospect, but also enables choices and decisions made along the way to be revisited and examined by those involved, and if necessary by others when this is required for governance purposes.

Both learners and facilitators benefit from keeping a learning log; this helps them to realize the full potential of the reframing-reperception cycles in scenario planning that we discussed in Chapters 1 and 3. The reframing impact of scenario planning will most likely challenge the established view of the status quo in power. The facilitator can help those challenged to engage in the reframing-reperception cycle—or at least prevent their killing the process—by encouraging them to reflect on what has been learned, by noting how they feel about the choices, and by explicitly keeping a record of the choices that determine what was put into or left out of the contrasting set of frames developed in a given iteration of the scenario planning process.

INTERVENTION LOGICS: CHOICE OF SCENARIO METHODS

The following generic types of plausibility based scenario planning methods appear most frequently in the literature. Any of them could be deployed in ways that are consistent with the OSPA to open a space for reframing and reperceiving the situation facing the scenario learner:

- *Deductive method.* This method involves mapping and analyzing uncertain factors in the contextual environment and how these might plausibly interact and have a disruptive or transformative impact on the transactional environment in the time horizon under consideration. These uncertain factors are then termed "key drivers" of change (that is, driving changes in the transactional environment). In the deductive method, two or three mutually independent drivers are selected, sometimes using some form of cross-impact matrix/fuzzy logic[2] (Jetter and Kok 2014) to produce a framework of logical combinations that best serves the purpose and learner. This framework is often in the form of a 2×2 or $2 \times 2 \times 2$ matrix, such as economic growth vs. environmental quality, or economic growth vs. societal cohesion vs. ecological sustainability. In the deductive method, the structuring of the scenario framework occurs before the development of the scenario content. (We discuss content in terms of system maps and storylines later in this chapter.) The axes can be either/or axes or more-or-less axes; this choice makes a significant difference in the scenario set that is produced, and affects the ontological nature of the potential reframing-reperception impact (Ramírez and Wilkinson 2014; see also our discussion of this choice in Chapter 6). For example, the either/or format that van der Heijden (2005) advocated makes it logically possible for only one of the four scenarios in a 2×2 matrix to emerge, meaning that reframing is achieved from contrasting mutually exclusive possibilities. On the other hand, the more-or-less axes make it possible for several scenarios to emerge simultaneously, such as in different parts of a market or product line, which enables a framing of the possibility of several incompatible futures arising at the same time.[3]

- *Inductive method.* Here the scenario planning also starts with identifying novel and uncertain factors in the contextual environment, which might be in the form of weak signals, emerging issues, or trend analysis. These are then combined either through the development of story snippets and/ or by converting them into a set of drivers of change that describe their combined impact on the transactional environment in the time horizon under consideration. In the inductive method, these factors need not be key drivers that are independent of each other and that can then be combined to form a structure, as in the deductive method described above. Instead, the structure of the scenario set is established (induced) *after* developing a number of relevant and challenging stories which contrast with each other. This allows the differences among the scenarios to be compared against each other. This was the methodology followed, for example, in the UEG and Shell interventions found in the Appendices. Once a set of viable and useful futures has been generated, they are compared; then the scenario planners develop a structure that helps the purpose and the uses in this comparison.

- *Abductive method.* This method iterates between the inductive and deductive approaches mentioned above. This might be done by producing various versions of deductive structures, or by developing several scenarios inductively and choosing a framework that contrasts them most helpfully, or by juxtaposing each of these two approaches against each other over several days or weeks.

- *Normative method.* In this method the starting point in developing the scenarios is to articulate a preferred future—a vision of a system of concern, such as a department, a firm, a country, or the whole world. The scenarios explore the sets of wider conditions that might occur, and are used to assess whether the preferred future can arise in any, some, or all of the scenarios— and to inform the pathways required for the vision to be progressed under each of the scenarios.

- *Incremental method.* The starting point in the incremental method is what can be described as the "official future." This is sometimes formally stated by the senior management team, but often it is the expected or assumed future context under which the existing strategy of the organization will be successful. It corresponds to what Wack referred to as the "ghost" or "phantom" scenario, as it is often implicit. Alternative scenarios are then developed by asking "what if" questions to identify plausible alternative future contexts.[4]

- *Alternative futures method.* This method was developed by futures studies researcher Jim Dator. The scenario framework is preset, structured around four archetypal narratives of systems change. These narratives are "Continued Growth," "Societal Collapse," "A Conserver Society," and "A Transformational Society" (Dator 2009; see also Bezold 2009).

- *Critical scenarios method.* This approach was developed by Sohail Inayatullah. It considers explicitly how a scenario planning intervention reflects and/or reinforces power relations, then asks how the intervention can instead attempt to redress some of the power imbalances in the system in which it operates. Inayatullah developed "Causal Layered Analysis" (1998) as a method to expose worldviews and their underlying myths, and to help those he works with to use these to construct alternative scenarios and develop new narratives compared to the dominant policy narrative.

- The so-called *Perspectives-based approach* to scenario planning (van Asselt and Rotmans 1996), and parts of our own work (see Wilkinson and Ramírez 2010), demonstrate how scenario planning can be developed to reveal and navigate between differing worldviews. Within each worldview it helps to reveal its assumptions and to help those who hold them to accommodate different perspectives.

One can expect that new varieties of "methods" will continue to emerge, perhaps through hybridization: the blending of practices from one method with those of another. This might occur in response to the demand for, and opportunities to develop, online approaches to wider participation.[5]

All of these different methods of building scenarios using plausibility as a guide to the future result in a set of two, three, or more scenarios. In the OSPA, the aim is to build the minimum number required to serve the purpose of the scenario learner. This is the opposite of methods that generate scenarios by permutating all variations in the combination of contextual factors, then "selecting" a more manageable number on the basis of probabilistic assessment and/or surveys of expert opinion to identify the most likely scenarios.

In the OSPA, the critical determinant for choosing the scenario building method is what best serves the purpose of the scenario planner, in their specific situation and context. The selection of the set of scenarios reflects the scenario learner's perception of its potential usefulness in revealing and reframing the different perspectives that are relevant to their situation. There is currently no overall contingency framework that captures all these factors and relates them to method choice. Each method listed earlier has merits and disadvantages.

In all of these methods, the initial building step is followed by the further development and refinement of the scenario set. In the OSPA, the two main ways of achieving this are system maps and storylines, which are best used in combination to ensure plausibility and memorability of the scenarios and their relevance for the learners' purpose. We discussed these matters in Chapters 2 and 3.

ONE-OFF INTERVENTIONS? OR ENGAGEMENTS THAT INVOLVE SEVERAL GENERATIONS OF SCENARIO SETS?

Scenario planning work can be conducted as a one-off intervention. Or scenario planning can involve a set of repeated, more or less cyclical processes which can become deeply embedded into how an organization's top managers think, strategize, and learn about their environment and about how they (tacitly, in some cases) frame that understanding. Royal Dutch Shell[6] and the Singapore Government are examples of organizations that sustain scenario planning activities and have developed capabilities in this area. The cycles are not quite "continuous"—that would be exhausting. But the cycles happen with some regularity, albeit typically less than the frequency of budget cycles. In such settings, scenario planning becomes embedded as a routine part of how the organization does its work (the WEF is an example), and/or is triggered when needed to inform its strategy (Wärtsilä, Statoil, DP World, and Eskom are examples). In some organizations which are repeat learners of scenarios, a new set of scenarios has to take into account the previous set, so a sense of continuity is built into the sensemaking that the scenarios provide for the company's executives. Shell is the archetypical example here; see Wilkinson and Kupers (2014).

Many private sector organizations and governments have started up scenario planning work on a one-off project basis and, in the process of doing so, discovered the value of reframing and reperception that the intervention stimulates and delivers. When organizations do several rounds of scenario planning they learn more about how they and others perceive and frame the key issues that shape the strategic agenda, underpin strategic choices, and influence which strategic options are considered (or not). Such organizations may end up institutionalizing scenario planning, and then have an in-house scenario planning capability that they can use not only internally but also with clients and other outsiders. The Harvard Business School case study on Morgan Stanley's scenario planning, and particularly its use in Japan, which we discussed in Chapter 4, is an example of this. Morgan Stanley reportedly did several rounds of scenario planning, each yielding interesting and actionable options, more than three-fourths of which were subsequently implemented.

Similarly, van der Heijden (2008) recounted his work in the Indian agricultural sector, where a first set of scenarios opened up lines of action and inquiry which were pursued. The lessons learned were recorded, and gave rise to a second round of scenario planning to further develop the learnings obtained through the original set.

Designing a scenario planning intervention: choices and key parameters

We have worked on scenario planning interventions with individuals and groups in many different organizations around the globe—as educators, researchers, and consultants. Our experiences all point to the importance of considering multiple elements in designing any intervention. We describe these in this section.

The scenario planner needs to make a number of choices in designing an effective scenario planning initiative. As we discussed in Chapter 4, those choices depend most importantly on the purposes of the intervention and the cultures (professional, organizational, national) of the learners, and also include all the factors around the edges in Figure 5.1.

In the OSPA, the scenario planner's choices mainly concern the three ovals in the Figure:

- *Intervention design.* At the "highest" level of the overall design of the intervention there are a number of factors to consider, relating to purpose, use, and authorizing environment; see the eight arrows impinging on the intervention design oval in Figure 5.1. Two main questions need to be addressed. First, how well do the methods, tools, and techniques that will be deployed fit with the chosen *epistemology*[7] that legitimizes the scenario learning? For example, the scenario planners in the AiA project (Appendix D) had to attend to and be able to incorporate multiple views of what knowledge means and involves—some were traditional and oral;

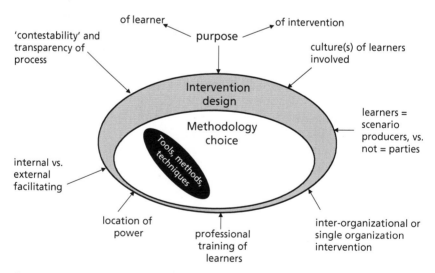

Figure 5.1. Elements in designing a scenario planning intervention

others positivist and evidence-based, as in Western medicine. Second, how well does the methodology that is chosen relate to the *ontological assumptions* (assumptions about what is "real") held by the scenario learners? These views on what is real are affected by the culture and professional training of the learners.[8] For example, the UEG scenarios in Appendix C had to take on board the way medical researchers deal with reality in the present and the future. These choices also must take into account the time and investment that will be dedicated to the scenario planning.

- *Choice of method.* At the "middle" level, how does the set of tools and techniques that comprise a method fit the chosen *methodological stance*? Recall from Chapter 3 that a given method consists of a collection of tools and techniques, whereas methodology reflects the epistemological principles that the learner and facilitator have taken up in designing the intervention. Moreover, the choice of method deals with the very practical issues relating to exactly how the learners, the purpose, and the timing will affect what is done, when, and by whom, as we discussed earlier.

- *Tools and techniques.* At the "lower" level, how do the tools and techniques to be used in a scenario planning intervention articulate the chosen *method*, and how do they come together as a coherent and useful set? Examples include interviews, surveys, desk research, trend-crashing, and causal layered analysis. The preferred techniques of an experienced consultant may or may not be the most appropriate for the scenario learner's situation. For example, in management consulting it is often expedient to define the "problem" with a clear question or set of questions to settle the scope of the intervention and enable the process to proceed to problem-solving activities as quickly as possible. In a scenario planning intervention, this equivalent of quickly closing in on a "focal question" may backfire if it is too narrow, shallow, artificial, or untested. Instead, as we described in Chapter 4, the painstaking effort involved in carefully listening to the scenario learners' concerns and establishing how the scenarios are going to be used, when, and by whom to reframe-reperceive the situation becomes a valuable investment of time. Indeed, a focal question might emerge *after* the scenario building cycle has started. If a focal question is tightly prescribed at the start (which we counsel against), it is very important to consider whether that question is going to be seen as manipulative in foreclosing considerations of the future in the present that might not fit with the orthodox view or dominant perspective in the organization.[9]

In the rest of this chapter we highlight eight issues that have arisen in our conversations in the classroom with executive participants as they learn how to work across these three levels. These are:

- Defining the purpose and intended use of the scenario planning engagement.
- Designing and scoping the engagement.

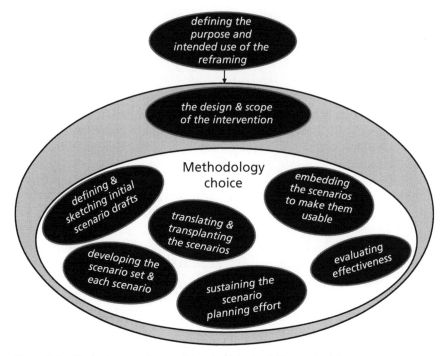

Figure 5.2. Choice issues to be considered within the OSPA methodology

- Defining and sketching the scenario drafts.
- Developing the scenario set and each scenario.
- Translating and transplanting the scenarios to make them usable.
- Embedding the scenarios to make them part of the organization's routines.
- Sustaining the scenario planning effort.
- Evaluating effectiveness.

We offer detailed, practical suggestions for each of them next. To clarify where they fit in terms of Figure 5.1, we have specified them in Figure 5.2.

DEFINING THE PURPOSE AND INTENDED USE—GETTING TO KNOW THE SCENARIO LEARNER

Refer now to Box 5.2. In devising a scenario engagement, we often find it helpful to imagine clearly the equivalent of Blank's "movie about the movie," *Burden of Dreams*, as we start working on the actual *Fitzcarraldo* scenario planning engagement. This is because imagining how the scenarios will be seen once they are done, and how the process of building them will be considered ex-post by learners not involved in their making, will enable the purpose of the engagement to become clearer. The "movie about the movie" will enable the scenario

---

BOX 5.2 *FITZCARRALDO*

Werner Herzog's movie *Fitzcarraldo* (1982) portrayed efforts by a would-be rubber plantation baron, an Irishman known as Fitzcarraldo, to transport a steamship in one piece over a steep hill to access an area rich in rubber trees in a Peruvian jungle. The story is apparently based on actual events. Making the Herzog movie was very difficult, even chaotic; and director Les Blank made another movie, a feature-length documentary called *Burden of Dreams*, to document these difficulties.

---

planner to better help the learner to clarify his/her purpose, and assess which tools and techniques in the method are most advisable to deploy and when.

A similar analogy is offered from the world of cuisine. A good chef does not simply follow the recipe book; instead, he is mindful of the quality of the dining experience. He does not just cook and serve up dishes. He is attentive to how the ambience of the restaurant and the design of the menu will be appreciated by his clientele. The emphasis is on service, and while quality of production matters, it is secondary to the design of the overall experience.

As we discussed at length in Chapter 4, in the OSPA it is the job of the scenario learner, supported by the facilitator, to do all that can be done, perhaps shy of hauling a ship over a steep hill, to ensure the reframing potential of the scenario set is both useful and put to use. To achieve this it is important to understand when and how scenario planning contributes to reframing and reperception of the situation, which we discussed in Chapter 1. From the facilitator's point of view, it is important to determine as specifically as possible how and when the scenarios will be used to reframe understanding (whose and when) before embarking on the building phase.

Similar to any organized activity involving more than one person, scenario planning requires resources, planning, and management. *Defining the purpose* includes appreciating why the scenario learner (who is sometimes "the client" in other literatures[10]) has decided to consider scenario planning, that is, why, why now, and what for? (Recall our discussion in Chapter 4 of the learner-defined purpose in the OSPA.) Defining the purpose benefits from getting to know the wider authorizing environment, because the learner is embedded in it and it can strongly affect the design and scoping of the engagement, as we discuss in the next subsection. This defining of the purpose in the context of the authorizing environment is done partly to determine who could kill the scenario planning intervention and why, and to determine how these people are related to the scenario learner. Scenario planning interventions can fail to be effective in situations where, for example, a senior manager in headquarters thinks a field manager in a region or a function such as risk management "ought to" use scenarios—but these learners might not see things that way! Instead, they may feel that the headquarters manager does not really understand the situation they are facing in the field. We have learned the hard way that the purpose has to be that of the actual scenario learner, not that of the learner's boss. This requires discipline on the part of the scenario facilitator—avoiding the tendency to elevate problematic situations to the attention of more senior decision-making levels for reasons of ego rather than practicality. It also requires considerable effort to clarify purpose and thus to "land an intervention." As we mentioned earlier in the book, fudging this key element is one of the most commonly reported reasons for failure in scenario planning.[11]

Recall the *Burden of Dreams* documentary. It is advisable for the facilitator to have a full movie (or rather, movie about the movie) in one's mind of how the intervention (the *Fitzcarraldo* movie, if you will) will actually be seen afterwards, and to do so *before* one starts the intervention and *alongside* the intervention itself. In the EPO scenarios described in Appendix E, it took a full day of very difficult discussion with some fifty senior staff to determine the different learners and the hierarchy of purposes that the scenarios needed to be responsive to in order to be effective. For the AiA project described in Appendix D, the scoping and launch of the initiative took over six months, due to the complexity of the stakeholders involved.

In the OSPA, a further challenge for scenario learners in mastering scenario planning is to move beyond the usual "end report" mentality in routine intervention planning (and basic good management practices), to also prepare the ground for the application of the new knowledge that has been generated in the reporting process. Furthermore, as we have noted, there can be several iterations of the steps within an entire cycle of scenario planning until the "aha" moment of reperceiving is realized. And if reperception happens, lots of new inquiry or prototyping and option development work might follow.

From our teaching, research, and engagement experiences, we have found that many scenario-based initiatives fail for one or both of two main reasons: (1) they have failed to clarify the learner and uses; or (2) they have used all the available time and resources trying to build what might erroneously be marketed as a "perfect" set of scenarios (this may be a result of failing to clarify learner and uses). Instead, the OSPA uses the 1/3–2/3 heuristic discussed in Chapter 4 for an effective allocation of available time and resources.[12]

Getting to know the scenario learner's current framing and perception of their situation, perhaps manifested as a mental map, is a main objective in designing the intervention and making choices about methods, tools, and techniques. The facilitator (preferably working with the scenario learner) also gets to understand the learners' preferences and values, their intent (and perhaps hoped-for legacy), what they want to achieve in their value creating activities, and how they see the scenario planning intervention helping them to do so.

Conventional project management assumes that once a problem has been clearly defined and assigned to an appropriate owner, then it will be dealt with, if not resolved. But in scenario planning, the engagement of key stakeholders tends to result in identifying new problems, issues, challenges, and/or questions; this is the essence of reframing. This is because scenario planning work tends to deal with the wicked situations in TUNA conditions referred to in Chapter 3. Moreover, reframing contributes new questions, and researching these often leads to the discovery of new stakeholders, who in turn can hold different perspectives. This process of iteration and feedback often continues throughout the scenario planning cycle as well as across cycles, and this is why scenario planning is not entirely suited to the one-off, time-bounded interventions that characterize the majority of organizational processes and team-based activities.

It is not uncommon that something "big"—such as a major natural disaster, a significant takeover, or a radical reorganization—may happen while the scenario planning engagement is underway. In such situations purpose, learner, and use should be redefined, and (more or less formalized) recontracting is called for. This is because such events upset the ground upon which scenario planning and its effectiveness rest, namely, the organization's standard operating procedures, social processes, and culture.

DESIGNING AND SCOPING THE INTERVENTION

Designing and scoping the scenario planning intervention concerns first and foremost establishing with the learner what the learner's system (what we have called the authorizing environment) is, and whether it matches the characteristics of those who will benefit from the learning if they include others. That is, is it one organization? Part of a larger organization? Several organizations working together, and if so permanently or just for this intervention? A meta-organization? The learner's system becomes more complicated from the first to the last of these situations, and thus requires more effort to ascertain purpose and learners. On this foundation, the transactional and contextual environments can then be formulated and explored.

At the lower level in Figure 5.1, several issues affect the choice of which techniques and tools might be used, such as whether quantifying the scenarios is required; and whether the scenarios need to be kept secret or reserved in-house for a select internal group, or whether they will be made publicly available. In addition, the format(s) for articulating the scenarios can vary. The scenario set at a given point in time can be produced in the form of a dedicated book or booklet, like the AiA, EPO, Wärtsilä, and Shell scenarios. (It should be noted that in all of those cases, structured strategic dialogues were also staged so that people could engage with the scenarios.) Scenarios can also be delivered as imagined newspaper or magazine articles; for example, a set of World Bank scenarios were communicated in the format of a daily newspaper that was distributed via the usual morning service of the hotel where the scenario learners were staying. Scenarios can also be delivered as a film, through theater (see the EPO case), as an online software release (see the UEG scenarios), or even as an "app" (see the 2014 Delta Lloyd scenarios[13]).

The design and scoping aspects also include ascertaining how much effort is going to be put into the engagement, by whom, and over what period of time. The number of people involved, the number of workshops, and roles and governance arrangements are all determined here. Expectations of who does what and when, and how progress is going to be documented, are also set here. The facilitator and the learners need to review this "contract" and, if necessary, adapt it periodically over the course of the engagement.

One of the key resources to be secured is the core team. The facilitator needs to identify who will use the scenario planning; and as precisely as possible, how, when, in what meeting, conference, workshop, seminar, negotiation, or encounter, and for what purpose. In our collective experience, in far too many instances these things remain unclear, making evaluation (the final issue below) difficult.

Beyond such contracting and documenting there are a number of other activities concerned with designing and scoping the engagement. These are explained in greater detail than we can do here in van der Heijden's *Scenarios: The Art of Strategic Conversation* (2005). They include: conducting initial interviews within the learner system, and if relevant, outside; determining the expected value and evaluation criteria; setting a timeline for actual use; and crafting an initial set of scenario research topics.[14]

Findings from the initial internal and external stakeholder interviews can be fed back in the form of a "chorus of voices" analysis. This analysis is presented by question or issue, and preserves interviewee anonymity. The feedback will help confirm, settle, or adjust what is known, unknown, agreed, and contested within the learner group. The interview findings are typically cross-checked and complemented with other inputs such as board meeting minutes, external reviews of the sectors, and published papers and books.

These initial data-gathering activities help to begin identifying remarkable people that could be brought into meetings or workshops; and to determine if an orientation workshop is required, and how it will be structured.

A situation which can benefit from a scenario planning intervention is typically not a clearly defined problem given the TUNA conditions in which such work is undertaken. Instead, it entails only a tentative, initial mapping of what the learners understand of their situation(s) and context(s), and which questions or issues they want to explore with the engagement. Several techniques that can be used to structure the initial situational mapping are mentioned in Box 5.3.

> **BOX 5.3** TECHNIQUES TO STRUCTURE SITUATIONAL MAPPINGS
>
> - Open-ended interview protocol ("seven questions") (van der Heijden 2005).
> - Clarifying the learner's business idea (van der Heijden 2005).
> - Using Vickers' judgment triangle to clarify which aspect(s) of strategic judgment will be most helped by the scenarios.
>
> These techniques were mentioned in Chapter 4.

The time horizon of the scenarios

An important methodological choice in designing a scenario set is determining the appropriate time horizon for the scenarios, which is the future point in time from which the reframing perspectives are to be held on the present. Determining this time horizon entails taking into consideration a number of elements and reconciling them to ensure that the reframing makes sense and is effective. This is more of an art than a science.

Considering the system and its context from future vantage points seeks to look back at the current context and its possible unfolding with "new" eyes, unhampered by past and current conditioning and opening new possibilities. Freeing one's mind in this way means conceptualizing perspectives beyond the usual time horizons used in policymaking, strategic planning, risk management, and issue management processes—the one-year budget, the 1–5 year financial planning cycle, the 3–5 year political cycle, the 5–10 year industrial business cycle, the 3–5 year strategic plan, and so on.

Longer time horizons seek to reconsider the organizational, societal, and/or technological status quo framing by placing the current "photo" in a longer "film," freeing the imagination. However, learners will find scenario horizons that are too long to be unhelpful for the purposes of reframing. The purpose as well as the nature of the industry can make a big difference in identifying how long (or far away) the "longer-term future" is. To define time horizons it is often helpful to consult with a diverse set of external stakeholders in the initial interview process, such as retired executives, non-executive directors, suppliers, clients, and regulators.

Our experience suggests that pushing the horizon as far away as possible is helpful, but without losing plausibility (10,000 years from now is probably implausible for all learners) or usability for the learners' intended reframing. Examples of criteria for setting these horizon times from our experience are: considering who might buy twelve-year-old Scotch whiskey thirteen years from now (or twenty-six years if it is twice that cycle, etc.); the date at which a new doctor will be in the middle of her career when it takes eight years to produce a new gastroenterology specialist (that is, twenty-five years hence, as in the UEG scenarios for 2040 found in Appendix C); and imagining what kinds of cars might exist in Europe three car generations beyond the current and planned model lifespans, given the current 5–6 year new product timeline from engineering model to showroom (that is, 15–18 years hence). The initial interviews can also help to identify key uncertainties that currently represent "unknown knowns" to intended learners, and some of these can help to define the time horizon. For instance, in the 1990s one of the authors worked on the future of paper, and one interviewee said that the time horizon that was being used tentatively at the beginning of the intervention was too short to consider whether genetic engineering might plausibly develop a process where the industry would no longer need chlorine to whiten the paper (a big game-changing reframer in that industry). So the time horizon was duly lengthened to consider that plausible option within the scenario set.

Issues to research

In the OSPA, the key uncertainties to be researched in a scenario planning intervention are those that arise in the contextual environment. The UEG scenario case study lists the eighteen uncertainties in the contextual environment which the members of the association's Futures Trends Committee researched and brought to the scenario definition workshop (see Figure C1). In the inductive method, a common next step is to do further research to assess how these uncertainties might combine to produce emerging factors "driving" the logic of each of the alternative scenarios being considered. In the deductive method the same is done once the axes have been defined, within each of the scenarios in the set. Through research, iterations of data gathering, new knowledge generation, and sensemaking help the scenario learners to construct collaboratively and assess plausibility. Connections among the uncertainties, always in reference to the specific reframing purpose and intended use, are proposed, tested, contested, and refined.

Sometimes it is necessary to revisit the time horizon to keep the unfolding story of how the uncertainties might interrelate plausible. At other times the interconnections lead to highlighting another uncertainty in the contextual environment that needs further investigation. For example, in the UEG scenarios, at some point in the future (2040 was the chosen time horizon in 2014) it became important not only to question what medical science, welfare economics, and politics might do to gastrointestinal care, but also what people might be eating and what a "family" might be in each scenario. With these newly gathered uncertainties, the research process can be run anew, with the insight about a particular critical uncertainty clarifying what the reframing is casting light on, and how it is clarifying the understanding of the futures under consideration.

The scoping, design, and uncertainty research work described here makes it possible to start mapping the transactional and the contextual environments referred to in Chapter 1. Here, the scenario facilitators and learners can begin to consider the critical uncertainties in the contextual environment that might become driving forces that could transform the more immediate transactional environment for the organization (or system of organizations) that the scenario learners are in.

Clarification of the boundary conditions that will make the scenarios useful reframing devices for the scenario set is another part of designing and scoping. By *boundary conditions* we mean how *im*plausible a set can be and still be helpful to learners, and how much challenge the organization's members can stand. For instance, in the EPO case (Appendix E) it was very difficult for some members to believe that what Greenpeace thought of some patents at the time was credible; yet in the end, they thought it *might* be credible and a version of this appeared in one of the scenarios.

Researching key contextual uncertainties helps the learners to map how each of the frames holds a distinct understanding and perspective of the situation of concern. This helps them to critically assess their mental maps and the assumptions they have been using, by capturing existing differences in opinion in the learner group about future developments and helping them to discuss those differences. Indeed, disagreements are an important source of information for constructing scenarios, so documenting and working through them is important, preferably by the scenario learners as well as by the scenario facilitators.

In some interventions we have used big poster canvasses (for European readers, A0-sized) to do this group model building, as was done in the Wärtsilä (Appendix A) and UEG (Appendix C) scenario interventions. One could also use flipcharts. Some practitioners (Hodgson 1992) suggest that using hexagonal Post-it notes helps to link factors to each other more easily in 3D than do rectangular ones, and many scenario workshops have adopted hexagonal formats. This is one area where technology is well positioned to transform practices and techniques; for example, Adrian Taylor has been exploring ICT-enabled 3D group system modeling spaces.[15] See also the brief discussion of modeling in scenario building in Chapter 3.

DEFINING AND SKETCHING THE SCENARIO DRAFTS WHILE ATTENDING TO THE COMPARISONS AMONG THE SCENARIOS

Having defined and researched the contextual uncertainties (and in the deductive method, chosen the driving forces that best serve the learner and reframing purposes), attention shifts to defining and sketching the scenarios and constructing the scenario set.

In the *deductive method*, one first determines a scenario framework by selecting two uncertainties that are causally independent over the chosen time horizon. The criteria for selecting these are those which best support the intended reframing, and which best "organize" the other uncertainties to support this reframing. The two mutually independent uncertainties that are selected are then turned into dimensions with contrasting end points (such as high–low climate change, or strong–weak government regulation), creating a 2 × 2 matrix.

In the *inductive method* the uncertainties are put together to create a large number (often over a dozen) of draft or sketch scenarios that are designed to challenge the current framing and to bring forth possible alternatives that manifest challenging and useful framings. This was how the UEG and Shell scenarios were produced. Then a small set of two to four draft scenarios is selected; they should contrast not only with the current framing but also with each other, and they should support the learning of the purposeful intervention. Then (or in some cases, at the same time) the framework that allows them to be compared is created.

In the *abductive method*, one iterates between the inductive and deductive approach; this was the method used in the EPO and Wärtsilä scenarios. Here, the framework and the scenarios are developed iteratively in relation to each other.

Once this research on and assembling of uncertainties is well under way, it is possible to begin developing storylines, system maps, and story maps. We describe these next.

DEVELOPING THE SCENARIO SET AND EACH SCENARIO

The main considerations in developing a set of scenarios include determining the level of detail, predetermined elements, plausibility, systems diagrams and event maps (which structure the storyline and story), and scenario names.

Like many aspects of scenarios, the *level of detail* of the scenarios in the set depends on the learner's reframing purpose. In some cases, such as in a crisis, "rough and ready" scenarios suffice; in other situations the scenarios need to be very carefully vetted by peers before they are rendered public. The AiA and EPO scenarios in the Appendices were of the latter kind—their learners expected them to be subjected to severe criticism by all kinds of stakeholders once the scenarios were made public.

Recall the concept of *predetermined elements* in Chapter 3. These are outcomes that will take place in *any* and all of the scenarios in a set. In developing a set of scenarios, it is important to clarify what is predetermined; in fact, it is one of the most important aspects of doing scenario planning, according to Wack.

Recall from Chapters 1 and 2 that *plausibility* has to be co-produced by people learning together to make sense. Plausibility becomes evident for the mind when the causal logic supporting the scenarios—as they are constructed—becomes clear. In building the scenario set, plausibility is established and checked in producing, critiquing, and refining both systems diagrams and the scenario storylines. It becomes confirmed in the absence of implausible inconsistencies within each story. Plausibility is also strengthened indirectly by other qualities, including relevance, challenge, and memorability of the reframing effort. The emphasis is not on plausibility based on present understanding but plausibility in terms of future developments (Ramírez and Wilkinson 2009a; Ramírez and Selin 2014).

In the OSPA, the development of the scenarios and the framework is supported by *systems diagrams* and *event maps* that become storylines. Systems diagrams are compilations of time-independent connections among the uncertainties as they relate to each other at the end of the scenario planning horizon. Typically, one is produced for each scenario. A good analogy is that it is the equivalent of the "destination guide" on a voyage. Say you are going to visit Prague for the first time and you buy a guide to the city. The guide can be read as a systems diagram; it tells you how the city features are connected to each other, and how they together make up the system for the city so it "works" as a tourist destination.[16] Its complement, event maps, link the uncertainties to each other in time. They are presented as time series of key developments that occur in the story, again, typically one for each scenario. Following this analogy, an event map would be the equivalent of a calendar for a guided tour of the city (Monday the church and the market, Tuesday the history museum and the bridge, etc.). It becomes a storyline when learners and the actors in the learners' transactional environment bring it to life, and would be the equivalent of a travel log or account. The stories of the scenarios were the heart of how the Shell, EPO, and AiA scenarios were presented, and the event maps played an important supporting role.

As we noted in Chapters 2 and 3, scenarios involve a social process of knowledge co-production, which renders intuitive and tacit knowledge into an explicit and contestable form. Systems diagrams are used to manifest the learners' understanding and insights about the structure of the system and to assess, with positive and negative feedback loops, whether or not the system's dynamics are stable or subject to lock-in or to sudden shifts.

The format of the scenario set should be designed to maximize impact, interest, and memorability in its reframing role. *Naming the scenarios* is an important consideration. Color coding, images, symbols, tables, and charts help to convey the story. For example, four colors were used in the EPO scenarios, three in the UEG and Wärtsilä ones, and two in the Shell ones to denote clearly each scenario as, for instance, the "Green" or the "Blue" scenario—and everyone involved knew what this meant.

A set of scenarios must be credible and comprehensible in the eyes of learners, as well as for those the learners work with, inside and outside their organization. A learner must be able to communicate a set of scenarios to his/ her counterparts if they are to be able together to use the scenarios for reframing effectively. This is obviously an important issue in ensuring the scenarios will be useful.

A usable scenario set is free of unexplained internal contradictions, with each scenario in the set being clear and distinctive. Each scenario in the set is clearly contrasted from the others, as well as from how the situation is seen today. Finally, each scenario needs to be memorable. The memory might be facilitated through the story, the name, the pictures used, or the examples given. See the thumbnail descriptions of the scenarios in each Appendix case for examples.

TRANSLATING AND TRANSPLANTING THE SCENARIOS

Recall that in Chapter 4 we considered translating and transplanting scenarios as a matter of technique. Here we focus on how translating and transplanting involves interpreting the scenarios in different ways so that a wider set of stakeholders can also learn with them and reframe their own understandings. Often this involves exercises where someone other than the main learner is put at the center of the learner system (see Figure 1.1), and the scenarios are reinterpreted accordingly. This can happen within a single organization as well as among organizations. Thus, when Ramírez helped the chief political scientist of Shell to take the 2001 Global Scenarios (Appendix B), primarily intended for the management board of the whole company, to Shell Mexico, the core team put Shell Mexico at the center of the picture, reinterpreted what the "global" scenarios meant for that particular group of learners, and ascertained what reframing this afforded for them. In another exercise, the same "global" scenarios were taken to "lower olefins," a department of Shell's chemical business, and again they were reinterpreted and made relevant for them.

As we saw in Chapter 4, we use the term "transplanting" based on insights of our colleague Trudi Lang. The saying "for a one dollar plant, dig a ten dollar hole" conveys the idea that preparing the ground is important for something to take root in a new setting. Transplanting a set of scenarios meant for learners in one role or situation, to be usable by another set of learners in a different role or situation, means that a lot of preparation in the host setting has to be undertaken for the "new plant" to be accepted. We said in Chapter 3 that a difference between scenarios and forecasts is that the latter are for "anyone," while scenarios are always for "some-one." If after serving that "some-one" they can serve "an-other," then they need to be translated to fit the specifics of that "other" and their framing challenges. One cannot assume that the reframing purpose, scope, definition, etc. of the first party will also serve the second one unchanged; that is why "translation" is also called for.

In the OSPA the stories told in scenarios are open, in the sense that they invite the learner to reinterpret them. The readers of a scenario that has been written up by someone else are not required to remember the plot of a good scenario story as presented. They are, however, encouraged to insert themselves into the story and explore what is going on and what this means for how they frame and can reframe the understanding they have of their context, their organizations, and themselves. This is what we mean by "immersion."

To aid memorability, the structure of the story of an effective scenario has just a few parts. Scenario storylines should be limited at most to three to five major, easy to recall segments. This narrative structure, whose plausibility is supported by systems diagrams, can be enhanced with event maps (see the online UEG and Wärtsilä shipping scenarios presentations for examples), and graphs and illustrations (the AiA, Shell, and EPO scenarios booklets do this very well). This can provide a powerful combination for communicating the scenarios in an efficient and effective manner.

Widening the usage of the scenarios makes the investment in scenario planning work more rewarding, as it can increase the returns on the resources invested in an intervention. For instance, working with an energy company, one of the authors found that in addition to the strategists (the intended primary learners), others in the company could find the scenarios very useful, such as purchasers, HR managers, risk assessors, and country managers. However, a translation and transplanting effort was required for each group to be able fully to use the reframing potential the scenarios offered.

EMBEDDING THE SCENARIOS TO ENHANCE THEIR REFRAMING EFFECTIVENESS

In the OSPA, issues associated with developing the scenarios and the set can be confused with how the intended learners engage with the scenarios, particularly if the learners have been intimately involved in the definition and production of the set. Here we explore how this engagement with the learning can be embedded as an ongoing activity within the learners' organization. Significant learning can be achieved by *test driving* the scenarios, as we discussed in Chapter 4, and this can be done not only once but on a regular basis—until the scenario set becomes obsolete and another set is needed to reframe again.

If the scenarios are not to be seen as a brief visitor to the organization's managers that brought a gift of a fleeting reframing of their situation, then a scenario planning *process* needs to be embedded as a way of thinking. When this is done, the scenario-enabled reframings can be more effectively used as ongoing inputs that support the other processes and activities which create value in the organization's or learner's system, as discussed earlier. Few organizations, however, seem to be able or willing to do so.

When scenario planning becomes embedded, a scenario set is no longer simply a "product" that the "producers" (scenario facilitators) eject out from their factory door on to unknown learners. Instead, scenario planning and the scenarios it produces become embedded in the way the organization's managers think about how they think. The Nokia and Statoil cases discussed in Chapter 4, in which scenario planning was used again and again to help competitive intelligence teams to direct their early warning radars more effectively, is an example of this (see Ramírez et al. 2013).

The successful embedding of scenario planning thinking means that the framing being used at any one time remains fresh, perhaps by being *re*freshed. This can make the pay-off role of reperceiving with scenario planning a powerful capability (Ramírez et al. 2013). As we stressed in Chapter 1, scenario planning is an important element of a strategic planning system, but is not itself strategy, nor by itself strategic planning.

Each scenario in a scenario set can be rehearsed as an alternative reality in which strategy teams can role play what it would be like for each competitor (as well as one's own organization) to live in such a world, and to assess if the expected behaviors actually unfold as such. Also, as mentioned in Chapter 2, in TUNA conditions collaborative strategy has as much of a role as competitive strategy. Ramírez and van der Heijden (2007) suggested that coming together to create a "larger actor" helps those involved to have their shared transactional environment take up what had been elements of each individual actor's contextual environment, to decrease the uncertainty of the contextual turbulence for all involved.

At a more fundamental level, scenario planning reframings can be used to articulate what different factions on the board and executive committee might expect, for instance by mapping assumptions about the wider business environment that different factions are using when they take strategic decisions and propose courses of action. This latter role was a key driver of the evolution of scenarios in Royal Dutch Shell (Wilkinson and Kupers 2014): the scenario planning process enabled the pet initiatives of individual executives to be safely and constructively challenged and checked, by exploring under which scenario(s) a particular initiative would succeed or fail.

Other examples of using scenario planning in strategic planning and management systems are shown in Box 5.4.

SUSTAINING SCENARIO PLANNING CAPABILITIES

The mastery of scenario planning benefits from reflective practice, which we discuss extensively in Chapter 6. While many organizations have invested in cultivating a skillful scenarios community of practice, few have managed to

---

BOX 5.4 EXAMPLES OF SCENARIO PLANNING IN STRATEGIC PLANNING SYSTEMS

- *Assessing strategic options*—as seen in the Wärtsilä Power scenarios (Appendix A).
- *Testing strategic innovation domains*—as used for innovation and R&D in Shell (Ramírez et al. 2011).
- *Rehearsing the future*—the use EPO made of its scenarios in "gaming" the future of patenting (Appendix E).
- *Developing new options and imagining new products*—as in the second of the Wärtsilä Ship Power scenarios (Appendix A).

---

sustain this community over many years. This is a shame, as scenario planning can be a powerful strategic capability in TUNA conditions.

Sustaining a scenario planning capability involves developing and testing new processes, techniques, and tools. Sometimes this is done internally; sometimes it involves doing it in different divisions within one company, as Wärtsilä did in its shipping division, then in its energy division, and then again in shipping, helping both its service and manufacturing functions as well (Appendix A). And sometimes it entails new ventures with outsiders, as Shell, EPO, and the French utility Electricité de France (EDF) collaborated to achieve with the Risk-World scenarios (Appendix F), and as Shell did with UNAIDS in the AiA scenarios (Appendix D).

Sustaining a particular scenario planning intervention also can involve *broadening* the learning and reframing by linking these to more learners. We see this happening when the reframings can be leveraged into a new platform for collaboration, which, as Emery and Trist (1965) asserted, can help to forge new shared understanding and to produce the common ground upon which effective collaborative action rests. In this sense, scenario planning provides a means to build trust and social capital, as we discussed in Chapter 2. Lang (2012) showed how this was achieved in the second round of scenario planning by the Vice Chancellor's Office of the Open University. Wilkinson and Kupers (2014) documented how Shell has used scenario planning as an outreach and engagement support. And the EPO scenarios (in Appendix E), also studied by Lang, used scenario planning to position the office as a thought leader and to help convene the first five-major-patent-office summit in Hawaii. Thus, reframing can also inform institutional innovation, which matters when new institutional arrangements seek to engage emerging issues, as in the Risk-World and AiA cases in the Appendices. The Risk-World scenarios highlighted the shifting contours and new types of risk facing companies, public bodies, and regulators alike. The scenarios were used by others to establish a new organization, the International Risk Governance Council.[17]

EVALUATING THE EFFECTIVENESS OF THE INTERVENTION

With more TUNA conditions in the contextual environments of organizations, one may expect that the value of scenario planning will be increasingly recognized not only within strategy consultancies but also within their client organizations.

If scenario planning were done more effectively, more experienced practitioners could exchange learnings, cultivate and deepen reflective practice, and contribute to the development of practical skills in others. Supporting this upgrading of practice is one of the main reasons we have written this book.

Setting out the criteria for evaluating effectiveness is, as we have noted, very often a missing aspect of scenario planning interventions. In the OSPA, this is an essential component in ensuring that the investments of attention, time, imagination, creativity, and resources to reframe understanding and create new options for action are worthwhile. Defining evaluation criteria is intimately related to setting a purpose that is achievable, and it helps in assessing under what conditions that purpose is met.

There is no agreed scientific basis for evaluating a set of scenarios, nor is there agreement on how to measure the effectiveness of scenario planning work (de Leon Ardon and de las Nieves Sanchez Guerrero 2012). Unsurprisingly, the topic of evaluation of scenario planning is of growing interest to scholars and researchers, as shown in the increasing literature relating to it. A wide variety of different schema have started to emerge, and a list is found in the endnotes to this chapter.[18]

As discussed in Chapter 4, we believe the criteria for a "good" set of scenarios are typically determined by how well they fit the specific reframing and reperception purposes they seek to serve. Typically, in the OSPA the evaluation includes assessing whether the learning that was supported by the scenario planning was actually used as intended, and determining whether the reframing and reperception enabled value to be created, often in terms of effecting change in one or more of the areas listed in Box 5.5.

Conclusion: reframing services, not products

The late management guru Peter Drucker (1961, 310) once remarked, "The most common source of mistakes in management decisions is the emphasis on finding the right answer rather than the right question." Scenario planning involves a search for better questions rather than the usual problem-solving approach. Like any organized activity, it takes time, resources, planning, and management to do it well.

BOX 5.5 SOME VALUE CREATING CHANGES FROM REFRAMING AND REPERCEPTION

- How a situation has been reperceived.
- How aware those perceiving the situation have become of the assumptions they had been bringing to the situation, and how useful the scenarios were in surfacing and challenging assumptions or navigating worldviews.
- How much the reframing enhanced the quality of judgment by decision makers in the organization or learner system.
- The extent to which the reframing affected how options are assessed.
- The number of *new* options produced to engage the situation as a result of the reframing.
- Whether the reframing improved the quality of the conversations about the situation, its future, and the strategies associated with engaging the situation.
- How well the multiple frames stimulated by the scenarios helped disagreement between different perspectives to be managed productively.
- How much the frames offered in each of the scenarios enhanced each learner's understanding of other points of view, and understanding of the situation, its context, and its possible future unfoldings.
- The extent to which the scenario planning contributed to creating new social capital.

As educators, researchers, and consultants, we have been concerned to learn that senior managers in some companies and government departments hold a poor opinion of scenario planning. Their varied complaints usually center on a time-consuming, stand-alone intervention, often delivered with the help of expensive outside facilitators or consultants who the client felt did not deliver value for money. As we have explained in this chapter, however, these opinions come as a consequence of poorly designed intervention, not from the methodology per se.

Some groups and organizations seem to turn to scenario planning work in TUNA conditions when established approaches designed for a more predictable and stable world have failed to deliver the expected results. Perhaps it is the very act of such "grasping at straws" that can doom a one-off scenario planning intervention, and perhaps this is an iconic case of the failure of unrealistic expectations.

We suggest that scenario planning, and the reframing and reperception it supports, are better thought of in terms of being services rather than products. As such, we conclude with reflections on the redesign and innovation of this "service."

The capacity not only to adapt, but also thrive, in an era of TUNA entails investments in resilience. This involves attention to shifting situations and potentially disruptive events and forces in the contextual environment, and also to the resources and relationships that comprise the core capabilities of the organization. It also involves understanding the "other," engaging interactively with the future, and co-creating common strategies (Normann and Ramírez 1993; 1994; see also McCann and Selsky 2012).

We suggest, in turn, that scenario planning can contribute to organizational agility and adaptability by maintaining a more open sense of future and delivering new and different coping and thriving options, all of which are key elements of resilience. Reflective practitioners of scenario planning should consider these choices, even though we believe it is not possible to provide a methodological contingency framework (if the situation is "x," then do "y").[19]

This chapter has explored the methodological choices in scenario planning that help scenario learners to develop a more active, testable, and contestable sense of future; and, in turn, frame and reframe their understanding of their situation, and reperceive their choices and options for action. This calls for scenario learners and facilitators to engage with each other deeply. As Flowers (in Senge et al. 2005, 54) noted, "empowerment starts with an instrument or organ of perception. You can't just analyze such systems from the outside to get to the root causes—you have to feel them from within."

We saw in Chapter 2 that engendering trust and forging new common ground among learners and organizations with different intellectual traditions and disciplines, cultures, and/or interests requires that the scenario facilitator and the scenario learners work together to open up a safe space for contesting multiple future contexts. This, in turn, contributes to learners reframing and reperceiving their current situation and discovering new options for action. As such, in the OSPA the design of a scenario planning intervention is not seen as an end in itself but a means to something else which requires an interim outcome, that is, the cognitive shift signaling reframing and reperception. The greatest value is realized when the reperceptions that the scenario planning has helped bring about are embedded as *inputs* to other processes, for example, the visualization of a viable, new value creation system (Normann and Ramírez 1993), or the assessment of a strategy. As such we suggest that scenario planning operates as a co-created service.

Sudhanshu (2012, 34) defined *co-creation* as "a generative process where ideas, opportunities and aspirations are studied by very different stakeholders in an interactive re-invention mode; co-creation does not assume primacy of knowledge, but is aimed at cross-sector innovation in order to allow the creation of new markets, new forms of organizations, new policy environments etc."

It is this "service" provided by scenario planning (and the reframing it enables) that must be foremost in the mind of scenario learners and facilitators. It is the equivalent to making the "movie of the movie"—recall the *Burden of Dreams* example earlier in this chapter—or the Michelin Star chef attending to the fuller experience of the customer in his restaurant.

This emphasis on the co-created service of reframing is key to the design of an effective intervention and central in guiding methodological choices.

▓ NOTES

1. The depth and breadth of engagement includes those involved from the learner side, wider stakeholders, and, in particular, the involvement of "remarkable" individuals, who can help open up the intellectual space to plausible, alternative logics.

2. Cross-impact matrix analysis involves a variety of approaches to identifying the hierarchy of drivers of change in terms of their potential for impact on the transactional environment and the nature of that impact—the timing, uncertainty in knowability or ignorance, familiarity or novelty—as perceived by the scenario learner. Fuzzy cognitive map (FCM) modeling was originally intended to make complex political, economic, or social problems accessible for a wider audience. FCM model building is a multi-step process that captures causal knowledge in the form of cognitive maps, formally describes these maps as adjacency matrices, and applies neural network computation to refine the model and analyze model results (Jetter and Kok 2014). It uses a mix of non-numerical and numerical approaches. It enables the inclusion of multiple and diverse sources to overcome the limitations of expert opinions; it considers multivariate interactions that lead to nonlinearities; and it aims to make implicit assumptions (or mental models) explicit. FCM models are useful for integrating expert, stakeholder, and indigenous knowledge by creating scenarios that bridge the gap between quantitative analysis and qualitative story lines.

3. Ramírez and Wilkinson (2014) analyzed the different interpretations of the 2×2 matrix, which is frequently cited as being the most common method, although with no empirical evidence to support such claims. We bring up this paper again in Chapters 6 and 7, but it is beyond the scope of this book to explain the authors' analysis fully.

4. We encourage readers to consult van der Heijden (2005) for detailed descriptions of the deductive, inductive, normative, and incremental methods.

5. At the time of this writing, in early 2015, we are aware of a journal special issue on this very topic having been launched.

6. See Angela Wilkinson and Roland Kupers' (2014) book *The Essence of Scenario Planning: Learning from the Shell Experience.* These authors provide one of the most "detailed, balanced and satisfactory account" of the fifty-plus-year history and evolution of the scenario planning practice of Shell, according to a book review by M. Jefferson in the journal *Technological Forecasting and Social Change.* The authors also note the nature of scenario planning as a service that responds to the needs of a specific set of decision makers.

7. Recall from Chapter 3 that epistemology refers to the theory of knowledge in philosophy; it deals with how we know (and can know) what we know. Epistemology is linked to ontology, which deals with the nature of what exists independently of our knowing it. See also the Glossary.

8. As depicted in Figure 5.1, other factors to consider when determining the right design and methodology include the following: (a) whether the scenario planning is intended to be definitive or more like a "beta" software release that can be and is expected to be updated regularly; (b) whether the scenario planning will be considered the "end product" for a intervention that will produce a set of contrasting conceptual frames, or as an ongoing service "input" that enables others to create value over time where the scenarios act as an ongoing process; (c) whether the learners are participating in the construction or not; and (d) whether

scenarios capabilities developed through the intervention are intended to be nurtured in-house for subsequent scenario opportunities.

9. See Shirin Elahi's (2008) chapter in *Business Planning for Turbulent Times*—"Conceptions of Fairness and Forming the Common Ground."

10. It is important to distinguish between the scenario planning *client*, namely, the party paying for the resources invested, and the scenario planning *learner* if they are not the same individuals. If they are different people it is important to clarify where their perceptions match and differ.

11. Wharton scenarios guru Paul Schoemaker cites failure to secure top management support and failure to link to other processes as two of the top twenty most common pitfalls in scenario planning. See Schoemaker (1998).

12. As we discussed in Chapter 4, single organization scenarios work will need to spend about one-third of the available time and resources manufacturing the scenario "client". In the multi-organization settings, as little as one-fifth of available time and resources is for building the scenarios, and as much as four-fifths for using the work and assembling, organizing, and coordinating the learner system.

13. <http://www.deltalloyd.com/en/about-delta-lloyd/strategy/scenarios/> (accessed September 2015).

14. In some settings this has been referred to as the "scenario agenda." We prefer not to use this term as it can be a catch-all phrase that loses the fine detail of what needs to be done to ensure success.

15. <http://www.4sing.com/en/index.php> (accessed September 2015).

16. See Vennix (1996) for a thorough explanation of this technique.

17. <www.irgc.org/> (accessed September 2015).

18. A sampling of the literature on assessing the effectiveness of scenario work includes the following: addressing cognitive biases (Schoemaker 1993); decision support tool—quality of judgment/strategic conversation (van der Heijden 1996); at the table rather than on the menu (van der Heijden 1996); improving performance (Chermack 2004); conflict resolution (Kahane 2012); managing disagreement as an asset (Wilkinson and Ramírez 2010); organizational/leadership learning (de Geus 1997; Jaworski and Scharmer 2000); reframing (Wilkinson and Ramírez 2010); surfacing assumptions and gentle reperception (Wack 1984; 1985a); and social capital (Lang 2012).

19. We think such a framework is impossible to offer based on the phenomenological under-pinning of the OSPA. Every situation is unique, and uniquely experienced by learners, so generalization and even categorization is fraught with difficulty.

6 Learning and teaching

Scenario planning in executive development

Introduction

In previous chapters we have laid out the underlying theory, methodology, and practical steps involved in scenario planning as a social and knowledge generation process. In this chapter, we describe what is involved in learning and teaching scenario planning. This returns us to the planner as learner theme introduced in Chapter 1.

It is now impossible for anyone to read the thousands of publications on scenarios and scenario planning produced every year. Even if that were possible, learning scenario planning is like riding a bicycle: you can read all the "how to" guide books and operating manuals, and someone can tell you how to ride it, but you only know how to ride after you get on to the bike, feel the balance and turn the pedals, and even fall off a few times. So too with learning scenario planning; like learning to cycle, it requires practice and reflection as well as engaged fun. These are the features of action learning, a method in social science research that focuses on learning through reflection on one's actions. In this chapter we describe how we have gone about designing educational programs to this effect.

Similarly, we suggest that learning about scenario planning benefits from scholars engaged in the practice. In our own work we have found that bringing scenario planning into contact with different fields of scholarship yields insights on why it works and how it can be improved. In this chapter we outline how we have done so through the four Oxford Futures Forums we have convened to date.

An important purpose of this book rests on a related view—that as a continually evolving field of practice, scenario scholars and practitioners need to engage actively with each other to keep abreast of new developments and review claims of better practices. We hope this book is useful to fellow scenario planners that also act as teachers, learners, and researchers.

This chapter is organized as follows. First, we outline a philosophy of learning that is explicitly based on Churchman's (1971) design of inquiring systems, which we introduced in Chapter 3. We relate this philosophy of learning to van de Ven's (2007) "engaged scholarship," to Trist's "social engagement of social science,"[1] and to Schön's (1983) "reflective practitioner."

We make the case that the design of executive education as an inquiry process seeks to bridge two important divides: one between scholarship and practice, and the other between scenarios and other fields of scholarly inquiry. We consider how these design choices work both in the pedagogy of the Oxford Scenarios Programme (OSP)[2] and in the action learning and research of the Oxford Futures Forum (OFF).

Second, we consider how the learning of scenario planning actually happens. We examine the advantages of collective learning while attending to individual learning styles. We then invite the reader to consider the implications of understanding that learning is cyclical; that it never ends; and that it can be enhanced by being friendly toward errors. Third, we situate learning scenario planning as reflective practice. Finally, we link learning scenario planning as reflective practice with designed inquiry. We examine how designs can attend to individual learning styles in a collective setting, and we consider how to design feedback to enhance learning.

Designing learning for scenario planning

The elements of successful learning presented in this chapter have been garnered from designing and repeatedly redesigning the OSP. The OSP is a key research and development facility and test bed for the OSPA. To date it has graduated nearly 500 alumni(ae), and has utilized some thirty-one live case studies (including four repeats).

The OSPA's pedagogic design has also benefited from what we learn about scenarios theory and practices through the OFF. The OFF is an invitation-only event held every three years where we invite scenario planning scholars and practitioners to compare their research and practice with the work of scholars and practitioners in other fields. Four OFFs have been held to date.[3] In the 2005 OFF we confronted scenario planning with the field of social ecology, and in particular Causal Textures Theory which we introduced in Chapter 1. It led to two co-edited books: *Scenarios for Success* (Sharpe and van der Heijden 2007), and *Business Planning for Turbulent Times* (Ramírez et al. 2008a), plus several academic papers. The first OFF was special not only because it showed the design to work ("proof of concept"), but also because we in Oxford were gifted the Pierre Wack Library, which now has dedicated facilities in the Executive Education facilities at Egrove Park.[4] In the 2008 OFF we confronted the field of sensemaking, largely drawn from organization studies, with scenario planning. Several conference papers and the monograph *Beyond the Financial Crisis: The Oxford Scenarios* (Flowers et al. 2010) were produced. In addition, exchanges during the forum led to a workshop on plausibility hosted by Arizona State University. The 2011 OFF confronted complexity theories with scenario planning. So far one paper has been produced from that event. The 2014 OFF brought design scholars and practitioners together with scenario planning scholars and practitioners, and several spin-off projects—notably a special issue of the journal *Futures*—are currently in development.

Two common divides are thus addressed in the OSPA pedagogy—that between theory and practice, and that between scenarios and other scholarly fields. In this section we discuss how the designs of the OSP and OFF address such divides in order to help people learn scenario planning.

ADDRESSING THE SCHOLARSHIP–PRACTICE DIVIDE: DESIGNING INQUIRING SYSTEMS FOR LEARNERS

In terms of the divide between theory and practice, prominent organization theorist Andrew van de Ven, in his influential book *Engaged Scholarship* (2007), proposed that academics are increasingly called upon to put their theories into practice, yet this is rarely done.[5] He suggested that evidence-based practices put forward by researchers are often not taken up. It appears that even other academics do not pick up their colleagues' work very often, citing each other's work less than might be expected.[6]

The lack of uptake of research outputs into practice is regrettable: "Abundant evidence shows that the civic and academic health of any culture is vitally enriched as scholars and practitioners speak and listen carefully to each other" (Boyer 1996, 15, in Van de Ven 2007, 7). It is this active, mutual listening that provides the focus of the design of the OFF, which supports a process of generative dialogue to facilitate new shared insights and encourage further collaborations.

The OFF design addresses some of van de Ven's suggestions for bridging the scholarship–practice divide. As the call for submissions to the 2014 OFF stated, it is designed to be "a form of inquiry where researchers involve others and leverage their different perspectives to learn about a problem domain." The OFF's design is centered upon "a relationship involving negotiation, mutual respect, and collaboration to produce a learning community." The OFF is concerned with "studying complex problems with and/or for practitioners and others," and is open to "many ways to practice engaged scholarship." Finally, the OFF's design helps to critically establish "identit(ies) of how scholars view their relationships with their communities and their subject matter."

Yet the OFF design intellectually predates van de Ven's influential work on engaged scholarship. It is based on designs for inquiry established several decades earlier. One of these traditions is action research and the "social engagement of social science" that Trist and his colleagues developed in the Tavistock Institute after World War II through to the 1970s.[7] Another, more specific reference point for the OFF design is Churchman's (1971) *The Design of Inquiring Systems*, which we discussed extensively in Chapter 3. Thus the

OSPA philosophy of learning, as reflected in the design principles of the OFF, pivots on the concept of "a system of appreciative inquiry" that confronts scenarios with other fields of scholarship.

As we discussed in Chapter 3, Churchman analyzed how major Western philosophers developed the field of epistemology (the study of how we know what we know) through different approaches for seeking "truth" and different methods for considering something "truthful." Here we link what we do in our programs with these different epistemological positions.

The designs of both the OFF and OSP invite those who participate in them to be open to new inputs; this is consistent with Lockean inquiry, which seeks truth through consensus among a community of inquirers. In the OFF we do not assume *a priori* information. Instead, we invite participants to follow an inductive process of inquiry which begins with an exchange of perspectives and selected literature jointly to build associations about scenario planning through active listening and generative dialogue.

The OSP pivots around a set of core concepts (Leibniz would call them "axioms"), grounded in working with senior professionals or executives who bring live cases, that is, a real company, municipal government, or NGO currently facing a major strategic issue or decision. The participants learn about the concepts from lectures given by the faculty and other experienced practitioners, and apply these to concrete, real-world scenario planning interventions. The executives who bring the live cases are in the role of learners, and sometimes the live case work leads to new concepts or variations on practices.

In the design of the OSP, two separate teams of six to eight participants work in parallel on the same live case. Each team constructs two or more strongly felt and conflicting draft (first iteration) scenarios, either with the deductive or the inductive method discussed in Chapter 5. The draft scenarios are presented and critiqued; this review helps participants discover how the framing in each scenario contrasts with those offered by the other scenarios, as well as with the frame currently used by the executives in the actual live case. After revision, the following day, the teams present at least two contrasting scenarios (second iteration) to executives of the live case study they worked on. This process is consistent with Hegelian inquiry, which centers on the clash of conflicting ideas. We discuss how these live cases enable learning later in this chapter.

To invite contrarian views into the classroom (and to countervail any bias or blindness in the faculty viewpoints), we have adopted a peer review and evaluation system. Thus, each iteration of the OSP is observed by two independent reviewers: an internal (Oxford-based academic) and an external (non-Oxford based) scenario planner, scholar, or experienced executive development practitioner.[8] They write reviews of the program for the faculty and this helps us continually to improve the program.

We saw in Chapter 3 that Singerian inquiry accepts multiple data sources, multiple interpretations of reality, and thus multiple truths; and that this resonates strongly in actual scenario planning interventions. We try to reflect this practice in both the OSP and OFF by emphasizing that any truth arrived at is temporary and context dependent.

As we have seen throughout this book, the appreciation of (sometimes dramatically) different framings of the future context of a system lies at the heart of how the OSPA operates in *conducting* scenario planning interventions. This idea also applies to *learning* scenario planning. Thus, in the OFF, participants confront (amicably but robustly) tenets held in the field of scenario planning with tenets held in another field of scholarship and practice— scenario planning with turbulence, or as we are now calling it, TUNA conditions (in 2005); with sensemaking (in 2008); with complexity (in 2011); and with design (in 2014). For example, in the 2014 OFF, participants came to disagree with van de Ven's views on the role of design. In his view, design is limited to designing the research itself and does not extend to the building of theories, the formulation of problems, nor to their solution. Yet in the 2014 OFF, the participants came to appreciate that the links between scenarios and design practices were extended to be *also* pertinent for scholarship seeking to explain and describe potential futures. This new appreciation extended the scope of the roles that design (and scenarios) can hold in engaged scholarship.

ADDRESSING THE SCENARIOS–OTHER FIELDS DIVIDE IN THE OSP

We have just described the constructive confrontation between scenario planning and another field which characterizes the design of the OFF. We also include this constructive confrontation in the OSP, and do so with our tradition of "Oxford briefings," whereby colleagues from different parts of the university come and speak about what they are doing. We have had colleagues from fields including cognitive psychology, biology, nanotechnology and physics, medicine, medieval theology, classics, migration studies, environmental change, transport studies, astrophysics, mathematics, and anthropology. The sessions invite learners of scenario planning to imagine and seek out new connections.

The learning this enables is two-fold. First, by bringing in perspectives outside the immediate focus of the concepts and live cases, our Oxford colleagues illustrate the challenges and opportunities of provoking those engaged in scenario planning to consider new and different perspectives. As we mentioned previously, Wack first noted the use of "remarkable people" in supporting executives to think "out of the box"; and such "throwing in things from left field" (as American baseball fans would put it) has become a well-accepted technique in scenario planning. We carefully select scholars that are both leading edge within their chosen field and curious about connections with other fields. Second, these sessions stimulate OSP participants to draw learnings about scenario planning practices from the new connections they may have made. This demonstrates the recursive linkages between reflective practice and reflexivity, which we discuss later in this chapter. We have in turn been invited to help some of these colleagues with their research in several of those fields: transport, environment, migration, retailing, etc. Thus, working with scenario planning can result in the creation of new possibilities.

Pedagogy and action learning

We have delved into the literature on adult learning as well as action learning (see Ramírez 1983; Morgan and Ramírez 1984), and concluded that scenario planning is best learned by doing it and reflecting on that action (see next main section, on scenario planning and reflective practice).

An important aspect of learning involves understanding the different implications of errors and mistakes. As we see in this section, *errors* are mismatches between expectations and outcomes; recognizing them and reconciling the mismatch is the essence of learning (Argyris and Schön 1978). So in the OSPA the capacity to notice and analyze *errors* is a key element of learning, and this is done in a space designed to be safe from the consequences errors often have in everyday organizational life. An example is failing to attend to the purpose of an intervention as a way to assess scenario planning effectiveness.

Mistakes, on the other hand, occur when a less experienced practitioner is unaware of, or repeats, actions that are already recognized by more experienced colleagues to be ineffective. An example is confusing scenario planning with strategy making. While scenario planning education can help less experienced scenario practitioners to avoid repeating mistakes, error contributes to new learning for the field as a whole.

COLLECTIVE LEARNING

Our experiences suggest that people learn scenario planning better in groups than alone. We have coached individual clients, but joint learning settings appear to works best. Perhaps our experiences align with the logic of Venezuelan parents trying to help their children learn how to play music; with the "El Sistema" pedagogy children are placed in orchestras early on, and they generally learn to play their own instrument faster and better while playing in an orchestra from the beginning than they would on their own.[9] So we organize participants in our programs in learning groups, with individuals taking on the role of group learning leader and learning observer in turns. Yet, we also attend to the fact that each individual learns in his/her own specific way, and we strive to foster conditions wherein these different learning styles can support each other. Graduate and senior staff teaching assistants keep the focus on the learning more than on the task; participants come to Oxford to learn scenario planning, not to complete tasks perfectly (as they must do in their home settings).

This is not without its challenges. We find that many OSP participants are strongly predisposed by their professional training to find what they consider "the" solution; this reflects normal operating practice and the usual demands of their everyday working lives. Many participants have a tendency to over-attend to completing each task and to perform well with the executives of the live case, striving for perfection at each stage, rather than enjoying a sufficiently rich practice session that is meant to enable their learning.

LEARNING SCENARIO PLANNING AS AN ONGOING CYCLICAL ACTIVITY

In our view, learning scenario planning never ends. This is for several reasons. First, practice can be continually refined, as one does in trying to master dance, tennis, or chess. Next, scenario planning has craft-like features which benefit from guild-like apprenticeship and peer feedback. This is because effective scenario planning relies on learners (as planners) embracing their hopes, fears, distress, discomfort, and inquiry[10] through action learning. Finally, so much is happening today, as the field of scenario planning[11] and futures studies more generally develops, that there is always something new to be learned.

In the OSP we have thus designed the role of faculty to be "on the same side of the table" as the participant in the inquiry process. How the learner will put the learning to use, how the purpose and evaluation criteria for the intervention are to be set, and the issue whose plausible futures are being inquired into, are positioned "on the other side of the table." That is, our primary role as faculty is one of facilitating or helping the participants to learn, much more so than merely conveying information by lecturing at them.

In addition, as teachers we find that teaching is an excellent form of learning: it requires our clarifying what we understand to ourselves, as well as helping to redirect our own attention to new challenges and interesting research questions. This is characteristic of action learning. So we suggest that executives, who come to our programs as participants, engage in a similar action-learning teaching process with their colleagues when they go back to their home organizations.

LEARNING SCENARIO PLANNING IS HELPED WHEN ERRORS CAN BE MADE SAFELY

We mentioned earlier that many years ago our late colleagues Chris Argyris and Donald Schön (1978) suggested that the gap between expectation and outcome ("error") is the source of all learning, but only when the gap can be considered safely, that is, without fear of sanctions. Error may come either from a performance anomaly or deficit, or from unrealistic expectations. We agree with Argyris and Schön that error is a normal part, if not an essential component, of learning. Yet the topic of error is rarely addressed in the scenario planning literature, and when it is the emphasis is typically on something other than the performance of the scenario facilitator.

For example, in a 2006 issue of *Organization Studies*, Richard Whittington engaged Gerard Hodgkinson and George Wright in a dialogue as to why a scenarios-based intervention by the two authors ostensibly failed. Hodgkinson and Wright blamed the failure on client related issues, and Whittington ventured that perhaps problems in facilitation were involved. They agreed that the intervention was "premature" (2006, 1898, 1905) in relation to the turbulence emerging in the client organization's environment (2006, 1898). Although the three scholars failed to venture any guidance as to when in the rising turbulence it would have been advisable for scenarios to be deployed, we applaud this rare and frank exchange on error in scenario planning work.[12]

CREATING A SPACE FOR EXPERTS TO MAKE MISTAKES SAFELY

In the OSPA, it is important to distinguish between the errors of scenario planning that are inherent in the continual evolution of the field of practice, and the individual mistakes that can be made by practitioners who may be less experienced, less attentive, or less professional. Regarding mistakes, we are interested here in offering guidance to those practitioners who want to learn and improve their practices.

To date most practitioners have not started their scenario planning work with formal education in that field. In effect, they have learned and honed their trade mostly on the job. However, several universities, including Oxford, offer programs for the interested but inexperienced beginner scenario planner. In addition, there are helpful guides to how to do things properly. For example, in a frequently cited paper Paul Schoemaker (1998) issued a list of twenty things that can go wrong with scenario planning interventions, along with suggestions about how to avoid each of them. Box 6.1 lists some of the most common traps and pitfalls noted by Schoemaker. These resonate with our own experiences.

Several of these traps and pitfalls reflect the fact that scenario planning practice often goes against the grain of conventional wisdom, particularly the "wisdom" held in professions such as law, medicine, or engineering, which is increasingly "evidence based," "factual," and narrowly "rational." Wack, one of the pioneers of Shell's scenario practice, recognized the political liabilities of executives exposing their ignorance, and suggested that to engage their interest some, but not all, critical assumptions could be challenged at the same time. If

BOX 6.1 SOME COMMON TRAPS AND PITFALLS IN SCENARIO PLANNING INTERVENTIONS

- Failing to incorporate the decision makers in the process.
- Operating in a context that is reluctant to change.
- Lack of clarity about purpose.
- Not allowing sufficient time to maximize the use of scenarios.

Schoemaker (1998)

all such assumptions were to be challenged at once, the scenarios would likely be rejected and the learning potential unrealized. Or as he so eloquently put it, "You take the piece of bread and you put it in front of the goldfish, but not so far that the goldfish can't get it" (quoted in Wilkinson and Kupers 2014, 67).

Mistakes can be made safely within what Winnicott (1962) first called "transitional spaces," which as we saw in Chapter 3 are designed to help an individual or a group test the "as yet unknown" safely within the confines of the "already known" (see also Amado and Ambrose 2001; Ramírez and Drevon 2005). Thus, while an expert may find it very hard to be caught being wrong, scenario planning can open a space for the future in the present that allows learners to notice and learn from mistakes.

To amplify the bicycle metaphor from this chapter's introduction, we design the scenario planning learning process for safe learning that allows for both errors and mistakes. One must try to stay on the bike and accept that inevitably one will fall off (that is, make errors and mistakes) several times until one "gets it." One can neither learn to ride a bicycle nor learn how to do scenario planning solely by being lectured at by someone. The participants that come to learn scenarios with us in Oxford are mostly "reflective practitioners" in the sense we describe it in the next section. We help them to reflect critically on their own practices with us, with each other, and with the help of our own reflections on how *we* learned and continue to learn to do scenario planning work.

Scenario planning and reflective practice

In the OSPA, mastery in scenario planning is enabled through *reflective practice*. This term was coined by Donald Schön (1983), and means taking time to stop and reassess how one is practicing something and why one is doing it in a given way. It also includes opening oneself to consider and try out alternative forms of that practice. Thus, this process involves making explicit what works and what does not. Dialogues among less and more experienced scenario practitioners enable the learners that come to work with us to assess what *might* work and to examine critically what *has* worked, and *how* and *why*. This also applies to dialogues between expert practitioners and the "users" in the live cases—the wider teams, communities, and organizations that need and use scenarios.

The OSPA incorporates several approaches to learn how to practice scenario planning that are consistent with reflective practice:

- A common approach to becoming an expert scenario planner is the "guild" model of apprenticeship that Schön articulated so well in his books on reflective practitioners and their education. Here individuals and teams gain experience by becoming "apprenticed" to a more experienced (and reflective) practitioner—or better, a *group* of practitioners. An example of the apprenticeship model of reflective learning is that of Royal Dutch Shell, which typically does not recruit qualified scenario planners from outside the firm, but maintains and develops in-house capabilities for scenario work in several ways. For example, Shell seconds experienced staff from other parts of the company as well as other organizations such as the World Bank into its corporate scenarios team. Shell also fosters learning through participation in scenario projects, as well as through engagement and exchange of its experienced scenario planners with experienced practitioners beyond the company via international networks and communities of practice. Finally, Shell's ample executive development budget allows staff to be sent on external education programs, including the OSP.
- As stated earlier, another very good way to learn scenario planning is to help others learn it better, or to teach it to others. We authors continue to learn scenario planning in doing it and in teaching it, and we all enable learning in our practices as faculty and as scenario planners. Being reflective about our practices as well as about the learning of those we teach has led us to deepen our inquiries. Many things that appear self-evident in scenario planning (as well as in normal life!) are in fact not, and some of these are actually quite problematic. Critically examining taken-for-granted aspects helps in the learning. For example, in this book we have probed such questions as: what is time? What is learning? What is the future? How does language shape our mind—or at least, the way we think and perceive the world? How does the future get used to help change one's mind and the client's mind? What does the "quality" of a conversation depend on, and how is it manifested? Such questions delve into the deeper ontological and epistemological roots of the OSPA, and we highlight those roots in Chapter 7. Examining such questions is explicitly incorporated into the work we do with program participants as well as with scenario planning clients, colleagues in our teams, and of course ourselves.
- Finally, a useful way to learn scenario planning is to write about what has worked and not worked well, and to describe this as honestly as possible to explore how and why this was the case. It is important that such reports and

case studies be peer reviewed so that the description, intervention logic, practice, and outcomes are critiqued (and debugged) before becoming public. This aspect of scenario planning learning has in our view been insufficiently featured in the scenario planning literature, and we point to this in Chapter 7 as a fruitful direction for research.

The OSP recognizes that scenario planning has always been a practice-led field, or perhaps craft, rather than a theoretically derived body of abstract knowledge. We thus have come to appreciate that iterated reflective practice is a most effective way for people—experienced or not—to learn and understand scenario work.

The OFF also incorporates reflective practice. That is, the practices of scenario planners can be critically assessed by scholars of scenario planning helped by perspectives brought in from those of another field. Thus, by confronting scenario planning with design in the 2014 OFF, we asked that scenario planning practitioners and scholars manifest through actual designs what they imagine before they can or will describe this in words; that is, to manifest their images of plausible future contexts with media other than words, as designers do. We also asked the designers to consider working more like scenario planners, so that they would lend more attention to describing the assumptions they make of the contexts their designs are meant to live in rather than letting these designs "talk for themselves." We have found this type of robust and amicable confrontation to be a fertile and powerful catalyst for learning, generating insight, and provoking experimentation.

Reflective practice, where one reflects critically on what one does, also invites *reflexivity*, that is, using one's advice and methods on oneself. In short, we seek to practice scenario planning in our own professional lives and use scenario thinking to develop new options, to understand alternative points of view, and to inform choices. For example, in 2005 one of us worked with academic colleagues at Oxford using scenario planning to consider the future shape of executive education in the University of Oxford. This informed a decision to sell the Executive Education business (then housed at Templeton College) to Oxford's Saïd Business School in 2006. One of the consequences of this activity was paving the way for the merger of Templeton with Green College to form Green-Templeton College.

Executive learning as designed inquiry and engaged scholarship

In the executive education programs we offer at Oxford, we distribute van der Heijden's (2005) book *Scenarios: The Art of Strategic Conversation* to participants. It provides detailed practical guidance on how to design, build, and use scenarios in planning. We do not seek to cover all of van der Heijden's inventory of choices in method. Instead, we support student participants to navigate the critical methodological choices open to the reflective scenario planning practitioner. To put it in culinary terms, rather than providing a good recipe in this book, we aim to cultivate chefs capable of delivering remarkable gastronomic experiences.

We also distribute learning logs (small personal diaries) to the student participants. At the end of the week-long program the material individual learners have "downloaded" as notes into their learning logs is "uploaded" into collective learning walls. These are photographed and made available to all participants, so each can benefit from the insights noted as important to remember by fellow learners. They are fascinating artifacts of group learning in action.

As we mentioned earlier, the OSP is designed as an inquiring system to enable learning on the part of student participants and faculty members alike. (Recall our discussion of Churchman's (1971) inquiring systems.[13]) In this spirit, the faculty, including ourselves, have produced several research studies based on our engagement in this inquiring system. A notable example is our article on the deductive scenario method called "Re-thinking the 2X2 Scenario Method: Grid or Frames?" (Ramírez and Wilkinson, 2014). This study arose from our noticing that we replied to comparable questions from student participants in incompatible ways when they asked how best to use the widely used "2 × 2" ("matrix" or "deductive") method. We reflected upon this and discovered that the scenarios literature and practices in the field were equivocal in how they treated the dimensionality of the axes of the 2 × 2 scenario framework. In brief, we found that while van der Heijden (2005) stipulates that those using this method describe the axes using "either/or" parameters, many scholars describing and analyzing different scenario planning experiences used "more/less" axes instead. So we set out to clarify the nature of this methodological conundrum and the choices made visible to practitioners based on our analysis.

This kind of learning can also be considered inquiry or research; it is useful for the program's faculty because it will help us improve our responses to participants' questions about the deductive building method. It is also useful for students because it helps them to make more informed choices about their scenario building processes so that those processes can better fit the intended purposes of the user(s).

This exemplifies how we think of the job of faculty in enabling adult learners to learn scenario planning effectively. The job centrally involves designing a system of inquiry for participants to do the inquiring, with the help of faculty, teaching assistants, and other participants.[14] (Also note that faculty are themselves in the same inquiring mode they want the participants to be in.) Hence, the job of faculty is to design and guide the inquiry, including defining and nurturing the transitional safe spaces (Winnicott 1962) in which learning can happen, as seen in Chapter 3. The classroom in this mode of "teaching" becomes a safe space to learn—where embarrassment is contained, and where errors, mistakes, and ignorance can be seen as learning vehicles. Criticism in the classroom is about *how* one is learning as well as *what* and *why* one is learning. This design for learning enables the participants to go into what Kurt Lewin referred to as the "unfreezing" process of unlearning one's way away from prior views and practices, then moving into spaces in which testing out alternatives to those they entered with can be assessed safely. By the end of the program participants "refreeze" on to another, hopefully richer set of concepts, methods, and understandings.

DESIGNING SO EACH INDIVIDUAL CAN LEARN HER/HIS OWN WAY

As will be obvious by now, we have learned that design plays a crucial role in effective scenario planning learning.

In the OSP, design begins with an appreciation of each participant's learning expectations. The OSP attracts a very wide range of learners: managers and consultants; policymakers and advisors; full-time academics; foundation, NGO, and intergovernmental agency executives; aid, resilience, and development experts; and analysts and researchers from all sectors, regions, and industries (for example, on the future of agricultural research, humanitarian relief, forestry research, mining research, medical research, and educational research).

Each individual learner has a different learning style. Many have attended other executive development programs at all kinds of institutions and universities, and have expectations on how executive learning sessions operate. Some are ICT-savvy and others not; many are jet-lagged or/and do not have English as their working or mother tongue. Some participants come with pressure to take something back to the organizations that employ or sponsor them, and to do something concrete with whatever they expect to learn very soon to ensure that the considerable investment in attending the program "pays off."

Despite these differences, the participants share one critical thing: each one aims to increase his/her mastery of the craft of scenario planning, and to become a more rigorous, more effective practitioner. So we offer many pedagogical supports, too many for any one participant. We think of ourselves as operating a bit like a ring master in a multi-ring (multi-piste) circus, drawing attention to the many different acts on display, so that each person finds something that moves him, interests her, and spurs their own learning. Our intent is that each participant finds a broad and varied-enough set of pedagogical supports to enable him or her to learn the craft of scenario planning.

Some of these supports are available only during the week they spend with us in Oxford, such as the help in one's learning group offered by the teaching assistant, or time with faculty members shared over dinner. Other supports, such as bibliographies and guides for steps to be pursued, can be taken home and worked with alongside colleagues or clients in the weeks, months, and years to come.

Thus, we design myriad learning routes people can take to learn scenario planning, practices, and thinking. In any one session we may offer multiple methods, processes, and routes each individual participant can take up in their learning. Moreover, we have designed ways to help participants learn *with* each other. Participants work in groups of six to eight with the help of teaching assistants (DPhil students, but also university staff colleagues), in parallel with other groups, sometimes on the same issue or problem as others, sometimes on a different one. Sometimes they are instructed to use the same scenario method on a particular task as another group, sometimes a different method. These different approaches, some experimental, are designed to enrich learning. The learning is iterative as is reframing in the OSPA: various iterations of scenarios are co-produced in the classroom, and we help those executives who have lent their live cases to our participants to be able to recap the lessons from the week in Oxford when they return to their office and recreate with their colleagues the scenarios and the process of developing them.

DESIGNING FOR FEEDBACK

The design of possibilities for feedback is central to learning. Feedback operates between experience and conceptualization, linking discovery processes involving observation and imagination with grounded testing and experimentation (Kolb 1984). We have built into the OSP deliberate feedback loops for individuals as well as groups. Each morning of a program, we like to open the day with a feedback review of the previous day's proceedings prepared by a different group of participants, in which they note both their learnings and new questions these have given rise to.

Participants learn a lot when asked to write down what they think they have learned (as do scholars). So we provide each person with a small diary (the learning log mentioned earlier) and time to write down what they have learned, and we encourage them to share their writings with each other. In encouraging individuals to jot down ideas in this way we support them not only individually, but also enable them to give feedback to each other at various times during the day.

On the last day of the program we design in a feedback session of the whole week that every individual contributes to from their own individual reflections as jotted in their learning log, where they write up "aha!" insights and questions and learnings on big whiteboards (one for each day of the program). As mentioned earlier, these are then photographed digitally and shared electronically with everyone.

Another feedback feature that has been designed into the OSP fosters our own learning; that is, each iteration of the program is reviewed by external experts as well as internal Oxford faculty. This peer review provides valuable feedback to faculty and helps us improve the program each time we deliver it. For example, one set of suggestions was to include one case as a point of common reference for all participants, who come from very different walks of life. This suggestion has been incorporated into the design of the program in the form of a presentation of a completed scenario intervention by an established practitioner. (Some of them are former students of the program.) We typically change 10 to 15 percent of the program from one iteration to the next.

EXECUTIVE EDUCATION AS ENGAGED SCHOLARSHIP

The design of the OSP is, as we stated earlier, consistent with the tradition of engaged scholarship. The late renowned social scientist Eric Trist, one of the key scholar-practitioners of the Tavistock Institute (and one of Ramírez' mentors[15]), believed strongly in the "social engagement of social science," that is, generating knowledge from concrete, systematic engagement with real-world problems. (Some refer to this approach to scholarship as *action research*.) The design of the OSP draws explicitly from this tradition, in that participant learning is centered on an actual engagement. Participants work with actual organizations and their executives over the course of the program. The thirty-one live case studies we have utilized so far have included: two National Health Service Trusts, the City of Helsinki, Titan (India's largest watchmaker and jewelry retailer), Selex Sensors, BMW, the Royal Mail Group, Music World (India's then largest music retailer), Discovery (a South African insurer), the Jordanian operations of telecom company Orange, Atkins, and the Swiss Public Broadcaster SSR. The cases have also included NGOs such as Chatham House, the Koestler Trust, Oxfam, the Global Footprint Network, the National Breast Cancer Coalition (US), and the J.W. McConnell Family Foundation/Social Innovation Generation of Canada.

Two or three organizations are selected for each iteration of the program, and two or three groups of six to eight participants work in parallel on each of them. At the time the organizations are used in the program, they are experiencing a real strategic conundrum, issue, or problem. The organization lends its conundrum—and one or more of its executives' time—to OSP participants with the full understanding that the primary and clearly expressed purpose is to help these participants to reflect critically upon and learn about scenario planning. In return, the executives have the benefit of the thinking of fourteen or twenty-one participants from around the world focused on the conundrum they have brought to the table for a full week, with a good method taught by expert faculty and facilitated in group learning. Most of the organizations used over the past decade have found the insights they receive from this work to be valuable and helpful; this is currently an ongoing research project led by one of us.

Engaged scholarship invites those of us who work in this way to pay attention to scholarship, not only engagement. Improvement in practice and contribution to scholarship are also the two hallmarks of action research. What does such scholarship consist of in terms of the OSP and more generally the OSPA? We have come to learn and now believe that one cannot "train" people to do scenario planning, as if scenario planning acumen was a question of bettering one's muscles (as in training for the triathlon, or for the Tour de France bicycle race). There is no doubt that experience helps, and the "guild-like" professional development apprenticeship in scenario planning with good reflective practitioners has always been important. But scenario planning now is a sizable and vigorous academic field in its own right, and we must work in ways that peers in related fields such as strategic management or public administration can also relate to. To this end, in the OSP we have sought clarity with our participants on the "deeper" aspects of scenario planning work seen in Box 6.2.

Thus, participants in the OSP learn with our help how ontological positions and epistemology affect methodological choice; and what implications these choices have for determining appropriate techniques and capabilities, and, in turn, the specific tools to be used. Thus, if I think time proceeds only from past to future I will likely use forecasting, but if I think the future may come toward me I may be more open to considering scenario planning.

BOX 6.2 DEEPER ASPECTS OF SCENARIO PLANNING WORK IN THE OSP

- Ontological positions—the branch of philosophy that assesses what "there is" or might exist in the world independent of ourselves, for example, what is "time" exactly?
- Epistemology—the branch of philosophy that assesses how we may perceive, conceive, or know what "there is" or might exist in the world, such as how do we know what time is, and how does our conception of time affect our stance toward the future?
- Methodology—the branch of scholarship that considers how choices of method are made, and how these choices affect the efficacy of scenario planning. For example, how might we account for and measure time?*

* For example, we use or refer to Gareth Morgan's (1983) *Beyond Method* and Paul Feyerabend's (1993) *Against Method*.

Conclusion

In this chapter we have outlined what we believe are the essential elements needed to enable adult learners to learn scenario planning effectively. We described a philosophy of learning that is explicitly based on designing inquiring systems (Churchman 1971). We then related it to van de Ven's views of engaged scholarship, to Trist's social engagement of social science, and to Schön's reflective practice/practitioner. These touchstones inform the design choices we have made in developing both the OSP and the OFF. We analyzed the advantages of collective learning while retaining designs that also enable attending to each individual's unique learning mode. We proposed that learning scenario planning is iterative and never-ending, and that it is fostered by creating transitional spaces that enable safe learning from errors and mistakes. We concluded that this learning happens best when considered as reflective practice and engagement as well as joint and ongoing inquiry.

In effect, we seek to design scenario learning so that the learner is in the same position as an aspiring and talented cook seeking to become a great chef. We are careful in how we lay out the kitchen and the restaurant, and how the menu for the learner is set up. We help the learner to understand how s/he might offer the insights s/he has produced so they can be digested by other learners. For example, in what ways can learners best convey their ideas and insights to the executives from the live cases, so that those executives can take those insights back to their colleagues (or bosses or subordinates) in their home organization?

As we have said elsewhere in this book, we do not believe scenario planning is simply a matter of following the steps in a recipe book. When everyone learns, each in their own role and style, the learning we have seen in the OSP classroom and the OFF seminar room can be replicated in the boardroom or away day, where the strategic planners who come to work with us to enhance their learning work every day.

▓ NOTES

1. Trist co-edited a three-volume set under the title *The Social Engagement of Social Science: A Tavistock Anthology*. The papers in the books are drawn from writings by Tavistock affiliated scholars and practitioners. They were published in 1990, 1993, and 1997 by the University of Pennsylvania Press, Philadelphia. They are available for download by permission from <http://www.moderntimesworkplace.com/archives/ericsess/ericsess.html> (accessed September 2015).

2. The OSP at the time of this writing is a five-day executive development program offered twice a year and capped at forty-two participants. The OSP has had various iterations in its development. We first offered a predecessor, the "Oxford Introduction to Scenarios

Programme" in 2004, from what was then Templeton College at Oxford University (which since 2007 merged with Green College to form Green-Templeton College). The first versions were designed and delivered under the direction of Rafael Ramírez, with Kees van der Heijden and Hardin Tibbs. Upon the transfer of executive education from Templeton College to the Saïd Business School in 2006, the program was extended and renamed the OSP, and Angela Wilkinson joined the teaching group. Wilkinson directed the program during 2006–9, and Ramírez has directed it since then.

3. The format of the OFF is an invitation-only event capped at seventy participants, held over two days, and requiring each interested participant to submit a 250-word abstract that is peer reviewed. The four OFFs held to date have been designed as an Open Space format to enable generative dialogue; see <http://www.oxfordfuturesforum.org.uk>. Far from the standard conference design of sequential "stand and deliver" speeches, each OFF is inter-active and participative, with the substance created and evolved by the participants themselves. The set of initial discussion topics is determined by the organizers from the selected pre-OFF inputs submitted by participants. Subsequent discussion topics are generated by the participants during the event.

4. The library was formally gifted by the estate of Pierre Wack to Templeton College, now Green-Templeton College.

5. This material is adapted from <https://www.liu.se/kite/dokument/1.117786/ESReflections. pdf> (accessed September 2015).

6. Starbuck (2005) noted that papers in management journals average less than one citation per year (0.82).

7. See note 1, this chapter.

8. Internal reviewers have come from various parts of the Saïd Business School (science and technology studies, international business, entrepreneurship, finance) and the wider university (medicine, social policy, physics, anthropology). External reviewers have come from non-academic institutions, including the OECD, WEF, FAO, EU, the Crown Prince Court of Abu Dhabi, Tata Group, LVMH, executive consultants, and an editor of a leading futures journal.

9. <https://www.elsistemausa.org/el-sistema-in-venezuela.htm> (accessed September 2015).

10. See Antonio Strati's (1999) fascinating study of these matters in assessing how roofers attend to each other's skills.

11. As we pointed out in Chapter 1, about 2,500 peer reviewed articles with the key word "scenarios" are published yearly in English alone.

12. See Hodgkinson and Wright's (2002) paper; and the 2006 dialogue about it in R. Whittington, "Learning More from Failure: Practice and Process." *Organization Studies*, 27(12): 1903–1906; and G. Hodgkinson, and G. Wright, "Neither Completing the Practice Turn, Nor Enriching the Process Tradition: Secondary Misinterpretations of a Case Analysis Reconsidered." *Organization Studies* 27(12): 1895–1901.

13. Professor C. West Churchman, late of University of California Berkeley, was one of Ramírez's doctoral dissertation supervisors.

14. Those familiar with "El Sistema" orchestras from Venezuela, mentioned earlier, will find similarities here.

15. Ramírez was Trist's graduate student and teaching and research assistant at York University, Toronto.

7 Conclusion

An incomplete guide to scenario planning and the beginning of a conversation

Introduction

Throughout this book we have offered a wide variety of concepts, methods, and techniques associated with the OSPA. However, there is so much happening in the field of scenario planning that the OSPA is necessarily incomplete. Thus, the subtitle of this chapter pays homage to Willis Harman's classic 1979 book, *An Incomplete Guide to the Future*.

In Chapter 1, we stated the premises which underpin the OSPA and overviewed the central features of our approach, which we have examined in some detail in the other chapters. Throughout, we have illustrated the OSPA through reference to six scenario planning interventions conducted by intergovernmental and public sector bodies and private sector corporations; these are found in the Appendices.

In Chapters 2 and 3 we explained scenario planning as a set of interactive and iterative social and intellectual processes. We showed how they support the development of an open, flexible, and explicit sense of future to frame and reframe how the present situation is understood by contrasting alternative future contexts. We showed that each scenario planning learning iteration involves two distinct but related types of learning: a higher-order reframing of the wider context and an immersive learning that rehearses action under alternative future contexts and contributes reperception.

In Chapters 4, 5, and 6 we described the practice of the OSPA in terms of its learner-centric emphasis, methodology, and pedagogy, and highlighted the choices concerning approaches and tools that contribute to effectiveness in and mastery of good practice. We explained there is no single "right method" or "best practice," and instead offered guidelines for more effective practice.

In this chapter we revisit the distinctive characteristics of the OSPA, then delve deeper to highlight their associated ontological, epistemological, and methodological qualities. We then direct attention to two aspects of the scenario planning field's incompleteness, both of which call for more "conversations" among practitioners, scholars, and other interested parties. First, we point to four "unresolved issues" that we think require the attention of scenarios scholars going forward. Then we look ahead and identify two "new directions" for scenario planning research.

Distinctive characteristics of the OSPA

In Chapter 1, we highlighted the main characteristics that differentiate our approach from other plausibility based schools of scenario planning. We saw these as "cats eyes" for astute scenario planning practitioners: they keep them on the road of effective work; ignoring them may lead to leaving the road and an accident. They mean that in the OSPA, scenario planning is:

- *Learner-centric in terms of methodological choices.* The strategist is in the role of learner when engaged in scenario planning. The learner-centric view of strategy and policy in the OSPA emphasizes that scenario planning is effective only when a given intervention is designed with a purpose for someone (s) and for something(s). To fully support learning, scenario planning is best thought of as a service and not a product. This service role, in turn, necessitates attention to engagement and communication issues from the initiation and design stages to every other step of the scenario planning intervention.
- *Designed to produce iterative learning through reframing and reperception.* We showed how reframing occurs at a higher logical order, through a process of upframing which invites the scenario learners to view their situation from a "macro" viewpoint that encompasses the context. A complementary down-framing process then helps the scenario learners to immerse themselves in the new contexts they learn. In downframing, a learner experiences the "micro," specific, "what if" implications for practice—sometimes referred to as the "aha!" moment (see Box 7.1).

BOX 7.1 A GORILLA IN THE MIDST?

Reframing and reperception help to open the mind to see something that has not been seen. There is a now famous video by Chabris and Simons (2010) that records a tight series of basketball passes among five players. When people watch this video and are asked to count the passes, most fail to see a gorilla that crosses the scene. The mind is literally primed not to perceive the 300-pound gorilla in the room!

A set of two to four scenarios offer alternative frames to help learners free their attention from focusing only on the existing mindset and to become open to the possibility of seeing something outside the focal frame of whatever she is attending to—perhaps even a totally unexpected gorilla.

Watch the video at <http://www.theinvisiblegorilla.com/videos.html> (accessed September 2015).

- *Explicitly designed to help strategists and policymakers find more and better options for coping and succeeding in TUNA conditions.* We saw that in TUNA conditions the applicability of existing factual evidence to forecast demand, competition, governance, or the state of one's industry is limited. So scenario planning complements and challenges an organization's existing strategy development. Yet importantly, scenario planning is *not* the same as a strategy—it examines the wider contexts that the strategy and its implementation might inhabit, independently of the will, influence, and control of the strategist.

In addition, we have analyzed the central role of plausibility as it guides and helps assess the development of a limited number of contrasting, relevant, and challenging scenarios. In Chapter 2, we explained why plausibility is preferable to probability in TUNA conditions, where the latter is either irrelevant or a logical impossibility.

Delving deeper: ontological and epistemological foundations of the OSPA

In the remainder of this chapter we reflect on the implications of the three distinctive characteristics above and their links with the deeper ontological, epistemological, and methodological foundations of the OSPA. We then survey some matters that remain unresolved at the time of writing (mid-2015), and conclude with suggestions regarding two research directions for the field of scenario planning going forward.

ONTOLOGICAL CHARACTERISTICS OF THE OSPA

The future is a dynamic sense that is inseparable from the present

The future is both plural and paradoxical. It is plural, in that many possibilities remain open. It is paradoxical, in that it is both held here and now and is yet to come, but not as an end point or destination. It is a fiction existing within the present.

There is more than one strategic context

The context which one (one's self, one's mind, a person, an organization) is in is only and exclusively for that one party, not for everyone or anyone. The *immediate* context one is in is that which one influences by interacting with it; in the OSPA this is called the "business" or "transactional" environment. In turn, this transactional environment is embedded in and surrounded by a *broader* context, called the "contextual" environment. The latter is the bigger picture.

An organization's strategy-making focuses on the way the self relates to the transactional environment. The focus of attention of scenario planning is on the plausible ways that the contextual environment might unfold and how it might impact the transactional environment.

Risk management is unsuited to deep uncertainty

In Chapter 3, we noted that a capability to differentiate situations involving calculable risk and unpredictable uncertainty becomes important for strategic success in TUNA conditions. The management and the strategic planning apparatus of any organization certainly cannot operate independently of risk, risk appetite, and governance cultures; management of risk is central to successful strategy. But perception, analysis, and governance of "risk" can often be enlarged to sweep in uncertainty—enabled, tested, and informed by the consideration of multiple, plausible future contexts, as shown by the Risk-World scenarios in Appendix F.

EPISTEMOLOGICAL CHARACTERISTICS OF THE OSPA

Learning *with* multiple, contrastable futures

OSPA-based scenario planning helps learners to attend to their sense of future as a way of knowing the present, rather than considering the future as something that is knowable in advance. Scenario planning helps redirect attention to *alternative* future contexts. Knowing is phenomenological; it derives from the concrete experience of the learner. As noted earlier, the broader contextual environment, which encompasses both the self and the transactional environment, is by definition beyond direct reach and influence; it can only be known indirectly. The contrasted framings of scenarios generate new, shared understanding on and in the present. Immersing oneself in these alternative frames allows one to perceive the limits and promise of each frame and opens up new possibilities for action.

Scenarios as flexible conceptual scaffolding

A set of scenarios can be used as conceptual scaffolding, or as a colleague of ours calls it, *bamboo scaffolding;*[1] that is, as temporary, resilient, and disposable reframing devices which act in the service of the learner. Bamboo is flexible; and scaffolding can be put up, kept up to support a structure being built for as long as needed, and then taken down once the building (a new conceptual frame, a new conversation) is standing on its own.

METHODOLOGICAL CHARACTERISTICS THAT DIFFERENTIATE THE OSPA

In the OSPA, each scenario planning intervention is for one set of learners, with one set of purposes, in specific circumstances. Therefore, each intervention requires a bespoke design.

The scenario planning process is *designed* to serve a specific purpose and set of actors

The OSPA scenario planning methodology helps learners to examine whether the sense of future they have been using to understand a current situation is the only frame able to guide their understanding and action, whether these frames operate subconsciously or as explicit and testable strategic assumptions. Consistent with the learner-centric emphasis of the OSPA, the resulting set of scenarios are not "subjectively selected" from an "objective" and finite set of possible combinations of contextual factors, even if that set is very large.[2] The design and manufacture of a limited and useful set of scenarios in the OSPA involves engaging scenario learners and listening for the stories that are already emerging in the present, while at the same time challenging those stories that most help learners to reframe and reperceive in ways that help their purposes.

Reframing is only partial learning until the scenarios incite *reperception*

The OSPA processes involve moving between storytelling (freeing the imagination) and disciplined system mapping (co-producing plausibility) to generate useful memories of the future. This iterative development is similar to debugging the development and release of new software. In each round, the (draft) scenario set is debugged and improved until the next version is made available for use: first, "beta" scenarios for the insiders; then version 1.0, then 1.1, 1.2., 2.0, etc. if the purpose is well served by successive versions until the release of a stable version to wider stakeholders is deemed helpful.

This approach to strategic innovation and renewal does not require knowing which future will come about[3] (or indeed, giving probabilities to each scenario), but rather considering a small range of different futures, none of which are right but which are useful nonetheless. As we saw in Chapter 2, the OSPA methodology suggests scenario planning as a process plays a similar "transitional" role as a teddy bear in helping young children cope with new awarenesses of their world. In providing a transitional space, scenario planning depersonalizes ignorance and enables smart people to learn from and with each other, helping expert disagreements to become productive.

Not a silver bullet: related with other methodologies and linked with other processes

In this book we have underlined that scenario planning as seen in the OSPA entails a distinctive methodology which seeks to work *alongside and together with* other methodologies, processes, techniques, and approaches—such as horizon scanning, visioning, forecasting, trend impact analyses, visioning, risk management, and backcasting. In this sense, the OSPA is a form of what social scientists call bricolage,[4] a rigorous approach of qualitative inquiry pragmatically making use of tools and techniques (including quantitative ones) developed in other fields. This also includes developments in such non-futures fields as systemic risk assessment, issues management, stakeholder analysis, competitive intelligence, and other strategy-related methods and tools.

How scenario planning operates in relation to other techniques and approaches is an evolving and unresolved issue in the scenario planning field, and we discuss it in the next section as "scenario-plus" methods.

Unresolved issues

As we have highlighted several times in this book, some unresolved matters in the scenario planning field have been brought to our attention by executives and senior professionals attending our programs as participants, as well as by those working with us in actual scenario planning interventions. In engaging with these issues, we signal that as colleagues, scholars, and fellow practitioners we are committed to continued learning.

We see four unresolved issues that persist at the time of writing this book in mid 2015:

- Different interpretations of the 2×2 matrix approach in the deductive method, which make using the method confusing if people are unaware of the problem.
- Implications for scenario planning practices in different kinds of settings (organizational, interorganizational, and "multi-stakeholder").
- Critiques of scenario planning from other fields, in particular social scientists and consultants working with "complexity."
- Ascertaining scenario planning's value, or "return on investment."

We treat each of these four issues in turn.

THE 2 × 2 MATRIX METHOD

As we noted in Chapter 5, we discovered a confusion in the literature concerning the way scenarios are manifested in 2 × 2 matrices in the so-called "deductive method" (Ramírez and Wilkinson 2014). In brief, while van der Heijden (2005, 2–5) counseled that each axis should be positioned in either/or terms, we found many examples in the practitioner and scholarly literatures where the axes had been positioned in "more or less" terms. Our paper highlighted that while this deductive scenario method is a well-accepted one, it can unexpectedly involve conundrums when looked upon as methodological choices. We proposed that each approach had advantages as well as drawbacks, and that the choices to be made depended on what the scenarios sought to help the learner do with the reframing they enable.

The confusion (compounded in some cases where one axis was either/or and another more or less) lies in the fact that in the either/or format the result is four incompatible future contexts, whereas in the more or less format: (a) the scenarios are not necessarily occupying the whole box; (b) multiple scenarios can arise simultaneously (e.g. in different parts of the market, or concerning different parts of the product range); and (c) the scenarios can appear sequentially—a given scenario may be a temporary transition to another scenario which may remain locked in for a longer period of time.

In our paper we suggested that further research is required to help determine appropriate evaluation criteria for each approach, and to clarify the extent to which each of the two interpretations of the deductive method (one with "either/or" axes, the other with axes that exhibit "more-or-less" dimensions) is being used.

NEED FOR ATTENTION TO THE WIDER SETTING IN WHICH SCENARIO PRACTICES TAKE PLACE

The scenario planning literature reveals the dominance of articles in the management sciences focused on firm-oriented practices (Varum and Melo 2010). The literature does not yet appear to have attended to the increasing phenomena of multi-stakeholder, cross-sectoral social partnership, open source, and inter- and multi-organizational scenario planning.

So an open question is: are the traps, pitfalls, and benefits encountered by scenario planning practitioners in these latter settings (such as the AiA, Risk-World, EPO, and UEG case studies in the Appendices) the same as those encountered in more traditional private sector, firm-level, corporate settings (such as the Shell and Wärtsilä case studies)?

Clearly, in the highly political contexts of governmental and public administrative situations it can be challenging for elected political officials and policymakers to clarify the boundary between their transactional and contextual environments. Indeed, who is "they" is also an issue! But even for highly influential multi-organizational institutions, such as the G20 or the International Monetary Fund, there is a world of contextual factors out there that the collective will of the interorganizational grouping cannot control—be it technological innovation, natural disasters, or nefarious elements in society. These are issues that even very powerful organizations in their own domains, such as the EPO in IP and the UEG in European gastrointestinal medicine (both cases in the Appendices), have had to engage with to make their scenarios work effectively for them.

Public policy initiatives often have to invest more heavily to coalesce, organize, and if necessary, refresh or broaden the skills of the learner community to be supported by the scenario planning effort. This is for various reasons, including: the dominance of forecast-based planning cultures; a misunderstanding of scenario planning and model-based baseline "scenarios" (often not scenarios in the sense we mean them in this book, but different runs of an econometric, climate change, or energy model); and confusingly calling a policy option a "scenario for decision making."

Locating the scenario planning intervention at the "right" level in such settings is very important. In the EPO case, for example, it was critical for senior staff to reach out to and engage with the Supervisory Board members.[5] This broadening of the initially imagined learner group was an essential component for the scenario planning to become more effective.

Governance matters clearly become more significant in these settings and there is an added requirement to conduct such interventions under the full gaze of public scrutiny and ensure transparency. So greater clarity is required on the roles and rights of different stakeholders—sponsors, scenario facilitators, scenario learners, and experts external to the process—especially in terms of who decides which set of scenarios is to be used and on what basis.

Further research is required to assess whether, and if so how, the future is colonized in cross-sectoral partnerships, and whether the ethical choices for scenario planning in such settings need different criteria than within single organizations.

"SCENARIO PLANNING PLUS" METHODS OR LINKING SCENARIO PLANNING WITH OTHER PROCESSES?

As we have argued in this book, we do not claim scenario planning is a magic bullet, and we have encouraged practitioners to recognize the limits of when and where it might be useful. We have also shown that scenario planning can be effectively and helpfully related to other methods and processes such as risk management, capability assessments, human resource development, visioning, forecasting, and modeling. This differs from what some of our colleagues in Singapore have called "scenario planning plus" methods,[6] which in fact incorporate much of what is included in the OSPA. However, they also include designing strategies, which we maintain is part of the strategy process and only one of the organizational processes that can be supported by, but is separate to, scenario planning.

However, for some observers that label and related ones, where techniques considered to be excluded from scenario planning are "added," have been taken to mean that they are disappointed with the limitations of what they consider scenario planning to be. Often this occurs because of their misconception that scenario planning is somehow restricted to deductive reasoning and 2 × 2 matrix methods, with little attention to implications for the planner's learning—often mentioned only in passing if at all. We believe that such critics might draw a different conclusion if they practiced scenario planning as a way to reframe understandings of contexts to guide learner reperception, as the OSPA suggests.

Over the years, in our consulting and teaching practices we have also found that many reflective practitioners, some of whom are quite experienced people, are not using scenario planning effectively. Far too many, instead of assessing why this is so and fixing it, appear to be seeking to replace scenario planning (or to complement it given misperceived limitations) with different approaches to "analyze complexity." (Both of the co-authors have been invited to conferences to this effect in recent months.)[7] Furthermore, their definition of complexity often seems oblivious to social theories of risk, to Knight's distinction between risk and uncertainty, to bounded rationality, and to the ineluctable reality of power and its workings in strategic framing contests.

Furthermore, we have noted that scenario planning is not an end in itself but connects with other organizational processes, methods, and techniques. This is a growing concern in the literature, so we have analyzed some of the interfaces; a good sample of our efforts is found in the endnotes.[8] This subject is important because scenario planning in practice never exists in a vacuum, and as a process of inquiry and reframing it *has* to work with other processes—those it supports, those it draws from, those it challenges, and those it competes with. More of this type of work is needed.

THE RETURN ON INVESTMENT OF SCENARIO PLANNING

We have explained how we see scenario planning helping strategy. But like many other inputs to strategy, the return on investment of a scenario planning effort is difficult to establish. This difficulty of establishing return on investment is also what executive development suppliers and many advisors face. Also, as researchers and consultants, we also face the issue of confidentiality in attempting to clarify and assess such matters.

Take some examples of value derived from investing in scenario planning:

- How much of Shell's long-term commercial successes is due to its scenario planning capabilities—and its global scenario practice described in Appendix B? Even if the top managers of those firms have views on this, they would be unlikely to share this commercially sensitive information.
- How much of the EPO's support for the signature of the London Protocol or for the creation of the five-office coalition of national patent offices is due to the scenario planning described in Appendix E? Would these things have happened anyway? Even if they had, is the timing of when they happened attributable to the scenario planning? A few individuals may have views on this, but again it would likely be difficult for them to share such matters.
- How much of new research and teaching in gastrointestinal medicine might be attributed to the UEG scenario planning work described in Appendix C? How many other factors will have contributed to such results, and how does one isolate the distinct contribution scenario planning will have made to that outcome?

All these examples illustrate one of the classic problems in social research and policy analysis: the inability, or at least great difficulty, to isolate the effect of an intervention when done in a "natural setting" (not in a laboratory), and therefore the difficulty of knowing what works or what might work. One "solution" to researching such issues is to examine case studies as and when they become available.

New directions for research

ASSESSING HOW SCENARIO PLANNING-INDUCED REFRAMING IS VALUED

Many companies do not invest enough attention or resources into scenario planning and are disappointed by it. In a paper entitled "Scenarios: Worth the Effort?" Graham Molitor (2009) echoed the view that the investment does not yield the expected results.

The reality is that to our knowledge, no one has done empirical research comparing scenario expectations with outcomes—in our view, perhaps this is because expectations are often not included in the scenario engagement, as we have argued in the book. Efforts have been made to ascertain if things like corporate culture or decision making are affected. But if affecting any of these in a predetermined manner was not the original intent of the scenario planning engagement, then the "dependent variable" used in the evaluation appears somewhat spurious.

We suggest that scenario planning ought to be studied as social, embedded processes of framing and assumption surfacing, as enabling sensemaking, as ways of reframing understanding, of enhancing the appreciation of another perspective, of enabling reperception, rather than as analytical products, techniques, or tools. Engaging learners in the assessment, as is done in development studies (Ramírez et al. 2015), is a direction of research that is promising and underdeveloped in scenario planning.

DEVELOPING AND SHARING CASE STUDIES OF FAILURE

We are not the first to note that the field of scenario planning practices tends to be dominated by literature that claims success without offering much supporting evidence regarding how the success pertains to the original purpose. In addition, the literature contains very few exchanges on failures in practice, such as those we mentioned in Chapter 6 between Hodgkinson/Wright and Whittington in the journal *Organization Studies*.

From our perspective of scenario planning as a reflective practice, we suggest that sharing failed scenario planning stories is an important missing ingredient to enable deeper learning and the development of grounded theory to guide more effective practices. The OSP participants have requested that cases of failure to be taught as an aid to their learning, and so far there is little published on the matter, particularly from a phenomenological perspective.

How the developing and sharing of case failures might be done in the future remains to be ascertained.

An incomplete guide to the future of scenario planning, and a better place to start

In Douglas Adam's now classic novel, *The Hitchhikers Guide to the Galaxy* (1979), one of the characters relates the story of a race of hyper-intelligent pan-dimensional beings who rely on a computer named Deep Thought. They built Deep Thought to calculate the Answer to the Ultimate Question of Life, the Universe, and Everything.

The answer was revealed to be "42."

Yet this answer was incomprehensible because the beings that built the computer did not understand the question they were asking, nor the response to it.

In the novel, Deep Thought then predicts that another computer, more powerful than itself, would be made and designed by it to calculate the question for the answer.[9] An iterative process is thus initiated in which the codification of existing knowledge is followed by recognition of new ignorance, which spurs a further search for new knowledge.

This is the spirit in which we offer this book to those already traveling through the universe of scenario planning, or those who are about to. We have offered our views and experiences of building and using scenario planning to enable individuals, groups, and organizations to learn with futures, and with this learning to ask better questions. We have marshaled and systematized these views into a coherent and distinctive approach to scenario planning which we have labeled the "Oxford Scenario Planning Approach." We have distilled seven premises that help explain the need for and effectiveness of scenario planning, and articulated three main characteristics that differentiate the OSPA from other scenario "schools." We have placed the learner at the center of scenario planning, and explained that what this planning enables the learner to do is the process of framing and reframing real-world situations to motivate and inspire new action. We have resisted the temptation to describe scenario planning as a panacea that will solve an organization's strategic problems, and we have highlighted the contingencies of practice. We have noted that good scenario planning is designed to be both useful and ultimately disposable.

As Slaughter (1993, 228) put it, prediction if taken in its fullest sense is "an impossible aspiration, which if fulfilled would logically cancel out the active role of humans in shaping history." Computing the future is not what strategists that create unique offerings and businesses depend on. Instead, they depend on bringing forth distinctive ideas that are actionable and scalable. In TUNA conditions this is what scenario planning is intended to do.

In doing, facilitating, and researching scenario planning, we have found that for many senior professionals it can be hard to break out of what for them are conventional, positivist, forecast-based planning cultures that have come to dominate strategic planning and policymaking. But we have found that these same individuals have been engaging scenario planning with a less conscious, informal approach in their everyday lives; for example, they very regularly run stories through their minds to attend to their hunches and gut feelings about the contexts they might be in when considering new future possibilities. They inevitably also make (often implicitly) assumptions about the context for their plans—whether planning for their families, their personal lives, or celebrations, even holidays. This book invites them to bring that part of themselves—that part of their routine, everyday operating and planning—back into the board room, to the meeting, to the decision table, and to attend to it more explicitly and use it more actively to reframe more creatively and imaginatively the situations they are paid to engage with. When we say to participants in an engagement that "scenario planning is not an 'extra' activity you must add to your busy life, but something you are already doing and can do far better," it has been helpful for many.

We hope that, like Deep Thought, this book will not give you "the" answer to everything, but instead prompt you to ask better questions and to make more informed choices in your own scenario planning practices. This is because we have found that practitioners who become *reflective* practitioners become more effective scenario planners.

None of us is ever fully developed as a scenario planning practitioner. Instead, there is beauty in reflective practice—in the incompleteness that motivates and sustains a culture of curiosity, reassessment, revision, and improvement. In our experience, tuning into this beauty is characteristic of the more effective scenario planning scholars and practitioners.

▨ NOTES

1. Our Singaporean colleague Ambassador Chuan Leong first introduced us to the idea of scenarios as bamboo scaffolding.
2. Considering the TUNA conditions that scenario planning helps to engage with, there are an almost infinite number of potential future states. Trying to calculate the likelihood of all of these in advance and then reduce them to the most probable futures using a process of expert judgments might create the comfortable impression of an "objective" and "scientific" process. But such an exercise would need to ignore questions about who decides what matters and on what basis, and how these choices determine which drivers of change and key linkages matter. Ignoring such questions and choices would mean that the futures kept on the table and the ones discarded were artificially skewed. Furthermore, that purportedly "objective" exercise would also fail to prevent an abstraction of reality being confused for the reality itself. Arguably, this is what happened when the "war on terror" ideology and modeling encountered reality on the ground, bringing forth what Ramírez and Ravetz (2011) called a "feral" future.
3. Engaging decision makers in thinking about *all* possible futures is nonsensical and impossible. Pretending that this could be possible is like believing a computer program could come up with all the possible paintings produced by a groundbreaking artist—a next Goya, Turner, or Picasso—who has yet to be born.
4. The notion of bricolage has been used in management studies for about twenty years to signify "the imaginative use of materials for previously unintended purposes" (McCann and Selsky 2012, 130). See also Kincheloe (2001).
5. There is sometimes a sense of either an institutional void or the need for a more interdisciplinary approach to avoid unhealthy competition between silos of expertise. The EPO colleagues struggled with such issues in developing and using their scenario planning.
6. See the glossary in <http://www.csf.gov.sg/our-work/our-approach> (accessed May 2015).
7. Some of these suggest that complexity practices involving computerized ("self-learning") algorithms, with automated horizon scanning supported by the collection of huge volumes

of micro-narratives and "big data" analytics, will do the job better and more cheaply than the time and effort involved in scenario planning's discursive-analytical process, with its disciplined imagination and storytelling. Clearly a combination of artificial intelligence, algorithms, and real-time "big data" can do much to free people from needing to process increasing volumes of information to make routine decisions. But can strategic framing contests ever become resolved, or even fully appreciated or engaged with, without attending to deeply held interpretive frames? How can a meta-frame for interpreting micro-narratives in multiple languages be developed without recourse to strategic conversation and attention to new common language? We do not think these are rhetorical questions; we think they are unresolved issues.

8. Mangalagiu et al. (2010) and Wilkinson et al. (2011) have explored links between visioning and scenario planning. Ramírez and van der Heijden (2007) and Ramírez and Selsky (2015) assessed links between scenarios and collaborative strategy. Some of our students in the insurance business have carefully prototyped links between risk analysis and scenario planning. Mangalagiu et al. (2011) have assessed the links between complexity thinking, climate change modeling, and scenario planning processes. Ramírez et al. (2013) assessed the links between scenario planning and competitive intelligence. Ramírez et al. (2011) looked at how scenario planning informed the relationship between innovation and strategy.

9. From the Wikipedia entry.

APPENDIX A WÄRTSILÄ CASE STUDY

Rafael Ramírez

Background

Wärtsilä was established as a sawmill in a location of that name in Karelia, eastern Finland, close to the current border with Russia in 1834. By the 1940s the company had diversified into steel production, diesel engine manufacturing, and ship building through a series of acquisitions and licensing deals.[1]

The company survived the 1920s Russian/Soviet crash through deep restructuring, cutting wages by 25 percent. In the 1930s, Wärtsilä acquired a ship-building business. In 1938 it licensed technology from Krupp in Germany and in 1942 manufactured its first diesel engine.

After World War II, Wärtsilä became Finland's largest industrial firm, and after disposing of many units in what had become a diversified conglomerate, the company refocused on engines as the core business. Over the years the company held a leading worldwide market share in ships engines. The engines used in ships had also been found to be useful for land-based power generation, and this application spawned a considerable business, starting in the 1980s. As of 2002, the company extended its marine product range in propulsion systems, then moved back into ship design based on its capabilities in power and propulsion systems.

Today Wärtsilä describes itself as "a global leader in complete lifecycle power solutions for the marine and energy markets." In 2013, Wärtsilä's net sales totaled €4.7 billion, and it had approximately 18,700 employees. The company has operations in more than 200 locations in nearly seventy countries around the world. Wärtsilä is listed on the NASDAQ OMX Helsinki, Finland.

The company is structured in three divisions, whose presidents have considerable autonomy:[2]

- *Ship Power*. The leading provider of ship machinery, propulsion, and maneuvering solutions. The division supplies engines and generating sets, reduction gears, propulsion equipment, control systems, and sealing solutions for all types of vessels and offshore applications. In this business it commands a strong position in all main marine segments as a supplier of highly rated ship machinery and systems.
- *Power Plants*. A leading global supplier of flexible base-load power plants of up to 600 MW operating on various gaseous and liquid fuels. The division also designs, builds, and delivers liquefied natural gas terminals and distribution systems. As of 2014, Wärtsilä had 55 GW of installed power plant capacity in 169 countries.
- *Services*. Support to customers throughout the lifecycle of their installations, optimizing efficiency and performance with a comprehensive portfolio of services and

(as it claims) the broadest service network in the industry, for both the energy and marine markets.

Scenario project work

Wärtsilä has used scenarios three times, twice in its Ship Power division and once in its Power Plants division.[3] But as we will see, these efforts have been widely used internally by R&D, manufacturing, and by the Services division. In this section we describe the projects, and in the next section the scenarios themselves that were generated in each project.

FIRST SHIP POWER PROJECT

The first Ship Power scenario planning effort occurred in 2002–3 as part of a broader business review, when the then head of the division, Mikael Makinen, sought to reconsider the business with his board of management as well as to consider the changes in the wider world that could impact its business. Through this work the division sought to inspire a joint appreciation among the top management of the opportunities and challenges these possible shifts entailed. Research on uncertain factors was done by interviewing thirty-one shipping insurers, financiers, regulators, operators, and industry and academic researchers. One hundred and three pages of transcripts were assembled, and the views of these stakeholders were fed back in a "chorus of voices" format to the division's managers. Ten of these interviewees were brought into a two-day scenario building workshop with four members of the board to construct the sketch scenarios, for a period stretching ten years (to 2013). The scenarios that resulted were used internally and not shared externally.

POWER PLANTS PROJECT

The Power Plant division's scenario planning effort began after Christoph Vitzthum was named head of the division in 2006, a position he held until 2009. There were two small scenario exercises: one on grid stability in the US and one on environmental regulations. Then came the global scenarios for power generation, "Power Scenarios 2023." The scenarios were undertaken to support the division's strategy work, to consider what might happen fifteen years hence (to 2023), to provide thought leadership through wide dissemination[4] externally as well as internally, and to initiate new conversations with customers and to reframe those it had with existing ones. Some fifteen uncertainties were considered in depth; and in this process nine factors that had been considered certain at the beginning of the scenario planning were first reduced to three and then to only two. This process increased management's appreciation of contextual uncertainty, and they began to reframe their understanding of the opportunities and challenges inherent in their business context.

SECOND SHIP POWER PROJECT

The second Ship Power division scenarios project was initiated in 2008, under the leadership of Jaakko Eskola, president of Ship Power.

The scenarios sought to enhance the understanding of the structural changes that might reshape the shipping industry with the intent of seizing opportunities that changing contexts presented to the company. Indeed, Eskola sought to reframe the conversations from being only a supplier of marine equipment to being a strategic partner to its customers. These scenarios have been by far the most widely disseminated.[5]

The three projects' scenarios

FIRST SHIP POWER SCENARIOS

This first set of scenarios in Ship Power has not been published and remains confidential. The role that China would play in the ship-building and shipping industry was a central consideration, and the four scenarios were built around the China issue.

POWER PLANTS SCENARIOS

The Power Plant division produced three scenarios with a fifteen year outlook to 2023:

- *Blue Globe.* Utilities have market power and living becomes increasingly electrified. There is energy abundance, and use of coal continues as carbon capture and storage rises as a solution to emissions.
- *Green Earth.* Individual consumers have market power and are focused on small-scale renewable power generation and sustainable use of energy.
- *Gray World.* Governments have market power and rely as much as possible on indigenous resources. The economy is not doing well.

SECOND SHIP POWER SCENARIOS

The second Ship Power division scenario planning project produced three scenarios with a twenty year outlook, that is, out to 2030:

- *Rough Seas.* Resource scarcity is paramount. Climate change and protectionism have really affected trade. Ports are controlled by governments and logistics are optimized regionally.
- *Yellow River.* China's dominance of world business is quasi-complete. But it is no longer the cheapest producer, which has moved elsewhere in Asia and particularly to Africa. Global agreements no longer exist and climate change is only tackled regionally.
- *Open Oceans.* Globalized firms and megacities are more important than national governments. Climate change has been addressed through business-led innovation and trade flourishes.

Scenario planning project results: uses, outcomes, consequences

FIRST SHIP POWER PROJECT

The first Ship Power division scenario planning engagement led the divisional management to appreciate that the context for its business was more uncertain than it had taken it to be. This new appreciation led to the realization that the uncertainty carried considerable business potential but also involved substantial risk. It also led management to realize that the way division had considered its business might no longer be relevant for a very significant part of that market.

POWER PLANTS PROJECT

The lessons from the Power Plants division scenario planning effort[6] were that when external interviews were contrasted with internal interviews, it makes the messages in the scenarios clear, and helps to avoid the Cassandra problem.[7] According to division president Vitzthum, the scenarios helped the division to create a network of experts, to let disagreement become an asset, and to accept uncertainty and diverse views. Because the division's senior management "owned" its scenarios, this helped its top professionals to value the discussions that arose as a result. Publishing the scenarios helped the division to open doors that contributed to developing its business in the following years. As a government official commented, "We would never have met with you if not for your interesting scenario work."

The scenarios also positioned the division as one of the thought leaders in its field. "Power Scenarios 2023" were awarded the best strategy paper in *Power-Gen Europe 2011*. Sheila Gailloreto, publisher and editor of *Diesel & Gas Turbine Worldwide*, commented:

This might just be the tool or basis to provide a level of comprehensive understanding regarding the energy issues and challenges we face on a global level—especially to those outside of the energy industry. So much of what gets picked up in the mainstream media it seems is taken out of context or ends up appearing to have political connections.

The Wärtsilä manager who conducted and championed this scenario planning work, Pauliina Tennilä, was promoted to head of investor relations for the corporation in 2011.[8]

The Power Plant scenarios were "tracked": "Wärtsilä developed a tracking framework for analyzing the unfolding of the scenarios to enable them to receive constant feedback about changes in the environment; and to recognize when the natural life of the scenarios has come to an end and when it is time to restart the exercise."[9]

These scenarios were later translated and transplanted, with processes like those described in Chapter 4, to guide strategy work both in the Services division (in 2010) and in the Industrial Operations (manufacturing) function shared by the Power Plant and the Ship Power divisions (in 2011).

SECOND SHIP POWER PROJECT

This set of scenarios has been widely shared, and for quite some time. At the time of this writing (February 2015), a Google search with keywords "Wärtsilä Shipping Scenarios" finds 10,300 items, and the public version of the scenarios is still accessible on Wärtsilä's website.[10] As Andrea Hernandez, the manager who led this scenario planning initiative, has put it in several external presentations:[11]

Scenarios are a powerful tool for stakeholder dialogue. They act as an important proof of Wärtsilä's leadership; we have found that they are a very effective discussion generator and a powerful way to build the employer brand. Scenarios (also) generate media hits when presented in a right way and help shape corporate image. Sharing the scenarios is possible with several potential "audiences":

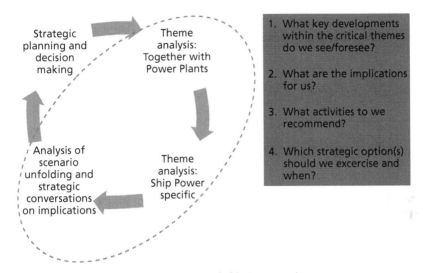

Figure A1. Cyclical process in Wärtsilä's second Ship Power project

(used with permission)

Present and potential customers; politicians and authorities; NGO's and think-tanks; researchers, teachers, students (university level); staff members; partners; and journalists.

Lloyd's List also suggested that this sharing has helped to make the company recognized as a thought leader in the industry:

One of the press announcements that did make me sit up and take notice was not a product or a service, but a vision. Finnish engineers at Wärtsilä revealed a set of possible shipping scenarios it thinks will materialise in the coming years, and the ship types that will evolve to meet them . . . it was, they said, an attempt to launch a dialogue to get people's thoughts about how the industry will develop.[12]

Internally, the scenarios were used to inform strategy, following an iterative process depicted in Figure A1 (also from Ms. Hernandez' 2014 presentation). Subsequently, in a division strategy document, a new and up to then unheard of type of ship—which one might expect to appear in each of the three project scenarios—was profiled, to call attention to the new product possibilities that the scenario planning heralded.

Implications

The repeated efforts for scenario planning in Ship Power and the influential scenario planning work in Power Plants helped Wärtsilä's senior managers to reframe their understandings of the contexts they were operating in. The scenario planning broadened the issues they paid attention to, lengthened the time horizons they used when considering alternative possibilities, and helped them to reposition their company from its role as a leading equipment and services designer, manufacturer, and supplier to also becoming involved as a strategic partner. The scenarios put the company "on the map" as a thought leader, and helped it become distinct in the minds of customers, suppliers, journalists, and industry analysts.

The structural changes described in each of the scenarios imply fundamental reorganizations for the roles that different players might hold in relation to each other, both in shipping and in power generation. The scenarios surfaced assumptions, clarified disagreements, and helped sharpen strategy.

■ NOTES

1. <http://www.wartsila.com/en/about/company-management/history> (accessed September 2015).
2. Adapted from the company website.
3. All with the support of NormannPartners.
4. See <http://www.img.fi/wartsila/Scenarios.pdf> (accessed February 2015).
5. <http://www.shippingscenarios.wartsila.com/> (accessed February 2015).
6. Christoph Vitzhum (2014).
7. The Cassandra problem is derived from ancient Greek mythology. Cassandra was granted the possibility of foreseeing the future by the gods, but in such a way that no one would believe what she said.
8. <http://www.wartsila.com/en/press-releases/pauliina-tennila-appointed-director-investor-relations> (accessed June 2015).
9. <http://www.icci.com.tr/dosya/2011sunumlar/o08_marco_golinelli.pdf> (accessed February 2015). See also Ramírez et al. (2013).
10. <http://www.shippingscenarios.wartsila.com/> (accessed February 2015).
11. Andrea Hernandez (2011; 2014).
12. Published in *Lloyds List*, September 16, 2010.

■ **APPENDIX B** SHELL 2001 GLOBAL SCENARIOS CASE STUDY

Angela Wilkinson

Background

Shell is a global firm in the energy and petrochemicals business with many subsidiary companies. At the time of this writing (January 2015) it employs around 92,000 people in more than seventy countries. The formal name of the parent company of the Shell group is Royal Dutch Shell PLC, which is incorporated in England and Wales, and the company is listed in Amsterdam, London, and New York.[1]

Shell has been building and using scenarios for nearly fifty years. Its "global" scenarios," which it produces regularly every few years, are designed to look further into the future than many other outlooks, and to highlight surprising possible developments. These global scenarios guide most of the more focused scenarios its scenarios team produces (relating to specific countries or issues), although every few years the company also produces even longer-term views, considering possibilities for periods that extend to almost a century, called "Long Term Energy scenarios."

This appendix describes the global scenarios and the (in Shell language) "round" of activity that produced them, which took place in 1998–2002. This round resulted in the publication of a public report, *Shell 2001 Global Scenarios: People and Connections*, as well as a guide book describing the Shell scenario building methodology, *Scenarios: An Explorer's Guide* (see Figure B1).

Scenario project work

Members of the company's Global Business Environment team (the "Shell scenario team") in Shell International develop long-term scenarios that examine how the world of energy and the overarching interests of the company—the "global scenarios"— might unfold. These scenarios inform corporate strategic planning and provide strategic analysis and advice to Shell executives. The scenario team also helps senior decision makers across the company to develop and use their own scenarios, which are translated and transplanted (see Chapter 4) to become refocused on business units and regional and country-specific operations, as required.

At the time of this case study (2000–1), the scenario team consisted of some seventeen professionals, who worked up to 50 percent of their time on the development of the global scenarios over this two-year period, following the inductive method described in *Scenarios: An Explorer's Guide*. As is common in a Shell scenario exercise, everyone on the team was encouraged to take a leap of faith at the beginning of the project and believe in the combined talent of the team. Arguably, this norm is more important in a scenario exercise than many other endeavors because of the ambiguity and creativity involved.

Figure B1. The Shell Scenarios *Explorer's Guide*
(used with permission)

Throughout the building process, the Shell scenario team worked closely with colleagues in the corporate strategy group and engaged with the members of the executive team, wider experts, and senior staff from across the organization. A lot of effort was put into grounding the scenarios by understanding the mindsets within the company and upcoming key decisions. It was not an arid academic exercise but a sharing of ideas and needs.

The project had three planned phases: orientation, building, and engagement and communication. The scenario building process began work in early 2000 with a series of open-ended interviews conducted in active listening mode by members of the scenario team, on a one-to-one basis with several dozen individual executives. Using these interviews, a "chorus of voices" analysis was prepared in the form of a 2 × 2 matrix which mapped Shell executives' ideas about changes and challenges within and beyond the organization, to identify areas of agreement and disagreement. This initial analysis provided a starting point for researching five cross-cutting themes that would underpin the definition of the scenarios and in a way that addressed the challenges facing senior managers and challenged existing views.

In parallel, starting in mid-2000, scenario team members began researching for relevant and interesting contextual developments which the team considered it needed to cover; these were in the general themes of society, technology, economy, environment, the changing nature of firms in society, and international relations. During this research phase, team members employed desk-based literature reviews and sponsored small-scale exploratory workshops involving wider experts. Throughout this phase, they also reflected on developments since the last round of global scenarios in 1998.

In these initial preparations there was intense inquiry and fierce competition among members of the Shell scenario team over which ideas would become central to the scenarios. The interview synthesis and the insights derived from the thematic inquiry were also shared with a cross-section of about forty Shell senior staff through a highly interactive, two-day "orientation" workshop. The workshop resulted in the creation of three possible scenarios, but the participants could not reach agreement as to which of these together involved the "best" set to fit the concerns identified in the chorus of voices analysis. The decision on which set to use was taken after this workshop by the head of the scenarios team. He decided to limit the scenarios to two contrasting ones; eventually one scenario was named Business Class and the other Prism. Once the team leader decided on the main ideas, the team rallied to complete the stories and share them.

Several drafts of the two scenarios were shared with staff across the organization; their feedback contributed to the further development, deepening, and clarification of each storyline, debugging contradictions and refining the core messages. When the storyline logics were sufficiently clear, the team customized existing macroeconomic models to test the internal logics and to illustrate quantitatively projections and impacts within each scenario, consistent with the system logic of each scenario story.

The final draft set of scenarios was tested for relevance, plausibility, and communicability at an interactive workshop with senior decision makers before being presented to the executive team for discussion.

The Shell 2001 global scenarios

Two scenarios were developed in 2000–1 with a time horizon of 2020. Each assumed that global economic growth would continue but with different patterns of globalization, each carrying different implications for the company.

The scenario framework reflected a set of critical but uncertain assumptions that were implicit in the strategic conversation across the organization but until that point had not been clearly articulated. These assumptions revolved around the basic question: will the resolution of dilemmas arising from globalization be dominated by global elites or by the people of the heartlands? Two contrasting answers to this question generated the two scenarios (see Figure B2).

The *Business Class scenario* offered a vision of "connected freedom" and greater economic integration. This was a world of efficiency, opportunities, and high rewards for those who could compete and innovate successfully. Established authorities would be continually challenged, and the power of nation states greatly reduced. In this world, globalization had brought tangible benefits to both rich and poor societies, and growing inequality was tolerated because people saw opportunities to improve their lives and had the freedom to pursue their own dreams. The world of Business Class was not run by big business, but it was run *like* a business with a focus on efficiency and achieving goals. Almost all organizations—companies, of course, but also national governments and international NGO's—would need to face the question of how to maintain their identity and purpose in a world of more open and fluid global networks.

The *Prism scenario* highlighted that human affairs were not inevitably going to be handled in a monochromatic globalized manner. This scenario articulated how an

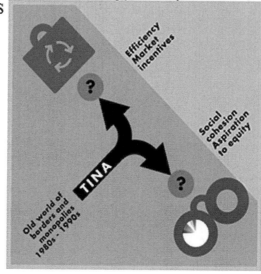

Figure B2. The two Shell 2001 Global Scenarios

Royal Dutch Shell PLC (used with permission)

alternative—many alternatives, in fact—would arise. They would arise because people in this scenario would have come to see and value the world, society, and institutions in very different ways. Prism was the story of how these alternatives played out over the next twenty years. The power of cultural values and the central role of belonging were stressed. What shaped the future in this scenario was not what people and peoples have in common but the interplay of their differences.

In effect, this round of Shell global scenarios attempted to reframe globalization away from the "accept or reject" reaction manifested in previous rounds of Shell scenarios. It focused instead on two contrasting perspectives: on the one hand, increasing competition and homogeneity (Business Class), and on the other the rise of emerging economies leading to a diverse pattern of multiple modernities (Prism).

A semi-public version of the scenarios was released to ambassadors and other dignitaries in the summer of 2001 in an event organized by Chatham House in London. A more public version of the scenarios was released in 2002. It included a reflection on how this set of global scenarios might help to interpret the terrorist attacks on the World Trade Center and the Pentagon, on September 11, 2001, as a defining moment, marking a new phase in the impact of globalization around world events. The global scenarios and 9/11 update had been shared in private with key governments in the months before the public booklet was launched. This followed the normal pattern of first using scenarios in-house to inform strategy, then sharing with key stakeholders, prior to publishing a public version and using the scenarios to reach out to wider stakeholders.

Project results: uses, outcomes, consequences

The Shell 2001 Global Scenarios were presented in Houston on May 30 as part of the 2001 Shell Business Week, bringing up to 300 Shell leaders together to work on issues relating to the group as a whole. The event marked the handover from then chairman, Sir Mark Moody-Stewart, to the chairman-elect, Sir Phil Watts. The meeting focused on considering a fresh approach to strategy and planning, along with the new set of global scenarios outlining challenges to the group.

Increased collaborative efforts between the Group Strategy and Global Business Environment teams led to further attempts to link scenarios to group strategy and portfolio analysis. The global scenarios were also communicated widely across the organization under a six-month embargo of external communication.

The new chief executive, Phil Watts, required individual businesses to test their business strategies against the scenarios. Even though Watts had mandated the use of the global scenarios as a context for the strategic plans of the businesses, the decentralized nature of the company meant that responses from some of the business units were often a matter of mere compliance rather than the result of deeper reflection. These business units adopted a "tick box" approach to using the global scenarios, preferring to harness specific elements of the supporting analysis involved in developing the global scenarios for their own scenario building and strategy processes.

In contrast, some businesses (including the major earners) translated, transplanted, and leveraged the global scenarios to develop more customized scenarios for their own strategic planning purposes. For example, Bill Colquhoun, head of Shell's chemical business, used the global scenarios as a starting point to catalyze an in-depth strategic review and restructuring of a business unit.

Many support functions also engaged the global scenarios to explore and inform elements of strategy. The group's HR director, John Hofmeister, was particularly interested in the global scenarios as a way to cultivate an "external mindset" as one of the core skills required by a Shell executive.

Implications

Scenarios are part of the corporate DNA of Shell. The scenario process is ongoing rather than one-off, and provides the opportunity for highly motivated and diverse leaders in the company to understand their differences and ultimately work together to achieve the goals of the company.

At Shell, the future provides a safe context in which to talk about challenges and their possible implications. The business people involved are also given license to focus on the bigger picture and the connections between aspects of their operating environment, as well as likely and possible future developments. The scenario planning process shifts the corporate conversation.

Some in the scenario team were long-term Shell people, and others had been hand-picked to join the team for the duration of the round, based on the personalities, perspectives, specialist knowledge, and connections deemed likely to be important by the team leader. A balance between people who want to continue exploring and those who want to get to the destination is a very important aspect of getting the team chemistry right. Designers were also involved at an early stage. The events of 9/11 happened after the 2001 global scenarios had been developed and were being used within the firm. The scenarios were not rewritten, but an addendum to the scenarios was quickly produced using the two global scenario frames, Business Class and Prism, as the starting point for developing much shorter-term crisis scenarios that provided alternative frames for making sense of this fast moving and unprecedented event, and for better interpreting different stakeholders' subsequent reactions. The speed with which the 9/11 addendum was produced demonstrated the value-added of the Shell scenarios culture which had been cultivated over decades.

Across the Shell Group, scenarios are developed focused on projects, countries, major investment decisions, and other strategic factors. By enabling the global scenarios developed on a centralized, top-down basis to "talk to" scenarios developed on a bottom-up, decentralized basis across the company, Shell is able to adapt quickly or build new scenarios when facing emerging risks and crisis situations, such as on the invasion of Kuwait, on Iraq, and on the prospect of a global influenza pandemic triggered by a new flu virus.

■ FURTHER READING

Shell 2001 Global Scenarios to 2020: People and Connections (Public Summary). <http://www.shell.com/content/dam/shell/static/future-energy/downloads/shell-scenarios/shell-global-scenarios 2020peopleandconnections.pdf> (accessed September 2015).

Shell Energy Scenarios to 2050. <https://s00.static-shell.com/content/dam/shell/static/future-energy/downloads/shell-scenarios/shell-energy-scenarios2050.pdf> (accessed September 2015).

Shell Scenarios: An Explorer's Guide. <http://s05.static-shell.com/content/dam/shell/static/future-energy/downloads/shell-scenarios/shell-scenarios-explorersguide.pdf> (accessed September 2015).

Wilkinson, Angela and Roland Kupers. 2013. "Living in Futures." *Harvard Business Review*, May. <https://hbr.org/2013/05/living-in-the-futures> (accessed September 2015).

Wilkinson, Angela and Roland Kupers. 2014. *The Essence of Scenarios: Lessons from the Shell Experience 1965–2013.* Amsterdam: Amsterdam University Press.

■ NOTE

1. <http://www.shell.com/global/aboutshell/at-a-glance.html> (accessed September 2015).

Shirin Elahi and Rafael Ramírez

Background

United European Gastroenterology, or UEG, is a professional non-profit organization in the health sector. It is actually an association of organizations (what Ahrne and Brunsson (2005) call a *meta-organization*), comprising all the leading European professional societies concerned with digestive disease, and also includes individual members. In total, UEG represents over 22,000 specialists, who work across medicine, surgery, pediatrics, gastrointestinal (GI) oncology, and endoscopy. This broad reach makes UEG the most comprehensive organization of its kind.[1]

UEG is therefore uniquely equipped as a platform for collaboration and knowledge sharing, enabling it to further its mission: to advance gastroenterology care and improve the prevention and care of digestive diseases in Europe. UEG acts as the united voice of European gastroenterology, delivering cutting-edge education and training; facilitating and disseminating world-leading research; and working to improve clinical standards and services and reduce health inequalities across Europe. To achieve these goals, UEG collaborates with healthcare professionals, scientists, patients, and the public, and liaises closely with politicians and policymakers.

UEG is funded by membership dues and the scientific activities and events it arranges. These include its annual congress, postgraduate teaching, publication of a scientific journal, and educational programs. It also enjoys sponsorship from industry.

Scenario project work

Current models (as at 2014) for healthcare delivery in Europe are unsustainable, with a rapidly aging population, rising health costs, reduced public budgets, volatile political and economic landscapes, as well as a shrinking workforce and increasing burden of lifestyle diseases. GI diseases contribute significantly to the healthcare burden in Europe, accounting for substantial morbidity, mortality, and cost.

For example, digestive diseases, that is, gastrointestinal and liver disorders, caused more than 500,000 deaths in 2008 in the twenty-eight EU member states, and more than 900,000 deaths in the whole of Europe, including Russia and other non-EU states (UEG 2014). Over one-third of all acute hospital admissions are due to GI diseases, and at least one in three Europeans will visit a gastroenterologist at least once in their lives.

It takes eight years to educate a gastroenterologist, so the UEG leadership considered that in 2040 the students entering medical school in 2014 to study this specialization would be half-way through a professional career that became active in

2022. The UEG wanted to examine how well the profession was educating these incoming colleagues for the conditions they might encounter in their future careers. To better anticipate and prepare for possibly new and very different future contexts, members of UEG's "Futures Trends Committee" and its then chairman, Professor Michael Farthing (now president of UEG), collaborated with Julia Frauscher from the UEG head office in Vienna, and hired the NormannPartners consultancy to explore how these future contexts might unfold:

"We know that the incidence and prevalence of most major GI disorders are rising across Europe and there is already poor access to care in many countries. Since changing the way we deliver healthcare in the future seems inevitable, we decided to take a bold approach and highlight possible scenarios, inspiring everyone to get involved and play their part in shaping a better future for digestive and liver disease healthcare," said Prof. Farthing. (UEG 2014)

The UEG scenarios-based strategic planning intervention set out to explore what the European healthcare system might look like in 2040; and to describe the future contexts for health "care" at home, in hospitals, and by oneself in 2040 and beyond.

The scenarios were produced for immediate use by the incoming president and for the members of the Future Trends Committee of the UEG he had chaired. He thought the scenarios would help them, as well as UEG members and stakeholders, in imagining future possibilities. The scenario planning process was thus designed to help these individuals inform UEG members and stakeholders about future possibilities; to challenge current thinking; and to inspire the gastroenterology community to work together to shape a better future for patients. An additional important purpose of the scenarios was to sharpen strategy, enabling UEG, its members, and stakeholders to have more courageous strategic conversations.

The scenario planning project was conceived in 2013 and took over a year to develop. Three scenario workshops were held over a period of several months, with substantial work by the scenario builders in between. The scenario building team comprised a diverse professional group of eighteen people drawn from across the various specialties, age groups, professional levels, and geographic regions of Europe.

The scenarios were built inductively from the eighteen key contextual uncertainties that were identified during the workshops (see Figure C1), and then further researched by the scenario building team. An initial set of eight scenarios were developed during the first day of the second workshop, with four others added in the second day. These twelve candidate sketch scenarios were then discussed, compared, merged, and reduced in plenary to produce three agreed final scenarios. The final set of three were tentatively entitled Meltdown, TechMed, and United States of Europe. The names were discussed and changed during the final workshop to those described in the next section. Following the final workshop, the stories and the formats for comparing the scenarios to each other were refined for sharing in a plenary hour-long session[2] in the annual meeting of the UEG held in October 2014. The scenarios were then made public through the UEG's website.[3]

The UEG scenarios

Three scenarios describe what the European healthcare system might look like in 2040. The final names were Ice Age, Silicon Age, and Golden Age.

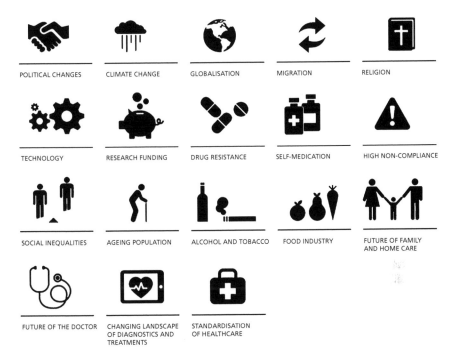

POLITICAL CHANGES	CLIMATE CHANGE	GLOBALISATION	MIGRATION	RELIGION
TECHNOLOGY	RESEARCH FUNDING	DRUG RESISTANCE	SELF-MEDICATION	HIGH NON-COMPLIANCE
SOCIAL INEQUALITIES	AGEING POPULATION	ALCOHOL AND TOBACCO	FOOD INDUSTRY	FUTURE OF FAMILY AND HOME CARE
FUTURE OF THE DOCTOR	CHANGING LANDSCAPE OF DIAGNOSTICS AND TREATMENTS	STANDARDISATION OF HEALTHCARE		

Figure C1. Driving forces in UEG's contextual environment

Used with permission; see <https://ueg.eu>

Ice Age. By 2040 European impoverishment has resulted in a two-tier system of medical treatments, which eventually triggers a collapse of public healthcare systems across Europe.

By 2040 natural resource shortages, climate change impacts, inactive aging, and economic crisis have contributed to the widespread impoverishment of Europe. The European Union no longer exists, most of the population is poor, unemployment is high, and membership of religious groups and alternative "health sects" is high. Environmental hazards, including pollution and increased exposure to potential carcinogens, contribute to this toxic mix.

Silicon Age. By 2040 advances in technology, science, and social interactions have led to extensive automation of diagnoses and treatment and redirected health behaviors, resulting in a shift to preventative health.

In Silicon Age, global trends and crises have led to changes at every level—in individual behavior, social priorities, industrial strategies, and government policies. Population growth has encouraged innovation and there is widespread acceptance of technology. Social media have become highly influential across the healthcare sector.

The European Union still exists and has contributed to the modernization of health legislation across Europe. There is a large non-EU immigrant population relying on social security, draining resources and escalating healthcare expenditure.

Golden Age. By 2040 a strong, well-coordinated, unified Europe has ensured access to high-quality healthcare to all European citizens.

An influx of immigrants and widespread cross-border movement of Europeans has resulted in a more multicultural and united Europe. Here we see a United States of Europe, with no internal borders, homogenized education, taxation, and legislation systems, and universal access to healthcare for all. Economic growth has slowed, environmental issues are being addressed, and preventative health is high on the agenda. The resulting peace and stability denotes a Golden Age for Europe.

IMPLICATIONS FOR HEALTHCARE AND THE ROLES OF HEALTHCARE PROFESSIONALS

Specific health and healthcare features of each scenario were drawn out, and these are summarized in Table C1. Each scenario also described how the role of the doctor and healthcare specialist might change in each future. In Ice Age, doctors are leaving Europe to seek better conditions and access to the latest technology and treatments elsewhere. In Silicon Age, doctors maintain a traditional role delivering patient-centered care supported by cost-effective e-health platforms. In Golden Age, doctors assist individuals with navigating and understanding their personal electronic patient cloud records.

Project results: uses, outcomes, consequences

These scenarios were made public at UEG Week 2014, an annual professional event that took place in Vienna and was attended by 13,000 delegates from 118 countries. The scenarios were presented at a special UEG Research Symposium, entitled Gastro-enterology and Hepatology: Past, Present and Future. Each of the scenarios was presented by the "champion" who had led the particular group of scenario builders who developed that scenario. This presentation triggered a widespread discussion that has subsequently moved online, with each of the scenario presentations described in a detailed video on YouTube.[4] At a press conference at UEG Week, the scenarios were also presented to leading medical journalists from all over the world.

In addition to the presentations, the scenarios resources that were prepared and have begun to be shared include a detailed section explaining why the world of healthcare will inevitably change. It argues why and how current models for healthcare delivery in Europe are unsustainable: a rapidly aging population supported by a shrinking workforce with limited public financing presents major challenges and requires new thinking. It describes the eighteen contextual driving forces shaping this transformation of the profession's transactional environment (see Figure C1).

The purpose of the scenario planning project was to encourage more courageous and informed debate, to support the UEG's external communications strategy, and to manifest the courageous conversations the scenarios enabled though different social media, particularly Twitter and Facebook.[5]

A tab on the UEG website called Starting the Conversation[6] announced that the scenarios were rendered public. It urged readers to help UEG plan for a better future for people with digestive and liver diseases by visiting the website and casting their vote on which of the three scenarios they thought was the most likely 2040 healthcare

Table C1. Health and healthcare features of the UEG scenarios

Ice Age	Silicon Age	Golden Age
A two-tier healthcare system has developed and led to the collapse of public healthcare in Europe.	While inequalities in healthcare still exist, the dominance of technology has provided a means of delivering high-tech, cost-effective care to the majority of Europeans.	Dictated by a strong, centralized public sector, the private sector has helped implement mandatory prevention programs.
An aging population with an increase in age-related chronic diseases like cancer, antibiotic resistance combined with a lack of new drugs, and outbreaks of infectious disease epidemics all threaten the population.	E-algorithms detailing risk profiles for multiple diseases are developed via genomic screening at birth.	Children are formally educated about the importance of health and to encourage all to have a positive attitude toward illness prevention.
Poverty and poor healthcare have led to high rates of morbidity and mortality within the general population.	Individuals take responsibility for self-monitoring, self-cure, and prevention assisted by comprehensive lifestyle and health data stored in their personal electronic patient cloud record.	Consistent Europe-wide prevention-based strategies, policies, and practices are in place.
Most individuals have little or no access to healthcare and are also plagued by diseases associated with alcohol, tobacco, and obesity.	Automated diagnostics and interventions, including robotics, are readily available by self-referral.	Good quality, cost-effective healthcare is available to all, delivered primarily via e-health initiatives, outpatient clinics, low-cost healthcare centers, and care at home.
In desperation, people are turning to alternative medicine and uncontrolled self-medication.	With the adoption of e-health, the role of the doctor has fundamentally changed from delivering healthcare to assisting individuals with navigating and understanding their medical e-data.	There is total European cohesion in healthcare with consistent medical education and training across the continent.
For the rich minority, there is excellent healthcare available in the private sector.	Collaborative ventures as well as innovative public and private partnerships work for the benefit of the patient.	Doctors continue to play a traditional role and deliver patient-centered care.
Science is market-driven, and healthcare services, primarily provided by profit-hungry insurance companies, are only available to those who can pay.	Widespread use of social media platforms has helped to integrate significant advances in medical research and data capture.	Patients increasingly use email and dedicated electronic platforms to liaise with their healthcare professional, and travel freely across the United States of Europe to access the best healthcare providers and specialist centers.
Healthcare workers are leaving Europe seeking better conditions and access to the latest technology and treatments.	Alongside e-health there has been a shift into an e-economy which includes novel monetary systems that carry the risk of using unofficial currencies and unethical or even criminal activities.	
Patients are increasingly seeking healthcare outside Europe or from offshore floating hospitals.	Social media and advanced technology bring with them privacy concerns.	
	Some poor-quality health practices as well as complex systems which are hard to navigate have arisen.	

scenario; or to post any thoughts and comments on the future of digestive and liver diseases throughout Europe.

At the time of writing (January 2015), the utilization of these scenarios in UEG is still in its early stages. To date they have opened a dialogue on some pertinent issues about the future of public health. They have enabled UEG's many constituents to broach a difficult subject, namely, that business as usual is unlikely to continue unimpeded into the future, and consequently that the profession—together with its education and research profiles, and healthcare in general—are bound to change in rather fundamental ways. According to UEG officials, a roadshow has been planned for 2015 and is likely to be taken up again in 2016 to present the scenarios to UEG members and stakeholders.

The scenarios have already begun to be used as a tool for policy engagement. For example, the UEG's top staff met with policymakers from the European Parliament and the Commission in late 2014 to assess current trends and future challenges in the field of gastrointestinal care for patients, and to discuss how EU health policies should be shaped in order to provide the best possible medical care to citizens.[7] The meetings sought to engage stakeholders in a structured debate about the future of public health policies in Europe, the challenges that accompany it, and adequate EU policy responses.

In addition to its *Scenarios for the Future*, in 2014 UEG also conducted and published a *Survey on Digestive Health across Europe*. This survey reflected the reality of the profession at that time. It included a detailed assessment of digestive and liver diseases in twenty-eight European countries, examined the clinical and economic burdens of these diseases, and evaluated the organization and delivery of gastroenterology services. It was the first study to compile all available data into a single comprehensive overview of gastrointestinal diseases and treatment in Europe, and identified concrete actions for further research and political action.

Implications

The UEG scenario planning initiative has enabled the organization to further establish its place as a thought leader and key player in the healthcare arena. It has helped it to remind policymakers of the critical role gastroenterology plays in public health. Each of the scenarios envisages very different roles for the patient as well as the doctor. These changing roles would have far-reaching impacts on the relationships among healthcare generalists, specialists, patients and their families, carers, clients/payers, and sources of funding. All of these relationships will require careful consideration.

UEG's analyses of inevitable change are meant to be a catalyst for further strategic conversations, and seek to help European policymakers to confront what might be unwelcome considerations about the future. The structural changes described in each of the scenarios imply fundamental reorganizations of the prevailing healthcare systems of Europe. In each of the three scenarios, the very nature of health is redefined, as are the actors who operate to provide healthcare in 2040.

In terms of healthcare, these changes impact social dynamics: they highlight the potential for a reinforcing health feedback loop and question the nature of public health. These dynamics also have political implications such as questioning the roles of the EU, how inequality might unfold, and what form the concept of "social solidarity" might take.

In addition to the public engagement, internally the scenarios entail a substantially different role for UEG, requiring it to acquire or develop different capabilities to remain strong and relevant. As such, the uptake of scenario thinking under the newly elected president will require a major rethinking of UEG's identity, how it relates to professional bodies and individual members, and even how best it can achieve its purpose. This could also include a reassessment of success criteria and ways for it to maintain its desired relevance.

▓ NOTES

1. <https://www.ueg.eu/about-ueg/who-we-are/> (accessed September 2015).
2. <https://www.ueg.eu/research/gi2040/#video2_ice> (accessed February 2015).
3. See <https://www.ueg.eu/research/gi2040/> (accessed September 2015).
4. The YouTube videos are publicly available. For example, see the Ice Age video at <https://www.youtube.com/watch?v=yBQPOdOIaqw> (accessed September 2015).
5. See <https://www.facebook.com/myUEG/posts/605534166218327> and <https://twitter.com/UEGMedia/status/530370395535577089> (accessed September 2015).
6. <https://www.ueg.eu/press/releases/ueg-press-release/article/ueg-week-press-release-what-will-the-european-healthcare-system-look-like-in-2040-ueg-launch-fu/> (accessed February 2015).
7. <https://www.ueg.eu/news/news/news-details/article/towards-new-frontiers-in-european-healthcare-scenarios-for-european-healthcare-in-2040/?tx_ttnews%5Bpointer%5D=1&cHash=c1a24f6f94b9b0d87609c82aad6ad693> (accessed February 2015).

Angela Wilkinson

Background

Human immunodeficiency virus infection and acquired immune deficiency syndrome (HIV/AIDS) emerged as a global health concern in the late 1980s.

AIDS in Africa: Three Scenarios to 2025 was a collaborative, multi-stakeholder scenario project which took place between 2002 and 2005.[1] It was aimed at developing a shared understanding of the possible course of the AIDS epidemic in Africa over the next twenty years across the diverse constituencies involved in a more coordinated response, such as the medical sector, development agencies, central governments, and people living with HIV/AIDS.

In 2001, after more than ten years of collecting data on HIV/AIDS, the Director of the Joint United Nations Programme on HIV/AIDS (UNAIDS), Peter Piot, was looking to move beyond defining the problem of HIV/AIDS to focus the debate on understanding the different patterns of infections that were emerging in different world regions. He also wanted to explore options for a sustained response to the spread of HIV/AIDS, which appeared to depend on a wide set of circumstances. UNAIDS was only one agent in a complex web of actors addressing HIV/AIDS. Supporting an effective response to the epidemic in Africa, and other parts of the world, was not, therefore, a simple case of a complete lack of action, but a challenge of engaging effectively with many organizations, spanning the public, private, and civic sectors.

Following a chance dinner conversation between Piot and the chairman of Shell, Phil Watts, agreement was reached to harness the Shell scenario method and deploy it to support the UNAIDS cause. Shell had a significant business presence in Africa and was concerned about the growing threat of an AIDS epidemic. The company had been developing and using scenarios for decades to appreciate and address new and emerging strategic challenges.

The two organizations entered into a Memorandum of Understanding in which Shell agreed to supply and underwrite its expertise in scenarios. Staff in the two organizations then co-developed a project prospectus, detailing the aims, proposed process, and governance structure for a one-year, multi-stakeholder scenario-based initiative focused on AIDS in Africa (AiA). The prospectus was used in joint fundraising, and another thirteen partners contributed the additional resources required to develop and use a bespoke set of pan-African scenarios.

The project was launched in February 2003 as an undertaking of UNAIDS in partnership with the United Nations Development Programme, World Bank, Economic Commission for Africa, and African Development Bank. It was financed by several development agencies, companies, and foundations:[2] DFID, CIDA, DCI, SIDA, USAID,

Merck, the Rockefeller Foundation, Pfizer, and the Gates Foundation. Shell International Ltd. provided the project with pro bono expertise in scenario building for the duration of the project, as well as office accommodation for the project team in London.

Scenario project work

The project had four distinct phases and was designed around three large, interactive workshops, with an ongoing element of supporting research, analysis, and numerous smaller meetings (see Figure D1).

ORIENTATION PHASE

Interviews were conducted with a range of stakeholders and participants to inform the design and preparation of materials for the first workshop. The initial target of fifty interviews was found to be insufficient in identifying repeating themes, and eventually nearly one hundred interviews were made. These open-ended interviews were synthesized by the core team to develop a "chorus of voices" analysis of the underlying issues, views, and perspectives that different individuals identified about the HIV/AIDS epidemic in Africa and its possible developments over the next twenty years. This analysis provided inputs to the discussions at the first ("orientation") workshop.

The orientation workshop took place in Addis Ababa, Ethiopia, in May 2003. Seventy participants met over five days to explore critical uncertainties about the future of AIDS in Africa. During this workshop there was a need to adjust the initial workshop design to accommodate a session on "undiscussible issues" perceived to be

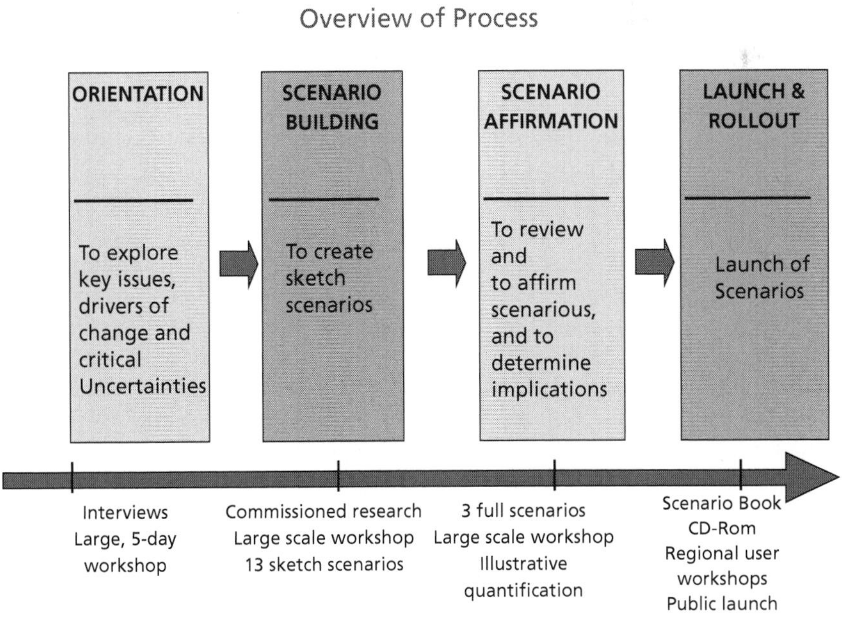

Overview of Process

ORIENTATION	SCENARIO BUILDING	SCENARIO AFFIRMATION	LAUNCH & ROLLOUT
To explore key issues, drivers of change and critical Uncertainties	To create sketch scenarios	To review and to affirm scenarious, and to determine implications	Launch of Scenarios
Interviews Large, 5-day workshop	Commissioned research Large scale workshop 13 sketch scenarios	3 full scenarios Large scale workshop Illustrative quantification	Scenario Book CD-Rom Regional user workshops Public launch

Figure D1. Four phases of the AIDS in Africa project

BOX D1 UNCOMFORTABLE AND UNDISCUSSABLE

One key aspect of the HIV/AIDS problem was the fact that it dealt with uncomfortable issues which society is unaccustomed to confronting. Because of the manner in which the virus is transmitted, there are trans-cultural forces and cultural taboos which make the problem undiscussable and therefore make it worse. Out of the best of intentions, groups and societies avoid conflict or embarrassment by not talking about HIV/AIDS infection. It can also be undiscussable to talk about why people don't talk about HIV/AIDS infection. This is a kind of double lock, which prevents deeper and more shared learning. There are also undiscussable issues around Africa's development and its relationship with the rest of the world.

---

part of the driving forces of the spread of the epidemic, and of the kind of Africa in which the epidemic was happening (see Box D1). These included: a culture of wife inheritance, taboos on discussing sex/sexuality, pressures from donor countries stifling African choices of development options, traditional medicines, and neocolonialism.

The workshop participants identified questions requiring further research by the core team. The initial framing of the spread of HIV/AIDS in Africa co-created by the workshop participants revealed the complexity of the situation: this was mapped in a form that included five levels of analysis (individual, community, national, pan-African, international) and six domains of policy (demography, economics, governance, HIV science, African cultures, and diversity).

After the workshop the core team conducted follow-up research on forty-one variables and 205 research questions identified from the workshop discussions: seventy-one research papers were commissioned from a wide set of experts. The findings of these commissioned papers were organized into six theme papers: Capacity to Learn/Behavior Change; Demography and People Movement; Ubunta/Jamaal (work on social capital); Africa in the World/The World in Africa; Virusology, Prevention, and Treatment; and Governance and Key Power Relationships. The six theme papers provided a starting point for recommencing discussions at the next workshop.

SCENARIO BUILDING PHASE

The second large-scale workshop took place over four days in Tunis, Tunisia, in September 2003. Participants engaged in discussions of the linkages among the six themes to develop an initial system mapping of the situation. The map sought to clarify deeper, structural dynamics (see Figures D2 and D3). They then turned their attention to clarifying the research agendas to be addressed by the scenarios. The scenarios explored the question: "In the next twenty years what factors will drive Africa (and the world's) response to the HIV/AIDS epidemic, and what kind of futures will there be for the next generation?" In seeking an answer to this question, two other questions emerged: "How is the crisis perceived, and by whom?" and "Will there be the incentive and capacity to address this crisis?"

Using these three questions, participants worked with an inductive methodology in parallel breakout groups and used the system map to create possible storylines. They grouped storylines to create sketch (i.e. crude and partial) draft scenarios. The plenary

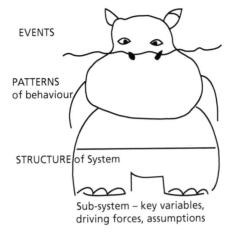

EVENTS

PATTERNS
of behaviour

STRUCTURE of System

Sub-system – key variables,
driving forces, assumptions

Figure D2. Graphic used to illustrate search for deeper structural dynamics of AIDS in Africa

(used with permission of author)

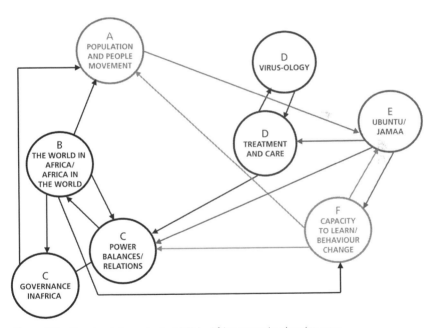

Figure D3. Structural dynamics in AIDS in Africa scenario planning case

sharing identified thirteen sketch scenarios. Following the workshop the core team worked with the materials developed by the participants and reorganized the sketch scenarios into three more developed scenarios as inputs for the next workshop. Each of the three was given a provisional name.

SCENARIO AFFIRMATION PHASE

A third large-scale workshop took place over four days in Johannesburg, South Africa, in February 2004. The core team's reorganization of the thirteen sketch scenarios into three more developed scenarios was vigorously contested by the participants, who could neither see nor agree on the logic used by the team in reorganizing their ideas.

A different set of three scenarios was thus restructured by the participants; even so, not everyone agreed with the final choice of three. A subset of participants wanted to progress a fourth scenario called "Mama Africa," in which the empowerment of women enabled the spread of the virus to be halted. But other participants considered that gender issues needed to be integrated into each of the other three scenarios, rather than considered alone.

Following the workshop, the core team tested and refined the plausibility, relevance, and challenges of the three scenarios in a series of regional workshops. The communicability of the scenarios in relation to different communities was enhanced through the development of illustrative quantification of each scenario by UNAIDS epidemiologists, and this helped to work alongside another form of presenting the scenarios so they could also engage the varied storytelling cultures of Africa. A workshop in Cairo in October 2004 reworked the three scenarios into Sufi tales. A set of African folk tales, commissioned from a published African author, were included in the final report.

A series of private briefings were held for different partners and stakeholders in the run-up to the public presentation of the scenarios. Briefing sessions for staff of UNAIDS, the African Development Bank, SIDA (in Africa), UNDP, Shell International, Merck, Pfizer, CSIS, and the Office of the United States Global Coordinator on AIDS. These briefings provided valuable feedback on how to present the scenarios and also generated interest among key partners.

PUBLIC PRESENTATION AND COMMUNICATION

The scenarios were rendered public in a high-level meeting in Addis Ababa in March 2005, attended by numerous African political and religious dignitaries. This signaled the start of a wider roll-out process of engagement and communication.

A book, *AIDS in Africa: Three Scenarios to 2025* (see Figure D4), was printed in English, French, and Portuguese. The initial print runs of 10,000 copies in each language were quickly exhausted. The scenarios book was widely distributed, including to UNAIDS offices and partners across the world, including of course the African ones.

A set of PowerPoint presentations which explained the scenarios was produced. These presentations used the visual materials contained in the scenarios book. The presentation materials were also available to download from the UNAIDS website. A CD-ROM containing the scenarios book, PowerPoint presentations, background research papers and report, and supporting audio-visual material, was made widely available. A dedicated UNAIDS webpage was created for the publication event. Most

Figure D4.   Cover image of the AIDS in Africa scenarios book

of the project documents and material were made available through the UNAIDS website.

The publication of the report received extensive media coverage from all parts of the world, with over 200 articles and placements written about it. Senior staff of UNAIDS gave several interviews to the media.

The AiA scenarios

The three scenarios that were developed and adopted were:

In *Tough Choices*, antiretroviral therapy has been scaled up, from less than 5 percent treated at the start of the scenario to just over one-third by 2025. The roll out of antiretroviral therapy has increased steadily, reflecting the continued investment in health systems and training, as well as drugs manufacturing capacity within Africa. Compared to Traps and Legacies, an estimated 24 million HIV infections are averted over the next twenty years. Initiatives to support children orphaned by AIDS also increase, but the number of children orphaned by AIDS almost doubles by 2025. This scenario applied the trajectory of the most successful response to date at that time (in Uganda), adjusted for respective national levels of the epidemic.

Traps and Legacies is a scenario where AIDS has depleted resources and weakened infrastructure. As a result, AIDS deepens the traps of poverty, underdevelopment, and inequality. In this scenario, the HIV prevalence across the continent by 2025 remains at around 5 percent of the adult population, with some countries above or below this level. Life expectancy drops across many countries, and the number of people living with HIV in Africa increases considerably. This scenario, in effect, extrapolated then current trends until 2025. HIV prevention efforts are not effectively scaled up. Efforts to roll out antiretroviral therapy continue (over 20 percent of people who needed anti-retroviral therapy have access to it), but huge obstacles remain, including a combination of underdeveloped and overwhelmed systems, and escalating costs.

In *Times of Transition*, AIDS is seen as an exceptional crisis requiring an exceptional response. AIDS is viewed in its broader development context. A series of transitions occurs in the ways Africa and the rest of the world approach health, development, trade, and security. External aid increases considerably and there is sustained social and infrastructural investment. This scenario illustrated what might occur if a comprehensive prevention and treatment response were rolled out across Africa as quickly as possible. In this scenario, Africa's adult HIV prevalence rate drops considerably, external aid to Africa doubles, and antiretroviral coverage is approximately 70 percent by 2025. Compared to Traps and Legacies, an estimated forty-three million HIV infections are averted by 2025.

Overall, Traps and Legacies showed what might happen if there were inefficient domestic AIDS policies in Africa and volatile or declining external aid; Tough Choices showed what was possible when there were efficient domestic policies but stagnant external aid; and Times of Transition showed what might happen if there were more efficient domestic policies and increased and high-quality external aid. The scenarios suggested that while the worst of the epidemic's impact was still to come, there was still a great deal that could be done to change the longer-term trajectory of the epidemic and to minimize its impact.

Project results: uses, outcomes, consequences

The AiA scenario initiative invoked the future as a means to establish common ground among the different groups involved in and affected by HIV/AIDS in Africa. It also acted as a way to learn more about current reality and as a platform for mobilizing collective action.

It was the hope of the project initiators, participants, sponsors, and core team that this material would provide an essential starting point, not only for exploring and expanding people's understanding of the epidemic, but also for sharing that understanding with others and clarifying the role of poverty in the spread of infection within countries and across the continent.

The initial agreement of the project involved a commitment to a formal follow-on phase aimed at using the scenarios. It had been envisaged that UNAIDS would conduct a structured use of the scenarios in a large number of countries. But this follow-up project, which included an element of capacity building on scenario planning, never materialized, although UNAIDS did advocate for national governments to make use of the scenarios.

The scenarios reportedly were used by individual counties and the African Development Bank on a serendipitous basis. The scenarios book was distributed through the UNAIDS offices across the world and one of the most surprising uses of the book was by educators.

Michel Bartok, one of the core team members from the UNAIDS organization, provided the following reflection in 2010, five years after the project concluded:[3]

The AIDS in Africa Scenarios for the Future project was challenging to UNAIDS. We were not used to thinking that far into the future, and it was not easy to persuade the epidemiologists or those estimating resource needs within UNAIDS to make their estimations that far into the future. However, since the involvement of UNAIDS in the scenarios project there have been a number of changes in perspective which are along the lines suggested by the project's outcomes. One is a significant emphasis on long term vision in responding to AIDS, including the creation of the aids2031 initiative which is seeking to explicitly bring about such a long term vision. Another is a greater attention to the financing needs and impacts of combined prevention and treatment responses to AIDS, with a focus on 2015 and the Millennium Development Goals. A third is the emphasis on universal approaches to AIDS with the adoption internationally of universal access targets for AIDS prevention, treatment, care and support. Finally, there has been a growing sophistication in addressing the link between poverty, other forms of social inequity and AIDS, including a more confident assertion by UNAIDS that poverty is not a straightforward driver of HIV. None of these responses have been directly or explicitly tied to the results of the scenarios work, but may reflect some of the changes in thinking that the project was intended to stimulate.

More recently, Peter Piot reflected on the project as follows:[4]

Scenarios for AIDS in Africa was a unique approach to AIDS in Africa. It identified very relevant foresight scenarios, which inspired UNAIDS' policy development when I was Executive Director. However, the work had little traction at the time, probably because it was clearly ahead of its time. A similar reflection is greatly needed today now that the AIDS response has made major achievements, but remains fragile with an uncertain future in terms of societal and financial sustainability.

Implications

The technical complexities, as well as cultural and political sensitivities of the issues of an international project conducted under the gaze of public scrutiny, required transparent governance mechanisms to be established.

Selection of participants. A three-month search process was needed to identify suitable participants using ten selection criteria: gender, nationality, age, education/profession, connectedness to wider stakeholders, open-mindedness, creativity, ability to leave institutional hat at the door, commitment, and availability. The scenarios were built by a group of over 200 participants; nearly 90 percent came from twenty-four different countries in Africa, and the remaining 10 percent from Europe and North America. They included politicians, musicians, dancers, ministers, heads of AIDS programs, former street children, journalists, religious leaders, doctors and care givers, people living with HIV, scientists, and policymakers.

Governance structure. Oversight of financial expenditures and project management was also provided by an independent international advisory board, comprising representatives of the fifteen sponsors. However, from the very beginning it was made clear that this group would not be able to determine the content of the scenarios. Similarly, while the core team shared the responsibility for the process, the workshop participants took the lead in the shaping of the scenario content.

Even so, the challenges of engaging multiple stakeholders with multiple perspectives using scenarios is not without problems, as highlighted in a paper by one of the core team, Pieter Fourie, which outlines a number of key impressions, insights, and lessons learned from this unique scenario building process.

Continuity challenges. The project was initially designed as a one-year project, but slow fundraising, complex stakeholder selection processes, and unpredictable project delays (e.g. rescheduling a key workshop that was planned to take place in Côte d'Ivoire, due to the outbreak of civil war) extended it to nearly three years. In the interim, many key players on the advisory board and within the co-sponsoring organizations moved on to other roles, as is common in the rotation of staff in international organizations. As a result, the project scope and purpose had to be renegotiated on several occasions.

▓ FURTHER READING

Fourie, Pieter. 2004. "Multi-Stakeholders with Multiple Perspectives: HIV/AIDS in Africa." *Development*, 47: 54–9.

UNAIDS. 2005. *AIDS in Africa: Three Scenarios to 2025.* <http://data.unaids.org/Publications/IRC-pub07/jc1058-AIDSinafrica_en.pdf> (accessed September 2015).

▓ NOTES

1. Dr. Wilkinson was one of the co-directors of the AIDS in Africa project.
2. DFID is the UK Department for International Development; CIDA is the Canadian International Development Agency; SIDA is the Swedish International Development Agency; USAID is the US Agency for International Development.
3. Private email communication.
4. Email communication to case author, June 5, 2015.

■ APPENDIX E EUROPEAN PATENT OFFICE CASE STUDY

Shirin Elahi and Rafael Ramírez

Background

The European Patent Office (EPO) is one of the largest intellectual property (IP) organizations in the world. It is a financially and administratively independent, intergovernmental public service entity governed by its own treaty with its seat in Munich, and offices in The Hague, Berlin, Vienna, and Brussels.

The EPO currently has thirty-eight member states, including all the member states of the European Union. The EPO was established in 1977 along with the Administrative Council, made up of representatives of the contracting states. The Council supervises the EPO's activities.[1] The EPO is the outcome of the European countries' collective political determination to establish a uniform patent system in Europe.

The mission of the EPO is to grant European patents. Its core activities are the examination of patent applications and the granting of European patents. The EPO also provides patent information and training services. European patents are granted on the basis of harmonized law, codified in the European Patent Convention of 1973, which laid down a single unified procedure for the member states of the European Patent Organisation.

At the time the scenarios were commissioned, the EPO had the largest civilian database in Europe and was the largest client for major ICT equipment and service providers on the continent. After the European Commission, the EPO is the second-largest pan-European organization, with an annual budget in excess of €1,700 million. In 2006, it received more than 200,000 applications, granted close to 63,000 patents, and had a staff of over 6,000. By 2015, annual applications received had reached 270,000, and the number of staff had risen to 7,000 from over thirty-five countries.

The EPO has grown in size and influence since its inauguration. The most important factors influencing this growth are largely external: the immense success and influence of scientific endeavors, the interlinked and exponential expansion in technological innovation, and perhaps most importantly, the growth in international IP protection as a basis to do business and safeguard returns on investments in R&D.

Scenario project work

The fourth president of the EPO, Professor Alain Pompidou, took office on July 1, 2004, for a three-year term. He decided to use a scenario planning process to help him and other senior managers take stock of the changing and unpredictable external environment in which the EPO was operating. He commissioned a three-year Scenarios for the Future project.

New perceptions of the role of patents—their status as financial and legal assets—had led to a growing interest in the workings of the patent system. The system was no longer accepted unquestioningly, and fundamental issues were being raised: does the system (really) support innovation? Is the balance between the interests of developed and developing countries fair? Is the interest of the applicant and that of society balanced? Should some scientific research remain a common good? How might politics and economics affect IP's legitimacy? Debates about ethical issues were on the rise; according to some reports the biggest single user of the EPO's database at the time were not the counsels of the biggest patenting corporations, but Greenpeace activists!

Despite the fact that these questions had arisen, there had been little coherent reflection on the future of the patent system when Professor Pompidou took office. As he commented:

A key concern for the managers of the system is how best to safeguard its future and its custodians. When I took office as President of the EPO one of my first goals was to initiate a fresh look at the world around us to see how changes outside the system would impact on its future.[2]

It was in this context that the scenario planning project was initiated, and it was completed within the three-year term of Professor Pompidou's presidency. Its intended success criteria were:[3]

- Producing a shared vision/future direction between the board and senior management.
- Progress on understanding of the business and political worlds' needs in terms of patenting; and development of strategies to deal with these needs.
- Progress and concrete action on developing critical competences needed by the EPO in the future.
- Developing and implementing a platform for debate on the needs of the patent system among lawyers, businesspeople, politicians, and other interested parties.
- Encouraging business plans which address possible futures and focus more on the concept of creating value.
- Assuring an understanding of the EPO scenarios throughout the Office by mid-2005.
- Developing clear criteria for making decisions.

The project sought to take all perspectives into account, and the in-house team[4] conducting the scenario planning initiative initiated wide-ranging consultations with key thinkers from around the world. This included people whose opinions could inform, challenge, and confirm the ideas prevalent within the EPO. More than one hundred extensive and wide-ranging interviews were conducted, and the divergent views they reflected formed the building blocks for the scenarios that were subsequently built.

The EPO scenarios

The EPO scenarios sought to help the EPO's senior professionals to address two key questions:

- How might knowledge regimes evolve by 2025?
- What global legitimacy might such regimes have?

The conclusion in each scenario was that the world of patenting and IP could evolve in one of four directions. We present these here in terms of how each scenario proposed plausible change.

Market Rules. A gray world where business has become the dominant driver in shaping the EPO's context.

This scenario is a story of the consolidation of a patenting system so successful that it is collapsing under its own weight. New forms of subject matter—inevitably including further types of services—become patentable and more players enter the system. The balance of power is held by multinational corporations; with their resources to build powerful patent portfolios, they enforce their rights in an increasingly litigious world and drive the patenting agenda. A key goal for these firms is the growth of shareholder value. Patents become widely used as a financial tool to achieve that end. In the face of ever-increasing volumes of patent applications, various forms of rationalization of the system occur, and it moves to mutual recognition of harmonized patent rights. The market decides the fate of the system, with minor regulation of visible excesses. Patent trolling, anticompetitive behavior, and standards issues all come under scrutiny. The courts become overburdened and patenting processes slow down.

Whose Game? A red world where geopolitics has become the dominant driver in shaping the EPO's context.

This scenario is the story of a boomerang effect which strikes dominant players in the patent world as a result of changing geopolitical balances and competing ambitions. The developed world increasingly fails to use IP to maintain technological superiority; new entrants try to catch up so they can improve their citizens' living standards. But many developing-world countries are excluded from the process, and work instead within a "communal knowledge" intellectual capital paradigm. Nations and cultures compete. The new entrants become increasingly successful at shaping the evolution of the IP system, using it to establish economic advantage, forcing an adaptation of the existing rules as their geopolitical influence grows. Enforcement becomes increasingly difficult, and the IP world becomes more fragmented. Attempts are made to address the issues of development and technology transfer.

Trees of Knowledge. A green world where society has become the dominant driver in shaping the EPO's context.

In this scenario story, diminishing societal trust and growing criticism of the IP system result in its gradual erosion. The key players are popular movements—often coalitions of civil society, businesses, concerned governments, and individuals—seeking to challenge existing norms. This "kaleidoscope" variety in society means that while the social fabric has become fragmented it also reunites, issue by issue, crisis by crisis—coming together episodically against real and perceived threats to human needs such as access to health, knowledge, food, and entertainment. Multiple voices and multiple worldviews feed popular attention and interest, with the media playing an active role in encouraging debate. This loose "knowledge movement" echoes the environmental movement of the 1980s, initially sparked by small, established special interest groups but slowly gaining momentum and raising wider awareness through alliances such as the A2K (Access to Knowledge) movement. The main issue has become how to ensure that knowledge remains a common good, while acknowledging the legitimacy of reward for innovation.

> *Blue Skies*. A blue world where technology has become the dominant driver in shaping the EPO's context.

This scenario story revolves around a split in the patent system. Societal reliance on technology and growing systemic risks force this change; the key players are technocrats and politicians responding to global crises. Complex new technologies based on a highly cumulative innovation process have come to be seen as the key to solving systemic problems such as climate change; and diffusion of technology in these fields is of paramount importance. The IP needs of these new technologies come increasingly into conflict with the needs of classic, discrete technologies. In the end, the patent system responds to the speed, interdisciplinarity, and complex nature of the new technologies by abandoning the one-size-fits-all model of patenting: the former patent regime still applies to classic technologies whereas the new technologies use other forms of IP protection, such as the license of rights. The patent system increasingly relies on technology, and new forms of knowledge search and classification emerge.

Project results: uses, outcomes, consequences

The EPO scenarios were made public in May 2007. As described internally:

> The results of the three-year Scenarios for the Future project will be presented to the public for the first time at the Forum, which will also kick-off the EPO's 30th anniversary celebrations.
> The interviewees from the Scenarios project have been invited to take part in the conference and the event promises to be a veritable "who's who" in the world of IP. German Chancellor Angela Merkel and Ged Davis, Managing Director of the World Economic Forum, have agreed to speak at the event.[5]

The published EPO *Scenarios for the Future* report was received with wide acclaim in professional IP circles. Some examples are:

- The IP journal *Intellectual Asset Management* commented that "the publication of the Scenarios Project . . . will inform patent policy making in Europe and beyond for years to come."[6]
- The Foundation for a Free Information Infrastructure described the EPO scenarios as a "grand report about the current state of the patent system and predictions for the next 20 years."
- A director of IT Corporate Standards wrote to say that the report "will become mandatory reading in my group—it is excellent and thoughtful presentation on a complex and contentious subject."
- A book on patents issued soon after said: "Whilst no one can predict with one-hundred percent certainty what the future entails, these scenarios provide key

illustrations as to what we can expect based on current trends and conceptions" (O'Connell 2008).

- In the midst of a debate about the impact of the patent system, the executive secretary of the Convention on Biological Diversity commented that the EPO scenarios project "is a very valuable exercise in gathering a large body of evidence and opinions in order to open space for creative thinking. In practice, the report highlights the desirability of an increasing range of choices and models through which knowledge and resources might be made available to serve a variety of purposes." (Oldham 2007).

The scenarios were widely cited and used. They were used in many different policy-making forums across the world—European, Japanese, Chinese, Brazilian, and others. They were translated by different groups into other languages, notably into Chinese[7] and Japanese;[8] in English, Google listed 7,910 results in January 2015. The EPO scenarios were used as a prism to guide reflections on where IP issues are a central concern by many other actors; for example, on synthetic biology (Rutz 2007) and regarding the role of standards.[9] In the academic field, in January 2015 thirty-six peer reviewed scholarly articles cited the EPO scenarios, and they have been the empirical basis of at least one doctoral dissertation (Lang 2012).

The scenarios also found a role in the civil society space, where they were used and disseminated in the field of development by various politically active NGO groups. For example, a major publication by Public Interest Intellectual Property Advisors (Wong and Dutfield 2011) analyzed them, and found that the scenarios demonstrated certain shortcomings and gaps that they considered limited their usefulness for developing countries and for future non-profit interventions, namely: the high level of abstraction rendering the application of concrete strategic solutions difficult; the peripheral focus on developing countries; the lack of acknowledgment of the dynamics of least developed countries within a IP global system; and including too little on the issue of capacity building necessary to enable these players and developing country stakeholders to act effectively within the IP arena. However, one group of authors concluded:

Despite these shortcomings, the EPO report stands alone as a uniquely detailed and creative evaluation, based on extensive research and a wide range of viewpoints on the options facing society and their potentially fateful consequences. Future scenario planning projects relating to IP will benefit greatly from the pioneering effort reflected in the EPO report. (Gollin et al. 2011)

According to a key EPO official who advised President Pompidou and his successor, the scenarios played a role in the EPO's strategic renewal, including a strategy debate with member states, establishing a European Patent Network, enabling the introduction of an internal Raising the Bar program to reduce the number of trivial patents clogging the IP system, accelerating and influencing the introduction of an end-to-end digitization program to produce patenting with zero paper emission. The scenarios project also prompted a rebranding of the EPO and a revision of the EPO's mission statement. The scenarios themselves appeared in countless (external) publications on IP and the so-called "IP5" coalition of five leading patenting offices (EPO, USPTO, the Japanese, Korean, and Chinese patenting offices) in several languages, and helped the case for cooperation among the five major patent offices.[10] Moreover, the scenarios were embraced by Pompidou's successor, Alison Brimelow, who gave them wider internal as well as external distribution.

The scenarios also played an important role in enhancing the EPO's reputation as a thought leader, and in bolstering the credibility of its role at a time when it was promoting major change to the patent system. The scenario planning effort of the EPO has been credited as having supported (according to some observers,[11] having had a "critical" role) the coming about of two major institutional innovations: (1) the London Protocol, an optional agreement aiming at reducing the costs relating to the translation of European patents;[12] and (2) the so-called Unitary Patent,[13] a European patent that would protect an invention in twenty-five countries with unitary effect and a unified European patent court, something that had been in protracted negotiations for several decades.

The contents of the EPO scenario planning that were rendered public also encouraged EPO senior managers to speak out on IP issues such as "global patent warming" and the conflict between IP and competition law; and helped the EPO to establish institutional links with the WEF, the OECD, and the United Nations (for green technology). As one IP journal commented:

Of course, setting policy is not the EPO's role; as the executive arm of the European Patent Organization, its main job is to examine applications and to grant European patents. But there is a sense that with these scenarios it is trying to set the agenda, to carve out a place for itself as a leader rather than a mere jobsworth.[14]

The EPO also took some substantive actions in the wake of its scenario planning project. For instance, the issue of technology transfer was so contentious, both politically and economically, in advance of the global climate change negotiations of 2010 that the EPO cooperated with the United Nations Environmental Program and the International Centre on Trade and Sustainable Development to produce a study on Patents and Clean Energy, and also to introduce a new patent classification system for climate change mitigation technologies.[15]

Implications

The EPO scenarios highlighted several key challenges to the patent system. One of these was the issue of patenting in an age of interdisciplinarity, and the Blue Skies scenario discussed a move from a "one-size-fits-all" model to a license of rights or "soft-IP" model.[16] The soft-IP approach created great interest, and companies such as IBM lobbied hard to create a modification of the patent system.

Traditionally, the world of patents had been predominantly, if not uniquely, viewed through the familiar lens of the gray Market Rules scenario. However, the scenario planning process with which the EPO engaged the IP world demonstrated that it could be quite unwise not to take a much wider perspective into account: the other three scenarios revealed further dimensions that had all too often been overlooked by the IP system, possibly bringing forth unnecessary distractions, and even dangers. The EPO scenario planning helped its senior staff to conclude that the patent system was far too complex, and the issues far too diverse, for any single group of stakeholders to decide its future. Some professionals found this disorienting, and were frustrated that the scenarios were not intended to prescribe solutions, but simply to provide the right questions for input into the policymaking process. The scenario planning exercise of the EPO achieved its goal of encouraging courageous reflection; it stimulated more informed debate, and it increased the understanding of a system where issues are not simple, but caught in a complex system linking a vast array of forces.

Yet the important political dimension that the EPO scenario planning achieved did not last as an ongoing process. Six years later, in 2014, after the two presidents had departed, the EPO retreated back to its core business—patent examination and granting—and its current management's attention is on efficiency, that is, delivering more value for money.

▩ NOTES

1. Technically, the overarching body is the European Patent Organisation. See <http://www.epo.org/about-us/organisation.html> (accessed September 2015).
2. Alain Pompidou (2006).
3. Scenario Proposal to EPO Board; December 17, 2003, by C. McGinley, Controller.
4. With support and advice from NormannPartners.
5. *EPO Gazette*, January 4, 2007.
6. *Intellectual Asset Management*, December 30, 2007. <http://www.iam-magazine.com/blog/detail.aspx?g=e07b99a6-7990-485a-a1a7-ac65402c4ab9> (accessed September 2015).
7. *EPO Gazette*, August 12–September 1: 12. The EPO scenarios were used as the basis for the NBER study *Standards, Stakeholders, and Innovation: China's Evolving Role in the Global Knowledge Economy*. Kennedy et al. (2008).
8. Initially published as IIP (2009) *Kiro ni Tatsu Tokkyo Seido (Patent System Stands in Front of Crisis)*; and later Ryo Shimanami (2012) *The Future of the Patent System*.
9. See note 7, this chapter.
10. C. McGinley, Presentation to Saïd Business School, University of Oxford, April 22, 2013.
11. (Anonymous) personal communication.
12. Agreement on the application of Article 65 EPC—London Agreement. <http://www.epo.org/law-practice/legal-texts/london-agreement.html> (accessed September 2015).
13. Refer to <http://www.epo.org/news-issues/issues/unitary-patent.html> (accessed September 2015).
14. *Intellectual Asset Management*, June/July 2007.
15. <http://www.unep.ch/etb/events/UNEP%20EPO%20ICTSD%20Event%2030%20Sept%202010%20Brussels/Brochure_EN_ganz.pdf> (accessed September 2015); see also Veefkind et al. (2012).
16. According to Wikipedia, *soft intellectual property* is a "proposed system that would enable [the] capture and protection of IP, with provision for making licenses available to all interested parties. This is particularly applicable to patents." The authors of the Wikipedia entry credit the EPO for the term, which was first introduced at the European Patent Forum in Munich in April 2007 when the EPO scenarios were launched. Refer to <http://en.wikipedia.org/wiki/Soft_IP> (accessed September 2015).

▪ APPENDIX F RISK-WORLD SCENARIOS CASE STUDY

Angela Wilkinson and Esther Eidinow

Background

In 2002, four organizations—two private firms and two from the public sector—established an informal partnership to develop a set of scenarios to cultivate a broader and shared understanding of a topic of common interest, namely, the shifting nature and role of risk in society.

The organizations involved were: the EPO; the UK Health and Safety Executive (HSE); Shell International, then part of the Shell Group of Companies and now part of Royal Dutch Shell; and EDF.

The initiative was conducted against the backdrop of what was then a recent spate of public and private sector risk-related scandals: for example, Enron, WorldCom, Brent Spar, the UK "mad cow" disease crisis, and the terrorist attack on the World Trade Center (9/11).

Scenario project work

Each of the organizations involved had a recognized source of expertise in risk management. The scenario work was conducted as a collaborative, interdisciplinary inquiry seeking to make sense of different perspectives on the inherently social conceptualization of risk. Available research on the topic was found to be fragmented across diverse fields of scholarship.

Shell International had achieved success in managing the technological, financial, and environmental risks of oil and gas extraction and production. It was, however, grappling with new forms of risk—including so-called "intangible" risk—and had recently suffered a crisis in reputational risk following public controversy in Germany and the UK over its decision to decommission Brent Spar, one of its North Sea oil platforms and storage buoys, in 1995.[1]

The intended scenario users at Shell were other members of Shell International's Global Business Environment team, who were themselves engaged in other scenario-based initiatives. They also provided strategic analyses and advice to Shell executives across the company. For example, the "Shell scenario team" were helping senior decision makers across the company to develop and use their own bespoke scenarios (often translated and transplanted from the global scenarios; see Appendix B) so that they could become (re)focused on business units, and on regional and country-specific operations. The Risk-World scenarios were also intended to inform the development of a new set of "global scenarios" to support the executive team and a process of corporate strategy.

The UK HSE was in the process of updating its policy framework on Tolerability of Risk, and was seeking a way to engage with wider expert perspectives on risk across a range of different disciplines and professions.

For the EPO, the main reason for its involvement in the project was a growing realization of the economic (as opposed to the technical) purpose of the patent system. This came at a time when the EPO was developing a new mission statement: "The mission of the European Patent Office—the patent granting authority for Europe—is to support innovation, competiveness and economic growth for the benefit of the citizens of Europe." The Risk-World project represented an opportunity for the EPO to explore the world of business purpose and how it could support the effective management of economic risks in the European economy.[2]

EDF's interest was to develop insights that could be fed into its corporate strategic planning process by members of its corporate risk management system. Despite their different individual situations and interests, there was agreement from the start among the four sponsoring organizations that shared insights from the project would also be made more generally available, that is, published in an academic and/or practitioner journal.

Scenario building process

The Risk-World scenario building project was conducted between February 2002 and February 2003 and consisted of four key phases:

1. *Orientation.* The first phase comprised an open search for relevant topics, themes, factors, assumptions, dilemmas, and questions. Project staff used a "snowball" process to identify key experts and stakeholders, starting with an initial email enquiry sent to a list of over 250 recognized experts drawn from across the fields of risk-related research. In parallel, the core project team, made up of two Shell scenario planning professionals and one senior professional from each of the other three organizations, conducted twenty-two open-ended interviews with selected representatives of the four sponsoring organizations.
2. *Exploration.* The second phase comprised a series of interviews with experts drawn from across the fields of risk-related research, coupled with a literature search. The aim was to broaden and deepen understanding of relevant factors, trends, and uncertainties. Interviews with thirty-eight experts explored in greater depth the drivers of change and uncertainties emerging from the analysis of the sponsor interviews. The expert interviews were also intended to help identify additional themes and topics not raised by the sponsor interviews.
3. *Building.* The third phase consisted of a two-day workshop involving representatives of the sponsoring organizations and invited experts. The aim of the workshop was to build a set of outline scenarios. Following the workshop, the project team engaged in follow-up discussions with participants to clarify and enrich the scenarios. The scenario building took place during a follow-up two-day workshop, held in late 2002 in Lincolnshire, UK. The core activity was small group work in which the participants first created a set of short stories about the future of societal risk, then in discussions focused on identifying the key factors and actors that would be

most influential in shaping societal risk perception and management over the next twenty years. Six critical uncertainties were identified. Finally, they agreed on three sketch scenarios. Following the workshop, the project team engaged in follow-up discussions with selected experts and sponsors in order to clarify and enrich the sketch scenarios, in a process that iterated between storyline development and systems thinking—see Figure F1. The scenarios were developed using the inductive building method; each was preceded by a scenario "vignette" evoking characters from that future.

4. *Engagement and communication.* The final phase involved publication of the three scenarios as the core content of a special issue of the *Journal of Risk Research*, and a public presentation of the scenarios. The final draft of the scenarios, including the dynamics, structures, and storylines, was circulated for comment among a number of leading experts in the fields of risk management. The comments returned provided the equivalent of editorial peer review and were published, together with the scenarios, in the special issue of the journal. In addition to publication, the scenarios were presented publicly in June 2003 at an event hosted by the King's Centre for Risk Management, King's College, London. The format of the presentation included actors performing scenes based on each scenario vignette.

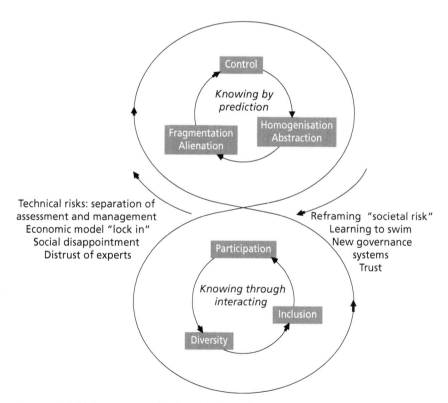

Figure F1. Initial system map developed in the Risk-World scenario planning project

The Risk-World scenarios

The three scenarios developed by the sponsors and workshop participants of the Risk-World project were called: Expert Rules, Common Sense, and Kaleidoscope. The time horizon was 2020. Each scenario depicted a different path society might follow as it copes with an environment characterized by increasing uncontrollable risks and awareness of risk. The following summaries are drawn from the 2003 *Journal of Risk Research* special issue.[3]

In *Expert Rules* the emphasis was on achieving global governance of man-made and natural systems in a world of increasing global connectivity and rapid technological innovation. Urban global society has come to perceive and experience similar risks across the world. Uncertainty about the effects of complex systems is acknowledged but considered too difficult to deal with. Society focuses on managing those risks for which there is concrete evidence of harm, relying on experts to assess what kinds of risks specific products or policies might bring and suggest general management approaches. It is accepted that unexpected events will happen, and crisis management has become a highly prized skill.

In this scenario, risk framing is separated from risk management. Risk *framing* takes place at two levels: the official expert analysis, and the "undertow" that is always preparing to challenge the status quo. Since the power base of the elite is under regular challenge, policy and regulation tends toward short-term results rather than sustained change. Risk *management* occurs at a very general level and no attempt is made to manage different kinds or levels of risks for individuals; increasing knowledge of individual genetics makes it clear that this would be impossible. Instead, people demand individualized risk-management options, such as personalized insurance policies. Although this is a world of expert opinion, evidence, and rules, the whole system depends on maintaining reasonable levels of trust between the different parts of society. At times, trust swings like a pendulum away from independent expertise to those espousing more emotive rationales—and then back again.

This scenario's vignette depicts the editor of a newspaper, the *People's Savior*, who regards his publication as "a guardian of the populace," publishing stories about companies that have failed to pay attention to all the potential risk aspects of any new product. The vignette describes one of his recent campaigns, against BabyBrain, a leading educational toy company which has not carried out the requisite tests on its latest doll. It also describes possible future campaigns, for example, against the development of the National Database for Genetic Diversity. In the course of this account, we hear about his perception of what the public wants—"it was the burning question of liability that fired people up!"—and the tools he uses to mine for information, including not only the patent office website, but also new organizations like ProductWitness.com, which lists products not properly labeled for the end-user.

In *Common Sense*, society has come to value cohesion and aspires to greater geopolitical cooperation. People expect that technology or scientific advances will allow them to fix risks, but they also understand these approaches will be considered legitimate if a wider range of people are involved in the decisions to use them. This creates an opportunity for direct citizen involvement in the framing and management of risks: panels or juries of citizens make the key decisions about what risks are important to society and how to approach them. It becomes a citizen's duty to take part in these processes. Rather than making decisions directly, regulatory agencies enable the decisions made by the panels. At a global level, panels comprising representatives of different cultures deliberate on risks.

The essential democratic processes, comprising direct involvement, mean that no single individual or organization is entitled to make trade-offs; the balance of opportunity for change and innovation is determined more broadly and inclusively. Broad recognition that there are many different perspectives and ways of knowing highlights the need to establish a common frame of reference (the new "common sense") to secure acceptable risk management for society. Rules and values determine trade-offs, and anyone in a position of power—whether legislator or artist—can act as an influential thought leader and behavioral role model.

Although recognizing the importance of different perceptions and contexts, risk framing is still separate from risk management. With risks seen as continually changing and evolving, decisions are revisited after a certain period of time. On the whole, governmental decisions have become much more widely accepted than previously (higher social efficiency), but can take quite a long time to complete (this became faster as information and communications technologies develop over time).

The role of the newly formed National Representation Agency is explored in this scenario's vignette. In the story, the Agency was started in order to institutionalize a new approach to risk, ensuring that risk-framing and risk-management decisions reflected society's expectations and norms. An example of its work includes organizing a number of culturally diverse global panels of representatives to participate in the creation of several agreements concerned with the risks and values of genetically modified crops. The vignette also raises the question of representation, focusing on a debate that has developed around the inclusion of fourteen-year-olds on the Risk Framing and Management Boards of the Agency.

In *Kaleidoscope*, people recognize the value of maintaining many different ways of perceiving and managing risks, and the dangers of uniform or imposed risk management approaches. There is widespread understanding and acceptance of the value of self-organization. Patterns of social and technological connectivity continually shift and change.

Communities develop portfolios of approaches to risk, many of which emphasize social innovation; that is, that a society can and should change and adapt itself in response to risks rather than seeking a single techno-fix. Precaution promotes, rather than inhibits, the pursuit of technological as well as social innovation. Since the need for ecological resilience has been established as the primary criterion for social and economic development, there is growing awareness of the inseparability of risk assessment and risk management, and the need for reflective adaptation.

Within each community of interest, risks are examined holistically, and approaches vary from community to community. Authority is decentralized and this releases innovative energy. Lots of local experiments erupt, exhibiting great social and technological diversity, and a wide array of different risk-coping mechanisms flourish. Communities unite around a vision rather than focusing on their individual vulnerabilities.

Such diversity does make more high-level risk management difficult, but most communities trade what they have learned about different coping mechanisms and do manage to negotiate mutually beneficial agreements about the risks they share. In addition, observing and learning from others in this way helps each community to remain aware of its own implicit assumptions about risk and become more prepared to change them, rather than becoming locked into one way of thinking.

The scenario vignette for *Kaleidoscope* is a section of an online thread, a discussion between members of the West Coast Network Community Resilience History Group. The group are introduced to Sasha, a spokesman for Membrain, an award-winning executive wetware training company offering a range of interactive programs, simulations, and educational packages. He describes some of their products, including The Dance of Resilience intended to help participants improve their perception and enhance their approaches to resilience. This is one of the first in Membrain's Catalogue of Products to Improve Approaches to Adaptation. Sasha's presentation becomes a discussion of the historical changes in attitudes toward uncertainty and risk; the Resilience Group looks back on how an increasingly turbulent global environment prompted the emergence of community-level action.

A comparison of the three scenarios, used in internal project presentations, is shown in Table F1.

Project results: uses, outcomes, consequences

The Risk-World scenarios were developed for the purpose of shared sensemaking, and—if necessary and relevant—reframing, rather than as quantified decision support tools. Furthermore, each participating organization applied the learning and insights they each derived from this collaborative inquiry to different processes internally. As such, there was no specific after-action evaluation process.

According to the EPO's principal director of patent administration, Ciaran McGinley,[4] for the EPO the most lasting impact of Risk-World and the whole idea of looking at the patent-granting process as a way of managing economic risks was evident in October 2002 in the EPO president's submission to the Administrative Council of EPO's member states. The strong influence of the Risk-World scenario work is especially evident in the early chapters (pages 4–8) of this extensive policy paper.[5]

The relevant insights derived by the Shell staff engaged in the Risk-World initiative were communicated and discussed with other Shell team members as part of the regular, ongoing research and exchange of the global scenario team. The fingerprints of the Risk-World's three alternative systems of future risk governance can be detected in the triangular trade-offs framework in the 2005 Shell Global Scenarios.

In addition, the participating Shell staff presented the Risk-World scenarios to various expert risk communities. Some groups were more receptive than others. Chris Bunting, former secretary-general of the International Risk Governance Council, said:[6] "Risk-World was an important effort. Several of IRGC's key players were impressed by the Risk-World scenarios report, and it certainly informed early IRGC thinking on where to focus and how best to add value." However, those wedded to

Table F1. Draft comparison matrix of the scenarios developed by the core team after the expert building workshop

Scenario name*	Expert Rules (Tower of Babylon)	Common Sense (Chorus of Voices)	Kaleidoscope
What beliefs and rationalities have most influence?	In an era of information overload, data abundance, and demand for individualized market-based coping mechanisms, independent experts are best placed to make wiser decisions about the most effective ways to achieve economic growth	There is monopoly on wisdom in a multipolar world and managing global concerns involves attention to the diversity of culture and values	In the search for ecological resilience, societal resilience is the key policy criterion and is defined in terms of the ability to self-organize, avoidance of technology monocultures, uninvesting in redundancy, and the ability to switch strategies
Who is entitled or empowered to shape the trade-offs?	Pendulum of trust swings between civil society-states-markets	Representation of societal diversity is essential to ensuring value-at-risk in global value chains relates to local societal needs and values	Bifurcation into more global and more local, with weaker role for leadership from central governments: transnational coalitions of global-to-local actor networks
How is issue framing driven and enacted?	Risk framing and risk management are separate processes to ensure truth speaks to power	Risk framing and management have to be integrated to identify acceptable trade-offs	Flourishing and diversity of new approaches and reflexive adaptation to coping with accelerating complexity and deep uncertainty

* Earlier title of scenario in brackets

conventional probabilistic modeling approaches to risk, such as financial analysts, tended to be resistant to the scenarios and their message.

Implications

If there was a key learning from the Risk-World process design, it was that the enrichment and clarification of sketch scenarios benefit from real-time, face-to-face exchange between the scenario builders and the users. In the project, the draft scenarios were sent to the workshop participants by email for comment. However, this process failed to catalyze the enrichment and clarification of the scenarios that can be more typically achieved at a workshop.

Furthermore, the project sponsors delayed discussing the possible implications of the final set of scenarios until after they were submitted for publication. Final drafting and discussion of the initial implications are usually brought together in a workshop to enable the scenario stories to be fine tuned, to create relevance and resonance with the community(ies) who will be using them. However, this was not possible given that the initial user community was dispersed across four different organizations.

Despite these limitations, the Risk-World scenario project enabled the communities of experts involved in academic risk research and those advising on risk management policy to be brought together and to reflect on what really matters concerning societal risk perception and management. Evidence of this is provided by expert reviews and comments on the scenarios included in the *Journal of Risk Research* special issue.[7]

■ FURTHER READING

The full set of scenarios, a description of the scenario building process, together with a summary of individual interviews conducted on this project, is available in the public domain.

Journal of Risk Research, 6(4–6), 2003. <http://www.tandfonline.com/toc/rjrr20/6/4-6> (accessed September 2015).

Mastering the Workload, EPO Report CA/132/02, Munich, October 8, 2002.

■ NOTES

1. There are several descriptions and analyses of this incident. See, for example, Elkington and Trisoglio (1996).
2. This is described in the EPO sponsor comments to the Risk-World project, co-written by Leo Giannotti and Cieran McGinley. See the *Journal of Risk Research* special issue on the Risk-World scenarios project (volume 6, issues 4–6, 2003: 591–4).
3. *Journal of Risk Research*, 6(4–6), 2003: 305–7.
4. Private correspondence by email, February 9, 2015.
5. *Mastering the Workload*, EPO policy paper CA/132/02, Munich, October 8, 2002.
6. Private correspondence.
7. See also the citations to the Risk-World scenarios in other journal articles at: <https://scholar.google.co.uk/scholar?biw=723&bih=520&bav=on.2,or.r_qf.&bvm=bv.85464276,d.d2s&um=1&ie=UTF-8&lr&cites=5022774840065166914> (accessed September 2015).

■ GLOSSARY

Italicized terms have their own definitions in the glossary.

Term	Definition
Backcasting	A process that starts by identifying a vision of the future and then working backward in time from that future to the present to identify what would have to happen—i.e. policies and programs—to make progress along the direction of change implied to achieve the vision. A scenario version of backcasting involves considering here and now implications of possible future scenarios. In this book this is done through *downframing*.
Boundary conditions	The context within which something is possible, beyond which it becomes impossible.
Business idea	Denotes the dominating logic of value creation that forms the backbone for a given business system and its context. In this book we suggest that this can be better appreciated through *upframing*.
Causal Textures Theory	Emery and Trist (1965) first proposed that various causal textures of an organization's environment are possible, depending on complexity and experienced uncertainty. Each texture—placid-random, placid-clustered, disturbed-reactive, turbulent—has distinctive features and implications for strategic responses. The most complex and most uncertain environment they termed the *turbulent* environment, although others later postulated the possibility of "hyper-turbulent" (McCann and Selsky, 1984) and "vortical" (Baburoglu, 1988) environments.
Contextual environment	The broader environment that is beyond the direct and indirect influence of a strategist—or more generally, an actor (or set of actors). It can only be appreciated as factors that comprise it in relationship to that actor(s). It is located beyond an organization's *transactional environment*.
Contradictory certitudes	These arise where differences, assumptions, or frameworks are incommensurable. They typically reflect deeper differences in underlying worldviews.
Critical uncertainties	Factors in the *contextual environment* that, alone or in conjunction, can drive significant change in the *transactional environment* of the scenario learner. They are used to develop a set of challenging, relevant, and plausible scenarios.

(*continued*)

Continued

Term	Definition
Cycle	A complete learning loop of *reframing-reperception*.
Downframing	Testing a newly framed perspective on the ground; rehearsing the future, perhaps through immersive role playing or war-gaming. Done, in particular, not only to verify how things work out by simulating actions and interactions as they unfold in a scenario, or developing the relevant prototypes, but also to assess how the scenario framing feels. See Normann (2001).
Epistemology	The branch of philosophy concerned with knowing, particularly its limits and validity. "An" epistemology refers to a particular theory of how minds know.
Forecasting	To throw (or "cast") the past forward (fore-ward); to extrapolate and project the existing knowledge about the present situation, or evidence from the past, into the future, typically with no breaks in logic allowed. In the OSPA, scenarios are not developed from forecasting, but can improve forecasting's assumptions.
Frame; framing	A lens, device, or type of filter that both includes and excludes. A frame and the process of framing directs what attention focuses on, and determines what remains peripherally attended to—and even out of the frame altogether. Frames and framing help the mind to order experiences; they also manifest what has been implicitly or subconsciously attended to—and not. *Reframing* involves considering alternative frames.
Horizon scanning	An aspect of the scenario planning process where attention is given to possible signals of change in the *contextual environment* relevant to the scenario learner's concerns. It involves search (looking for signals that might disconfirm what is known) and scanning (identifying more unfamiliar developments which may be awkwardly labeled and difficult to interpret).
Iteration	A repeat or successive round of the scenario planning *reframing-reperception* loop.
Knightian uncertainty	Economist Frank Knight proposed the term "uncertainty" to differentiate it from calculable "risk." Uncertainty is not measurable and thus cannot be calculated. In this book it is taken to be unpredictable in this sense, but uncertain events and states of a system can be imagined. A key feature of *turbulent* environments.
Memorability	The quality or state of being easy to remember or worth remembering. Stories and pictures make descriptions more easily memorable.
Memories of the future	A term coined by Ingvar (1985) to demonstrate that scenarios are housed in the same part of the brain as memory of past events, and thus lend themselves to *memorability*.

Method	A set of techniques, tools, and processes that articulate a *methodology* in practice.
Methodology	A process or procedural manifestation of a given *epistemology* comprised of a particular set of methods, rules, techniques, tools, procedures, and/or ideas.
Mind	The functioning of perception and conception with the central nervous system. Mind tends to focus on the brain but extends to other parts of the body as well (includes gut feelings).
Mindfulness	The attending to the working of the *mind*, typically associated with attention and focus. It can redirect, attending explicitly to what is within a *frame* and how this shapes perception. Mindfulness can help to "change one's mind."
Ontology	The branch of philosophy concerned with being and existence independent from a knowing mind. Related to metaphysics, this part of philosophy is concerned with the basic causes and nature of things.
Perception	See *reperception*.
Phenomenology	The philosophical study of structures of consciousness and experiences from the first-person point of view. It seeks through systematic reflection to determine the essential properties and structures of experience and the phenomena that appear in acts of consciousness. It is important for ascertaining the possibility(ies) of free will and intentionality—or, as argued in this book, for learners to be purposeful.
Plausibility	In the OSPA, plausibility refers to a shared perception that a future situation—i.e. something yet to occur—is considered to be a credible possibility in the absence of conclusive evidence. In the OSPA, plausibility is established by two or more scenario learners with the help of *storylines* and *system maps*.
Predetermined elements	Assumptions about what will happen in future that are maintained as common to all the scenarios in a set. For example, continued trends such as population aging or the assumption that the spread of the HIV/AIDS virus does not become airborne in the next twenty years. Pierre Wack (1985b) also used the term "sticky tendencies" to describe the elements of change assumed within the scenario planning process to be a common feature of all the scenarios.
Reframing	A learning process in which contrasting *frames* are used in a process of strategic conversation to develop new, shared insights about an existing situation. Reframing involves at least two frames, and the comparison helps scenario learners to attend to the deeper assumptions of how the world works which is implied by each frame. To enable reframing, the contrasting frames must be perceived as plausible by the *scenario learner*.

(continued)

Continued

Term	Definition
Reperception	Perception is a continuous sensemaking process, a subliminal human cognitive activity that contributes to tacit knowledge. A perception has to be "wrapped" or "held" with symbols (pictures, music, words, etc.) to be cognized and shared as in-form-ation. Perception is enabled within a pre-existing interpretive schema, or *frame*, which takes the form of a mental model, worldview, or myth that usually remains implicit. *R*eperception thus involves a cognitive shift (in scenario planning helped with *reframing*), where the mental model held by a given learner can be altered. Reperception is sometimes referred to as the "aha" moment in a scenario planning intervention. Pierre Wack (1985b) called scenario planning the "gentle art of reperceiving." In this book we suggest that reperception happens when scenario learners have the opportunity to immerse themselves in each scenario *story* to explore new and better options, i.e. what Normann (2001) referred to as *downframing* in strategy.
Scenario learners	The active participants in a scenario planning process. They may include people who can learn with and from a set of scenarios but who were not involved in their development. In the OSPA, "learning" is a process where new understanding is obtained when mismatches between outcomes and expectations are reconciled; the new understanding is obtained either by revising how outcomes are produced, how expectations are made, or how the two are made to align (based on Argyris and Schön 1978).
State domain	The description of a situation that uses variables (i.e. stocks and flows) to develop an understanding of causal linkages of the relevant system, i.e. to develop a systemic understanding. A description of variables at a specific point of time, e.g. the end of the scenario time horizon. See also *system map*.
Story	A recounting of a sequence of events. In the OSPA, a scenario is a story of what might happen, and it is in the form of an "open" story, i.e. it's not designed to be remembered verbatim but to provide a sense of a different context into which the scenario leaners can conceptually immerse themselves to *reperceive* something. Learners can further develop or adapt the story to share it with other *scenario learners*.
Storyline	A description of the sequence of events (including who is doing what to whom) that provide the narrative and plot of a story, i.e. the logic in/of the story of how actors, events, and things relate to each other in time and space.

Story map	A series of events (typically a combination of factors and actors) in a scenario story displayed in a time sequence; also called an "event map," where the interlinked elements make up the scenario's *time domain*. Story maps are the "bones" or "skeleton" of a story and often feature in the published manifestation of the scenario, as in the Wärtsilä and UEG examples in Appendices A and C of this book.
Strategic framing contest	A situation in which those who adhere to two (or more) seemingly incompatible frames disagree, and make the disagreement a zero-sum game because each party fails to understand the *plausibility* of the alternative frame(s).
System map	A diagram showing how a set of factors and (from the factors, as needed) actors in a scenario relate to each other logically or causally. The map links factors as a *state domain*, which helps to establish if such a domain might be plausible, and how it might lock-in and become stabilized.
Time horizon	The interval of time over which the *storyline* of each scenario needs to be developed to meet the purpose of the scenario learner; the endpoint date of the scenario storylines.
Tacit knowledge	Knowledge derived from a form of *mindfulness* of which one is unaware, but which can be elicited and made explicit.
Time domain	The description of a situation that uses time intervals to punctuate causal logic, e.g. what happens at the start, middle, and end of the scenario *storyline*. See *story map*.
Transactional environment	The immediate environment one (self, organization, multi-stakeholder body) is in, which one can influence by interacting with the other actors that comprise it. It is held by and is surrounded by the *contextual environment*.
TUNA	An acronym describing a type of context that scenario learners might find themselves in, involving *turbulence*, uncertainty (see *Knightian uncertainty*), novelty, and ambiguity.
Turbulence	The most complex *causal texture* postulated by Emery and Trist (1965), where conditions in the *contextual environment* overcome the *transactional environment* and prevailing ground rules governing interactions among actors (including interfirm competition) no longer apply or are questioned deeply. For anyone in turbulence, their perceived capacities to adapt are compromised.
Upframing	A conscious process to *reframe* understanding at a higher level of abstraction—or higher order of logic—that sweeps the wider context of the business landscape into *mindfulness*. See Normann (2001).

(continued)

Continued

Term	Definition
Uncertainty	See *Knightian uncertainty*.
Weak signals	Socially situated indicators of change that are not "noisy," i.e. which emerge as unclear in significance of implied change, as well as timing and impact (such as signals of emerging changes and latent possibilities); characterized by ambiguity, i.e. their meaning is open to different interpretations. Such signals are weak compared to the supposedly "strong" signals seen in quantified, evidence-based trends because they remain ambiguous; and also weak if different from and potentially challenging for the *dominant frame* in use in an organization at a particular time.
Vision	A description of a normative conceptual future. In the OSPA, scenarios are not the same as a vision since they describe what might happen rather than what should or what one wants to happen.
Visioning	The process of developing a *vision*.

REFERENCES

Ackoff, Russell. 1981. *Creating the Corporate Future*. New York: John Wiley.

Adam, Barbara, and Chris Groves. 2007. *Future Matters: Action, Knowledge, Ethics*. Leiden: Brill.

Adams, Douglas. 1979. *The Hitchhikers Guide to the Galaxy*. Reissued mass paperback, 1995. New York: Del Rey.

Adler, Paul, and Seok-Woo Kwon. 2002. "Social Capital: Prospects for a New Concept." *Academy of Management Review*, 27(1): 17–40.

Ahrne, Göran, and Nils Brunsson. 2005. "Organizations and Meta-organizations." *Scandinavian Journal of Management*, 21: 429–49.

Alcamo, Joseph, and Thomas Henrichs. 2008. "Towards Guidelines for Environmental Scenario Analysis." In Alcamo, Joseph (Ed.) *Environmental Futures: The Practice of Environmental Scenario Analysis*. Vol. 2. Philadelphia: Elsevier. pp. 13–35.

Alvesson, Mats, and Jörgen Sandberg. 2011. "Generating Research Questions through Problematization." *Academy of Management Review*, 36(2): 247–71.

Alvesson, Mats, and Jörgen Sandberg. 2013. "Has Management Studies Lost its Way? Ideas for More Imaginative and Innovative Research." *Journal of Management Studies*, 50(1): 128–52.

Amado, Gilles, and Anthony Ambrose (Eds.). 2001. *The Transitional Approach to Change*. London & New York: Karnac.

Argyris, Chris. 1991. "Teaching Smart People How to Learn." *Harvard Business Review*, 69(3): 99–109.

Argyris, Chris, and Donald Schön. 1978. *Organizational Learning: A Theory of Action Approach*. Reading, MA: Addision Wesley.

Arvidsson, Niklas. 1999. *The Ignorant MNE: The Role of Perception Gaps in Knowledge Management*. Doctoral dissertation. Stockholm School of Economics. <http://www.diva-portal.org/smash/get/diva2:369975/FULLTEXT01.pdf> (accessed September 2015).

Ashby, William R. 1956. *An Introduction to Cybernetics*. London: Chapman and Hall.

Baburoglu, Oguz. 1988. "The Vortical Environment." *Human Relations*, 41: 181–210.

Baghai, Mehrdad, Stephen Coley, and David White. 2000. *The Alchemy of Growth: Practical Insights for Building the Enduring Enterprise*. Boston: Da Capo Press.

Bartunek, Jean, Sara Rynes, and Duane Ireland. 2006. "What Makes Management Research Interesting, and Why Does it Matter?" Academy of Management Editors' Forum. *Academy of Management Journal*, 46(1): 9–15.

Berger, Peter, and Thomas Luckmann. 1966. *The Social Construction of Reality: A Treatise in the Sociology of Knowledge*. Garden City, NY: Anchor Books.

Bernard, Mary. 2008. "New Forms of Coherence for the Social Engagement of the Social Scientist: The Theory and Facilitation of Organizational Change from the Perspective of the Emery-Trist Systems Paradigm and the Ilya Prigogine School of Thought." In Rafael Ramírez, John Selsky, and Kees van der Heijden (Eds.) *Business Planning for Turbulent Times: New Methods for Applying Scenarios*. London: Earthscan. pp. 65–84.

Bezold, Clement. 2009. "Jim Dator's Alternative Futures and the Path to IAF's Aspirational Futures." *Journal of Futures Studies*, 14(2): 123–34.

Bohm, David. 1980. *Wholeness and the Implicate Order*. London: Routledge.

Bohm, David. 1985. *Unfolding Meaning: A Weekend of Dialogue with David Bohm*. London: Psychology Press.

Bohm, David. 1996. *On Dialogue*. London: Routledge.

Boyer, Ernest L. 1996. "The Scholarship of Engagement." *Bulletin of the American Academy of Arts and Sciences*, 49(7): 18–33.

Bradfield, Ron, George Wright, George Burt, George Cairns, and Kees van der Heijden. 2005. "The Origins and Evolution of Scenario Techniques in Long Range Business Planning." *Futures*, 37(8): 795–812.

Bridger, Harold. 1990. "The Discovery of the Therapeutic Community." In Eric Trist and Hugh Murray (Eds.) *The Social Engagement of Social Science—Volume 1: The Socio-Psychological Perspective*. Philadelphia: University of Pennsylvania Press. pp. 68–87.

Burt, George, and Kees van der Heijden. 2008. "Towards a Framework to Understand Purpose in Futures Studies: The Role of Vickers' Appreciative System." *Technological Forecasting and Social Change*, 75(8): 1109–27.

Calhoun, Craig. 1995. *Critical Social Theory: Culture, History, and the Challenge of Difference*. Oxford: Blackwell.

Cassirer, Ernst. 1964. *Philosophie des Symbolischen Formen*. Darmstad: Wissenschatliche Buchgesellschaft.

Chapman, Graham P., and Michael Thompson. 1995. *Water and the Quest for Sustainable Development in the Ganges Valley*. London: Mansell.

Checkland, Peter, and John Poulter. 2008. *Learning for Action: A Short Definitive Account of Soft Systems Methodology, and its Use for Practitioners, Teachers and Students*. Chichester: Wiley.

Chermack, Thomas J. 2004. "Improving Decision-Making with Scenario Planning." *Futures*, 36(3): 295–309.

Chermack, Thomas J. 2007. "Disciplined Imagination: Building Scenarios and Building Theories." *Futures*, 39: 1–15.

Churchman, C. West. 1967. "Wicked Problems." *Management Science*, 4(14): 141–2.

Churchman, C. West. 1971. *The Design of Inquiring Systems: Basic Concepts of Systems and Organization*. New York: Basic Books.

Ciborra, Claudio. 1996. *Teams, Markets and Systems: Business Innovation and Information Technology*. New Edition. Cambridge University Press.

Cornelissen, Joep, and Mirjam Werner. 2014. "Putting Framing in Perspective: A Review of Framing and Frame Analysis across the Management and Organizational Literature." *Academy of Management Annals*, 8(1): 181–235.

Coulson, Elizabeth. 1985. "Using Anthropology in a World on the Move." *Human Organization*, 44(3): 191–6.

Damasio, Antonio. 2000. *The Feeling of What Happens: Body, Emotion, and the Making of Consciousness*. New York: Vintage Books.

Dator, Jim. 2009. "Alternative Futures at the Manoa School." *Journal of Futures Studies*, 14(2): 1–18.

De Geus, Arie. 1997. *The Living Company: Habits for Survival in a Turbulent Business Environment*. Boston: Harvard Business School Press.

De Leon Ardon, Victoria, and Gabriel de las Nieves Sanchez Guerrero. 2012. "Scenarios Evaluation: A Criteria Categorization." Presented at the 5th ISPIM Innovation Symposium, Seoul, Korea, December 9–12.

Dennett, Daniel. 1995. *Darwin's Dangerous Idea: Evolution and the Meanings of Life*. New York: Simon and Schuster.

Drucker, Peter. 1961. *The Practice of Management*. London: Mercury Books.

Dufva, Mikko, and Toni Ahlqvist. 2015. "Knowledge Creation Dynamics in Foresight: A Knowledge Typology and Exploratory Method to Analyse Foresight Workshops." *Technological Forecasting and Social Change*, 94: 251–68.

Economist, The. 2015. "There's an App for That." January 3. <http://www.economist.com/news/briefing/21637355-freelance-workers-available-moments-notice-will-reshape-nature-companies-and> (accessed September 2015).

Eden, Colin. 1988. "Cognitive Mapping." Invited review. *European Journal of Operational Research*, 36: 1–13.

Eden, Colin. 2004. "Analyzing Cognitive Maps to Help Structure Issues or Problems." *European Journal of Operational Research*, 159: 673–86.

Elahi, Shirin. 2008. "Conceptions of Fairness and Forming the Common Ground." In Rafael Ramírez, John Selsky, and Kees van der Heijden (Eds.) *Business Planning for Turbulent Times: New Methods for Applying Scenarios*. London: Earthscan. pp. 223–42.

Elkington, John, and Alex Trisoglio. 1996. "Developing Realistic Scenarios for the Environment: Lessons from Brent Spar." *Long Range Planning*, 29: 762–9.

Emery, Fred. 1977. *Futures We Are In*. Leiden, Netherlands: Martinus Nijhoff.

Emery, Fred, and Eric Trist. 1965. "The Causal Texture of Organizational Environments." *Human Relations*, 18(1): 21–32.

Emery, Fred, and Eric Trist. 1973. *Towards a Social Ecology: Contextual Appreciations of the Future in the Present*. London: Plenum.

Feyerabend, Paul. 1993. *Against Method*. New York: Verso.

Finkelstein, Sidney, Jo Whitehead, and Andrew Campbell. 2013. *Think Again: Why Good Leaders Make Bad Decisions and How to Keep it from Happening to You*. Boston: Harvard Business Press.

Flowers, Betty Sue. 2007. *The American Dream and the Economic Myth*. Kalamazoo: Fetzer Institute.

Flowers, Betty Sue, Roland Kupers, Diana Mangalagiu, Rafael Ramírez, Jerome Ravetz, John Selsky, Chris Wasden, and Angela Wilkinson. 2010. *Beyond the Financial Crisis: The Oxford Scenarios*. Monograph. February. pp. 1–82. <http://www.insis.ox.ac.uk/fileadmin/InSIS/Publications/financial-scenarios.pdf> (accessed September 2015).

Forrester, Jay. 1961. *Industrial Dynamics*. Cambridge, MA: MIT Press.

Fox Keller, Evelyn. 2002. *Making Sense of Life: Explaining Biological Development with Models, Metaphors, and Machines*. Cambridge, MA: Harvard University Press.

Fuentes, Carlos. 1993. *Geografía de la Novela*. Madrid: Ediciones Santillana.

Funtowicz, Silvio O., and Jerome R. Ravetz. 1995. *Science for the Post Normal Age*. Netherlands: Springer.

Gollin, Michael, Gwen Hinze, and Tzen Wong. 2011. "Scenario Planning on the Future of Intellectual Property: Literature Review and Implications for Human Development." In Tzen Wong and Graham Dutfield (Eds.) *Intellectual Property and Human Development: Current Trends and Future Scenarios*. Cambridge: Cambridge University Press. pp. 329–66.

Gugan, A. 2008. "Successful Scenario Planning," JISC infoNet, available at: <http://www.jisc.ac. uk/publications> (accessed September 2015).

Hama, Noriko. 1996. *Disintegrating Europe: The Twilight of the European Construction.* Santa Barbara, CA: Praeger.

Harman, Willis. 1979. *An Incomplete Guide to the Future.* New York: W.W. Norton.

Harvey, Jerry B. 1988. *The Abilene Paradox and Other Meditations on Management.* Lexington: Lexington Books.

Heckscher, Charles, Michael Maccoby, Rafael Ramírez, and Pierre-Eric Tixier. 2003. *Agents of Change: Crossing the Post-industrial Divide.* Oxford: Oxford University Press.

Heifetz, Ronald, Alexander Grashow, and Marty Linsky. 2009. "Leadership in a (Permanent) Crisis." *Harvard Business Review,* 87(7/8): 62–9.

Hernandez, Andrea. 2011. "Exploring a Completed Scenario Set—Wärtsilä Shipping Scenarios." Invited Oxford Briefing lecture, Oxford Scenarios Programme, May 16.

Hernandez, Andrea. 2014. "Wärtsilä Learns from the Future." Presentation at the Information Intelligence Summit, Helsinki, March 5.

Hirschhorn, Larry. 2012. "Backcasting: A Systematic Method for Creating a Picture of the Future and How to Get There." In John Vogelsang, Maya Townsend, Matt Minahan, David Jamieson, Judy Vogel, Annie Viets, Cathy Royal, and Lynne Valek (Eds.) *Handbook for Strategic HR: Best Practices in Organization Development from the OD Network.* New York: AMACOM.

Hodgkinson, Gerald, and George Wright. 2002. "Confronting Strategic Inertia in a Top Management Team: Learning from Failure." *Organization Studies,* 23(6): 949–77.

Hodgson, Anthony. 1992. "Hexagons for Systems Thinking." *European Journal of Operational Research,* 59(1): 220–30.

IIP. 2009. *Kiro ni Tatsu Tokkyo Seido (Patent System Stands in Front of Crisis).* Tokyo: Institute of Intellectual Property.

Inayatullah, Sohail. 1998. "Causal Layered Analysis: Poststructuralism as Method." *Futures,* 30(8): 815–29.

Ingvar, David. 1985. "Memories of the Future: An Essay on the Temporal Organization of Conscious Awareness." *Human Neurobiology,* 4(3): 127–36.

IPCC (Intergovernmental Panel on Climate Change). 2007. *Fourth Assessment Report: Climate Change 2007: Synthesis Report.* Geneva: IPCC. <https://www.ipcc.ch/publications_and_data/ publications_ipcc_fourth_assessment_report_synthesis_report.htm> (accessed September 2015).

Jameson, Frederic. 2002. *A Singular Modernity: Essays on the Ontology of the Present.* London: Verso.

Janis, Irving, and Leon Mann. 1977. *Decision Making: A Psychological Analysis of Conflict, Choice, and Commitment.* New York: Free Press.

Jaworski, Joseph, and Claus Otto Scharmer. 2000. *Leadership in the New Economy: Sensing and Actualizing Emerging Futures.* Beverly, MA: Generon Consulting.

Jetter Antonie, and Kasper Kok. 2014. "Fuzzy Cognitive Maps for Futures Studies: A Methodological Assessment of Concepts and Methods." *Futures,* 61: 45–57.

Journal of Risk Research. 2003. *Journal of Risk Research* 6(4–6), special issue on Risk-World scenarios.

Kahane, Adam. 2012. *Transformative Scenario Planning: Working Together to Change the Future.* San Francisco: Berrett-Koehler Publishers.

Kahn, Herman. 1962. *Thinking about the Unthinkable*. New York: Horizon Press.

Kahneman, Daniel, and Gary Klein. 2009. "Conditions for Intuitive Expertise: A Failure to Disagree." *American Psychologist*, 64(6): 515.

Kay, John. 2013. "A Story can be More Useful than Maths." *Financial Times*, February 26. <http://www.johnkay.com/2013/02/27/a-story-can-be-more-useful-than-maths> (accessed November 2014).

Kennedy, Scott, Richard P. Suttmeier, and Jun Su. 2008. *Standards, Stakeholders, and Innovation: China's Evolving Role in the Global Knowledge Economy*. <http://www.nbr.org/publications/issue.aspx?id=116> (accessed September 2015).

Kincheloe, Joe L. 2001. "Describing the Bricolage: Conceptualizing a New Rigor in Qualitative Research." *Qualitative Inquiry*, 7(6): 679–92.

Knight, Frank H. 1921. *Risk, Uncertainty, and Profit*. Boston: Hart, Schaffner & Marx; Houghton Mifflin Co.

Koeppel. Dan. 2008. *Banana: The Fate of the Fruit That Changed the World*. New York: Hudson Street Press.

Köhler, Jonathan, et al. 2015. *Concurrent Design Foresight: Report to the European Commission of the Expert Group on Foresight Modelling*. Brussels: European Commission. <http://ec.europa.eu/research/swafs/pdf/pub_governance/concurrent_design_foresight_report.pdf> (accessed September 2015).

Kolb, David. 1984. *Experiential Learning*. Englewood Cliffs, NJ: Prentice Hall.

Lakoff, George, and Mark Johnson. 1980. *Metaphors We Live By*. Chicago: University of Chicago Press.

Lang, Trudi. 2012. *Essays on How Scenario Planning and the Building of New Social Capital are Related*. Unpublished DPhil dissertation. University of Oxford.

Lang, Trudi, and Lynn Allen. 2008. "Reflecting on Scenario Practice: The Contribution of a Soft Systems Perspective." In Rafael Ramírez, John Selsky, and Kees van der Heijden (Eds.) *Business Planning for Turbulent Times: New Methods for Applying Scenarios*. London: Earthscan. pp. 47–64.

Langer, Suzanne. 1942. *Philosophy in a New Key*. Boston: Harvard University Press.

Latour, Bruno. 2010. *On the Modern Cult of the Factish Gods*. Chapel Hill, NC: Duke University Press.

Lloyd, Elizabeth, and Vanessa Schweizer. 2014. "Objectivity and a Comparison of Methodological Scenario Approaches for Climate Change Research." *Synthese*, 191: 2049–88.

Mangalagiu, Diana, John Selsky, and Angela Wilkinson. 2010. "Beyond Unrealistic Dreaming to Creating a Better Future: The World Business Council for Sustainable Development Vision 2050 Initiative." 2nd International Symposium on Cross Sector Social Interactions, London, April.

Mangalagiu, Diana, Angela Wilkinson, and Roland Kupers. 2011. "When Futures Lock-In the Present: Towards a New Generation of Climate Scenarios." In Klaus Hasselmann, Carlo Jaeger, Gerd Leipold, Diana Mangalagiu, and Joan David Tàbara (Eds.) *Reframing the Problem of Climate Change: From Zero Sum Game to Win-Win Solutions*. London: Routledge. pp. 160–75.

March, James G., Johan P. Olsen, Søren Christensen, and Michael D. Cohen. 1976. *Ambiguity and Choice in Organizations*. Bergen: Universitetsforlaget.

Marchais-Roubelat, Anne, and Fabrice Roubelat. 2008. "Designing Action Based Scenarios." *Futures*, 40(1): 25–33.

McCann, Joseph, and John Selsky. 1984. "Hyperturbulence and the Emergence of Type 5 Environments." *Academy of Management Review*, 9(3): 460–70.

McCann, Joseph, and John Selsky. 2012. *Mastering Turbulence*. San Francisco: Jossey-Bass.

Michael, Donald. 1973. *On Planning to Learn and Learning to Plan*. San Francisco: Jossey-Bass.

Molitor, Graham. 2009. "Scenarios: Worth the Effort?" *Journal of Futures Studies*, 13(3): 81–92.

Morgan, Gareth (Ed.). 1983. *Beyond Method: Strategies for Social Research*. London: Sage.

Morgan, Gareth, and Rafael Ramírez. 1984. "Action Learning: A Holographic Metaphor for Guiding Social Change." *Human Relations*, 37(1): 1–27.

Naisbitt, John. 1984. *Megatrends: Ten New Directions Transforming Our Lives*. New York: Warner Books.

Normann, Richard. 2001. *Reframing Business: When the Map Changes the Landscape*. Chichester: Wiley.

Normann, Richard, and Rafael Ramírez. 1993. "Designing Interactive Strategy." *Harvard Business Review*, 71(4): 65–77.

Normann, Richard, and Rafael Ramírez. 1994. *Designing Interactive Strategy*. Chichester: Wiley.

Nowak, Michael. 2006. "Five Rules for the Evolution of Cooperation." *Science*, 314(5805): 1560–3.

Ocasio, William. 1997. "Towards an Attention-Based View of the Firm." *Strategic Management Journal*, 18(Summer): 187–206.

O'Connell, Donal. 2008. *Inside the Patent Factory*. New York: John Wiley.

Oldham, Paul. 2007. *Biodiversity and the Patent System: Towards International Indicators*. CESAGen, Lancaster University, United Kingdom. Report no. UNEP/CBD/WG-ABS/5/INF/6, September 26, 2007. <http://www.cbd.int/doc/meetings/abs/abswg-05/information/abswg-05-inf-06-en.pdf> (accessed September 2015).

Orru, Anna Maria, and David Relan. 2013. *Composing a Scenario Symphony*. The Resilients website. <http://libarynth.org/resilients/scenario_symphony> (accessed September 2015).

Perrow, Charles. 1984. *Normal Accidents: Living with High Risk Systems*. New York: Basic Books.

Polanyi, Michael. 1966. *The Tacit Dimension*. Chicago: University of Chicago Press.

Pompidou, Alain. 2006. *Preface: Interviews for the Future*. Munich: European Patent Office.

Popper, Karl. 1959. *The Logic of Scientific Discovery*. New York: Basic Books.

Ramírez, Rafael. 1983. "Action Learning: A Strategic Approach for Organizations Facing Turbulent Conditions." *Human Relations*, 36(8): 725–42.

Ramírez, Rafael. 2008. "Scenarios that Provide Clarity in Addressing Turbulence." In Rafael Ramírez, John Selsky, and Kees van der Heijden (Eds.) *Business Planning for Turbulent Times: New Methods for Applying Scenarios*. London: Earthscan. pp. 187–206.

Ramírez, Rafael, and Caroline Drevon. 2005. "The Role and Limits of Methods in Transitional Change Process." In Gilles Amado and Leopold Vansina (Eds.) *The Transitional Approach in Action*. London and New York: Karnac.

Ramírez, Rafael, Malobi Mukherjee, Simona Vezzoli, and Arnoldo Matus Kramer. 2015. "Scenarios as a Scholarly Methodology to Produce Interesting Research." *Futures*, 71: 70–87.

Ramírez, Rafael, Riku Österman, and Daniel Grönquist. 2013. "Scenarios and Early Warnings as Dynamic Capabilities to Frame Managerial Attention." *Technological Forecasting and Social Change*, 80(4): 825–38.

Ramírez, Rafael, and Jerome Ravetz. 2011. "Feral Futures: Zen and Aesthetics." *Futures,* 43(4): 478–87.

Ramírez, Rafael, Leo Roodhart, and Willem Manders. 2011. "How Shell Domains Link Innovation and Strategy." *Long Range Planning,* 44(4): 250–70.

Ramírez, Rafael, and Cynthia Selin. 2014. "Plausibility and Probability in Scenario Planning." *Foresight,* 16(1): 54–74.

Ramírez, Rafael, and John Selsky. 2015. "Strategic Planning in Turbulent Environments: A Social Ecology Approach to Scenarios." *Long Range Planning.* Forthcoming.

Ramírez, Rafael, John Selsky, and Kees van der Heijden (Eds.). 2008a. *Business Planning for Turbulent Times: New Methods for Applying Scenarios,* 2nd edition 2010. London: Earthscan.

Ramírez, Rafael, John Selsky, and Kees van der Heijden. 2008b. "Conceptual and Historical Overview." In Rafael Ramírez, John Selsky, and Kees van der Heijden (Eds.) *Business Planning for Turbulent Times: New Methods for Applying Scenarios.* London: Earthscan. pp. 17–30.

Ramírez, Rafael, and Kees van der Heijden. 2007. "Scenarios to Develop Strategic Options: A New Interactive Role for Scenarios in Strategy." In Bill Sharpe and Kees van der Heijden (Eds.) *Scenarios for Success: Turning Insights into Action.* Chichester: Wiley. pp. 89–119.

Ramírez, Rafael, and Johan Wallin. 2000. *Prime Movers: Define Your Business or Have Someone Define it Against You.* New York: John Wiley.

Ramírez, Rafael, and Angela Wilkinson. 2009a. "How Plausible is Plausibility as a Scenario Effectiveness Criterion?" Paper presented at the Joint Arizona State University-InSIS Plausibility Project Workshop, Arizona, November.

Ramírez, Rafael, and Angela Wilkinson. 2009b. "Business Planning in Turbulent Times: Relating Scenarios and Strategy; or Using the Future as a Safe Space to Consider the Present." Invited keynote, Risk Capital conference, Brussels, Spring 2009.

Ramírez, Rafael, and Angela Wilkinson. 2014. "Re-thinking the 2X2 Scenario Method: Grid or Frames?" *Technological Forecasting and Social Change,* 86: 254–64.

Ramírez, Ricardo, Galin Kora, and Daniel Shephard. 2015. "Utilization Focused Developmental Evaluation: Learning Through Practice." *Journal of Multidisciplinary Evaluation,* 11(24): 37–53.

Rittel, Horst W.J., and Melvin M. Webber. 1973. "Dilemmas in a General Theory of Planning." *Policy Sciences,* 4(2): 155–69.

Robert, Glenn, John Gabbay, and Andrew Stevens. 1998. "Which are the Best Information Sources for Identifying Emerging Health Care Technologies?: An International Delphi Survey." *International Journal of Technology Assessment in Health Care,* 14(4): 636–43.

Rosen, Robert. 1985. *Anticipatory Systems: Philosophical, Mathematical and Methodological Foundations.* Exeter: Pergamon.

Royal Dutch Shell. 2003. *Scenarios: An Explorer's Guide.* <http://www.shell.com/global/future-energy/scenarios/explorers-guide.html> (accessed September 2015).

Rutz, Berthold. 2007. "Synthetic Biology Through the Prism of Scenarios." *Biotechnology Journal,* 2(9): 1072–5.

Sardar, Ziauddin. 2010. "The Namesake: Futures; Futures Studies; Futurology; Futuristic; Foresight—What's in a Name?" *Futures,* 42(3): 177–84.

Scarry, Elaine. 2001. *Dreaming by the Book.* Princeton, NJ: Princeton University Press.

Schacter, Daniel, Donna Rose Addis, and Randy Buckner. 2007. "Remembering the Past to Imagine the Future: The Prospective Brain." *Nature,* 8(September): 657–61.

Scharmer, C. Otto. 2007. *Theory U: Leading from the Future as it Emerges.* San Francisco: Berrett-Koehler.

Schein, Edgar. 1999. *Process Consultation Revisited: Building the Helping Relationship.* Reading: Addison-Wesley.

Schein, Edgar. 2013. *Humble Inquiry: The Gentle Art of Asking Instead of Telling.* San Francisco: Berrett-Koehler Publishers.

Schlag, Pierre. 2002. "The Aesthetics of American Law." *Harvard Law Review*, 115(February): 1047–118.

Schoemaker, Paul J.H. 1993. "Multiple Scenario Development: Its Conceptual and Behavioral Foundation." *Strategic Management Journal*, 14(3): 193–213.

Schoemaker, Paul J.H. 1998. "Twenty Common Pitfalls in Scenario Planning." In Liam Fahey and Robert M. Randall (Eds.) *Learning from the Future: Competitive Foresight Scenarios.* Oxford: Wiley. pp. 422–32.

Schoemaker, Paul, George Day, and Scott Snyder. 2013. "Integrating Organizational Networks, Weak Signals, Strategic Radars, and Scenario Planning." *Technological Forecasting and Social Change*, 80(4): 815–24.

Schön, Donald. 1983. *The Reflective Practitioner.* Basic Books.

Schön, Donald A., and Martin Rein. 1995. *Frame Reflection: Toward the Resolution of Intractable Policy Controversies.* New York: Basic Books.

Schumpeter, J.A. (1994). *Capitalism, Socialism and Democracy.* London: Routledge.

Schwarz, Michiel, and Michael Thompson. 1990. *Divided We Stand: Redefining Politics, Technology, and Social Choice.* Philadelphia: University of Pennsylvania Press.

Schwartz, Peter. 2004. *Inevitable Surprises: Thinking Ahead in a Time of Turbulence.* New York and London: Gotham/Penguin.

Schweizer, Vanessa, and Elmar Kriegler. 2012. "Improving Environmental Change Research with Systematic Techniques for Qualitative Scenarios." *Environmental Research Letters*, 7(4): 044011.

Selsky, John, James Goes, and Oguz Baburoglu. 2007. "Contrasting Perspectives of Strategy Making: Applications in 'Hyper' Environments." *Organization Studies*, 28(1): 71–94.

Selsky, John, and Joseph McCann. 2008. "Managing Disruptive Change and Turbulence through Continuous Change Thinking and Scenarios." In Rafael Ramírez, John Selsky, and Kees van der Heijden (Eds.) *Business Planning for Turbulent Times: New Methods for Applying Scenarios.* London: Earthscan. pp. 167–86.

Senge, Peter. 1990. *The Fifth Discipline: The Art and Science of the Learning Organization.* New York: Currency Doubleday.

Senge, Peter, C. Otto Scharmer, Joseph Jaworski, and Betty Sue Flowers. 2005. *Presence: An Exploration of Profound Change in People, Organizations, and Society.* New York: Crown Business.

Sharpe, Bill. 2014. *Three Horizons: The Partnering of Hope.* Axminster: Triarchy Press.

Sharpe, Bill, and Kees van der Heijden (Eds.). *Scenarios for Success: Turning Insights into Action.* Chichester: Wiley.

Shimanami, Ryo (Ed.). 2012. *The Future of the Patent System.* Cheltenham: Edward Elgar.

Simon, Herbert. 1978. *Rational Decision-Making in Business Organizations.* No. 1978-1. Nobel Prize Committee. <http://EconPapers.repec.org/RePEc:ris:nobelp:1978_001> (accessed September 2015).

Slaughter, Richard A. 1993. "Futures Concepts." *Futures*, 25(3): 289–314.

Smithson, M. 2008. "Social Theories of Ignorance." In Robert Proctor and Londa Schiebinger (Eds.) *Agnotology: The Making and Unmaking of Ignorance.* Stanford: Stanford University Press.

Starbuck, William H. 2005. "How Much Better are the Most-Prestigious Journals? The Statistics of Academic Publication." *Organization Science,* 16(2): 180–200.

Starbuck, William. 2009. "Perspective-Cognitive Reactions to Rare Events: Perceptions, Uncertainty, and Learning." *Organization Science,* 20(5): 925–37.

Strati, Antonio. 1999. *Organization and Aesthetics.* London: Sage.

Suddaby, Roy. 2006. "What Grounded Theory is Not." *Academy of Management Journal,* 49(4): 633–42.

Sudhanshu, R. 2012. "Working to Understand Co-Creation." *Scenario,* 4: 34–7.

Sutcliffe, Kathleen, and Klaus Weber. 2003. "The High Cost of Accurate Knowledge." *Harvard Business Review,* 81(5): 74–82.

Thompson, Michael. 2008. *Organising and Disorganising: A Dynamic and Non-Linear Theory of Institutional Emergence and its Implications.* Axminster: Triarchy.

Trompenaars, Fons, and Charles Hampden-Turner. 1998. *Riding the Waves of Culture.* New York: McGraw-Hill.

Tuomi, Ikka. 2013. "Foresight in an Unpredictable World." *Technology Analysis & Strategic Management,* 24(8): 735–51.

Tversky, Amos, and Daniel Kahneman. 1986. "Rational Choice and the Framing of Decisions." *Journal of Business,* 59(4): S251–S278.

UEG (United European Gastroenterology). 2014. "What Will the European Healthcare System Look Like in 2040?" Press release. Vienna, October 21. <https://www.ueg.eu/press/releases/ueg-press-release/article/ueg-week-press-release-what-will-the-european-healthcare-system-look-like-in-2040-ueg-launch-fu/> (accessed January 2015).

Van Asselt, Marjolein, Nina Faas, Francke van der Molen, and Sietske Veenman. 2010. *Out of Sight: Exploring Futures for Policymaking.* Amsterdam University Press, Scientific Council for Government Policy (WRR), Explorations 24.

Van Asselt, Marjolein, and Jan Rotmans. 1996. "Uncertainty in Perspective." *Global Environmental Change,* 6(2): 121–57.

Van de Ven, Andrew H. 2007. *Engaged Scholarship: A Guide for Organizational and Social Research.* Oxford: Oxford University Press.

Van der Heijden, Kees. 2005. *Scenarios: The Art of Strategic Conversation,* 2nd edition. Chichester: Wiley.

Van der Heijden, Kees. 2008. "Turbulence in the Indian Agriculture Sector: A Scenario Analysis." In Rafael Ramírez, John Selsky, and Kees van der Heijden (Eds.) *Business Planning for Turbulent Times: New Methods for Applying Scenarios.* London: Earthscan. pp. 87–102.

Van der Heijden, Kees, Ron Bradfield, George Burt, George Cairns, and George Wright. 2002. *The Sixth Sense: Accelerating Organizational Learning with Scenarios.* Chichester: Wiley.

Van Notten, Philip, Jan Rotmans, Marjolein van Asselt, and Dale S. Rothman. 2003. "An Updated Scenario Typology." *Futures,* 35(5): 423–43.

Varum, Celeste A., and Carla Melo. 2010. "Directions in the Scenario Planning Literature: A Review of the Past Decades." *Futures,* 42: 355–69.

Veefkind, Victor et al. 2012. "A New EPO Classification Scheme for Climate Change Mitigation Technologies." *World Patent Information,* 34: 106–11.

Vennix, Jac A.M. 1996. *Group Model Building: Facilitating Team Learning Using Systems Dynamics.* Chichester: Wiley.

Vickers, Geoffrey. 1965. *The Art of Judgment: A Study in Policy Making*. London: Chapman and Hall.

Vitzhum, Christoph. 2014. "The Practical Use of Scenarios." Invited plenary presentation to the Oxford Scenarios Programme, September 29.

Volkery, Axel, and Teresa Ribeiro. 2009. "Scenario Planning in Public Policy: Understanding Use, Impacts and the Role of Institutional Context Factors." *Technological Forecasting and Social Change*, 76(9): 1198–207.

Wack, Pierre. 1984. *Scenarios: The Gentle Art of Reperceiving*. Harvard Business School Working Paper 9–785–042.

Wack, Pierre. 1985a. "Scenarios: Uncharted Waters Ahead," *Harvard Business Review*, September–October: 73–90.

Wack, Pierre. 1985b. "Scenarios: Shooting the Rapids," *Harvard Business Review*, November–December: 131–42.

Walton, John. 2008. "Scanning Beyond the Horizon: Exploring the Ontological and Epistemological Basis for Scenario Planning." *Advances in Developing Human Resources*, 10(2): 147–65.

Weick, Karl. 1979. *The Social Psychology of Organizing*. Reading: Addison-Wesley.

Weick, Karl. 1995. *Sensemaking in Organizations*. Thousand Oaks, CA: Sage.

Weick, Karl. 2006. "Faith, Evidence, and Action: Better Guesses in an Unknowable World." *Organization Studies*, 27(11): 1723–36.

Weick, Karl, and Kathleen Sutcliffe. 2007. *Managing the Unexpected*. San Francisco: Jossey-Bass.

Weick, Karl, Kathleen Sutcliffe, and David Obstfeld. 2005. "Organizing and the Process of Sensemaking." *Organization Science*, 16(4): 409–21.

Westrum, Ron. 1994. "Thinking by Groups, Organizations, and Networks: A Sociologist's View of the Social Psychology of Science and Technology." In William Shadish and Steve Fuller (Eds.) *The Social Psychology of Science*. New York: Guilford. pp. 329–42.

Wilkinson, Angela, and Esther Eidinow. 2008. "Evolving Practices in Environmental Scenarios: A New Scenario Typology." *Environmental Research Letters*, 3(4): 045017.

Wilkinson, Angela, and Roland Kupers. 2014. *The Essence of Scenarios: Learning from the Shell Experience*. Edited by Betty Sue Flowers. Amsterdam: Amsterdam University Press.

Wilkinson, Angela, Roland Kupers, and Diana Mangalagiu. 2013. "How Plausibility-Based Scenario Practices are Grappling with Complexity to Appreciate and Address 21st Century Challenges." *Technological Forecasting and Social Change*, 80(4): 699–710.

Wilkinson, Angela, Diana Mangalagiu, and John Selsky. 2011. "Challenges of Using Futures Methods in Sustainable Development Projects." Academy of Management national meetings, ONE Division, San Antonio, August.

Wilkinson, Angela, and Rafael Ramírez. 2010. "Canaries in the Mind: Exploring How the Financial Crisis Impacts 21st Century Future-Mindfulness." *Journal of Futures Studies*, 14(3): 45–60.

Winnicott, Donald W. 1962. "Ego Integration in Child Development." In Donald W. Winnicott (Ed.) *The Maturational Processes and the Facilitating Environment*. London: Hogarth Press.

Wong, Tzen, and Graham Dutfield (Eds.). 2011. *Intellectual Property and Human Development: Current Trends and Future Scenarios*. Cambridge: Cambridge University Press.

Zurek, Monika, and Thomas Henrichs. 2007. "Linking Scenarios across Geographical Scales in International Environmental Assessments." *Technological Forecasting and Social Change*, 74(8): 1282–95.

■ SUBJECT INDEX

■ NAME INDEX

Hegel, F. 55
Heifetz, R. 27
Henrichs, T. 48, 113
Hernandez, A. 176–8
Herzog, W. 123
Hirschhorn, L. 49
Hodgkinson, G. 26, 42, 148, 158, 169
Hodgson, A. 129
Hofmeister, J. 183

Inayatullah, S. 47, 118
Ingvar, D. 44, 60, 107

James, W. 83
Jameson, F. 37
Janis, I. 35
Jaworski, J. 140
Jefferson, M. 139
Jetter, A. 116, 139
Johnson, M. 58

Kahane, A. 49, 114, 140
Kahn, H. 83
Kahnemann, D. 28, 30, 66, 84
Kant, I. 54
Kay, J. 100
Kennedy, B. 62
Kennedy, J. F. 62
Khrushchev, N. 62
Kincheloe, J. L. 171
Klein, G. 66, 84
Koeppel, D. 47
Kok, K. 116, 139
Kolb, D. 154
Kriegler, E. 83
Kuhn, T. 69
Kupers, R. 42–3, 45, 68, 74, 113, 119, 134–5, 139
Kwon, S.-W. 46
Köhler, J. 84

Lakoff, G. 58
Lang, T. 46, 76, 106–7, 132, 135, 140, 205
Langer, S. 83
Latour, B. 6
Leibniz, G. 54
Lewin, K. 153
Lloyd, E. 74, 83
Locke, J. 54
Luckmann, T. 56

McCann, J. 9, 21, 137, 171
McGinley, C. 207, 213, 215

Makinen, M. 174
Mangalagiu, D. 73, 172
Mann, L. 35
March, J. G. 32
Marchais-Roubelat, A. 72
Melo, C. 165
Merkel, A. 204
Michael, D. 3
Molitor, G. 168
Moody-Stewart, M. 183
Morecroft, J. 84
Morgan, G. 65–6, 83, 146, 156
Morris, I viii

Naisbitt, J. 85
Newland, E. 92
Normann, R. viii, 9, 11, 13–14, 29, 37, 39, 49, 63, 70–1, 84, 95, 137–8
Nowak, M. 2

Ocasio, W. 44
O'Connell, D. 205
Oldham, P. 205
Orru, A. M. 114

Perrow, C. 28, 49
Piot, P. 192, 199
Polanyi, M. 53
Pompidou, A. 201–2, 207
Popper, K. 55
Porter, M. viii
Poulter, J. 77
Prigogine, I. 8

Ramírez, R. xv, 3, 9, 14, 26–7, 29, 36, 44, 46, 49–51, 54–5, 58, 63–4, 67–8, 70, 77, 79–80, 83–4, 90, 95, 100, 113, 116, 118, 134–5, 137–8, 140, 142, 146, 149, 152, 158, 165, 169, 171–2, 178
Ravetz, J. R. 51, 57, 63, 80, 171
Rein, M. 3–4
Relan, D. 114
Ribeiro, T. 113
Rittel, H. W. J. 32
Robert, G. 80
Rosen, R. 84
Rotmans, J. 118
Roubelat, F. 72

Sandberg, J. 68–9, 84
Sardar, Z. 55, 58
Scarry, E. 44

Printed and bound by CPI Group (UK) Ltd, Croydon, CR0 4YY